INUYASHA

VOL. 48

Shonen Sunday Edition

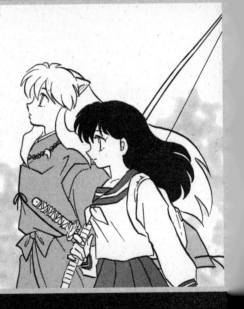

STORY AND ART BY
RUMIKO TAKAHASHI

CONTENTS

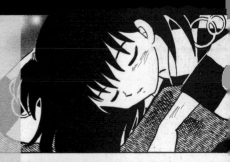

Long ago, in the "Warring States" era of Japan's Muromachi period, dog-like half demon Inuyasha attempted to steal the Shikon Jewel—or "Jewel of Four Souls"—from a village. The village priestess, Kikyo, put a stop to his thievery with an enchanted arrow. Pinned to a tree, Inuyasha fell into a deep sleep, while mortally wounded Kikyo took the jewel with her into her funeral pyre. Years passed...

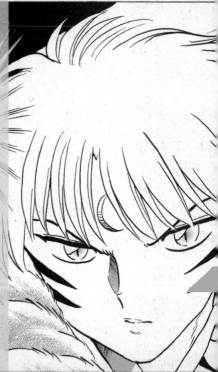

In the present day, Kagome, a Japanese high school girl, is pulled down into a well and transported into the past. There she discovers trapped Inuyasha—and frees him.

When the Shikon Jewel mysteriously reappears, demons attack. In the ensuing battle, the jewel *shatters*!

Now Inuyasha is bound to Kagome with a powerful spell, and the grudging companions must battle to reclaim the shattered shards of the Shikon Jewel to keep them out of evil hands...

LAST VOLUME Naraku transfers the Shikon Jewel into Kikyo. After Kagome shoots a Sacred Arrow to cleanse it, Kikyo propels the purified jewel back at Naraku. This releases Koga from his grasp, but not before Naraku steals his shards. A struggle between good and evil ensues within the jewel. Naraku escapes. Mortally wounded Kikyo reassures Inuyasha that her soul has been purified, then dies once more.

Meanwhile, Sesshomaru's mother gives him a Meido Stone bequeathed to him by his father. Rin and Kohaku are swept into the Meido. Sesshomaru rescues Rin and Kohaku, but only

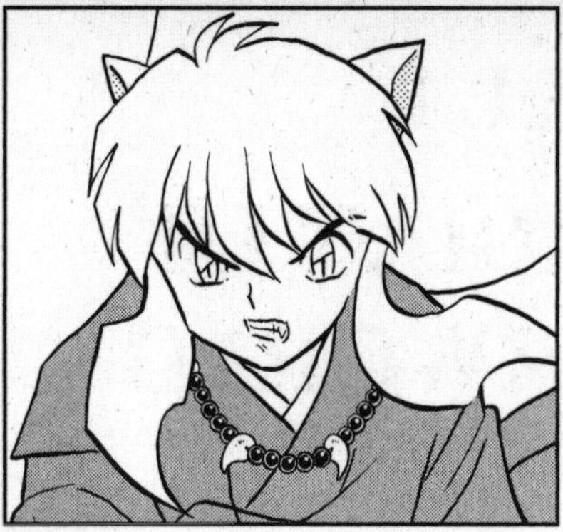

INUYASHA
Half-demon hybrid, son of a human mother and demon father. His necklace is enchanted, allowing Kagome to control him with a word.

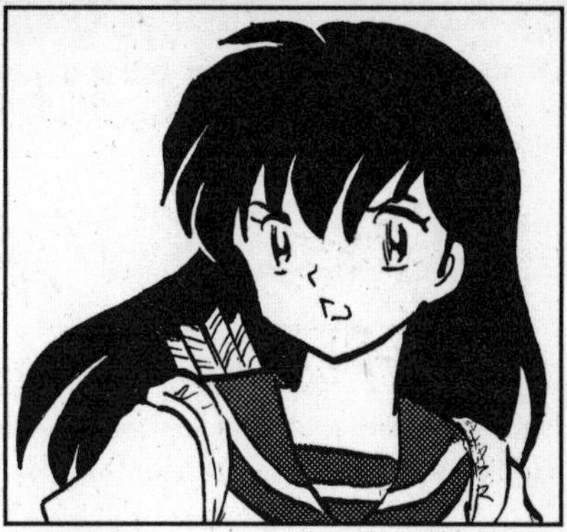

KAGOME
Modern-day Japanese schoolgirl who can travel back and forth between the past and present through an enchanted well.

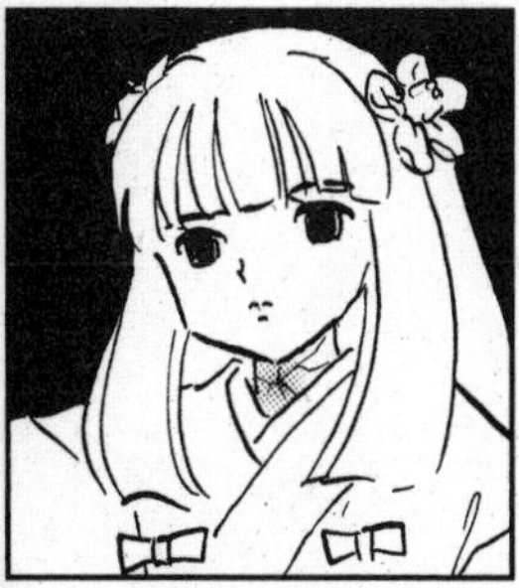

KANNA
Kanna is Naraku's first double. Her demonic mirror steals souls. Her loyalty to Naraku seems to be wavering.

SESSHOMARU
Inuyasha's completely demon half brother. Sesshomaru covets the sword left to Inuyasha by their demon father.

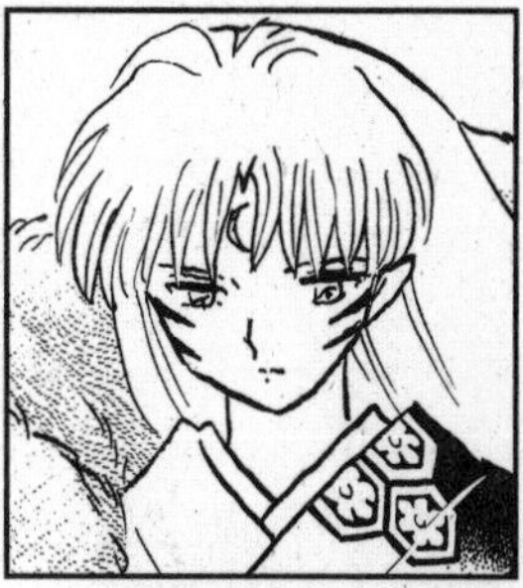

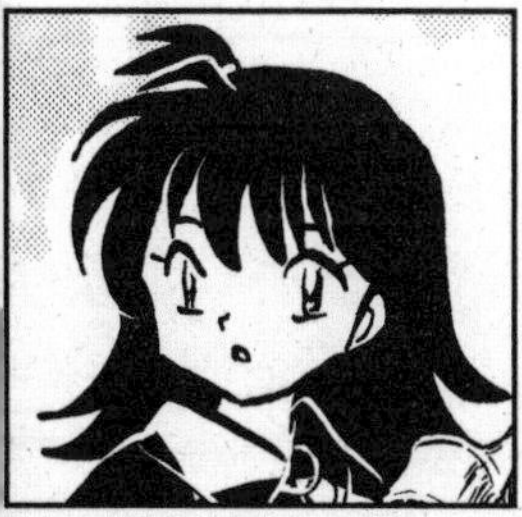

RIN
An orphaned girl devoted to Sesshomaru. He once resurrected her with Tenseiga. She brings out the best in him.

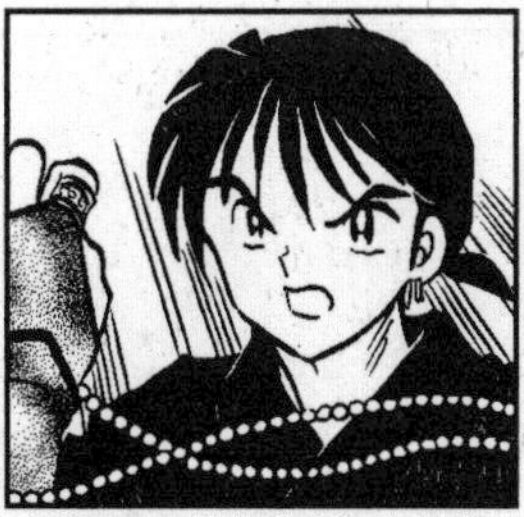

MIROKU
Lecherous Buddhist priest cursed with a mystical "hellhole" in his hand that is slowly killing him.

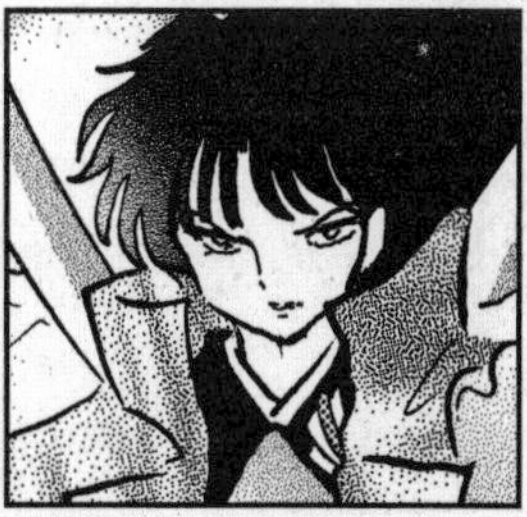

NARAKU
Enigmatic demon mastermind behind the miseries of nearly everyone in the story. He has the power to create multiple incarnations of himself from his body. He will stop at nothing to obtain all the shards of the Shikon Jewel.

SCROLL 1
THE GUARDIAN OF THE UNDERWORLD

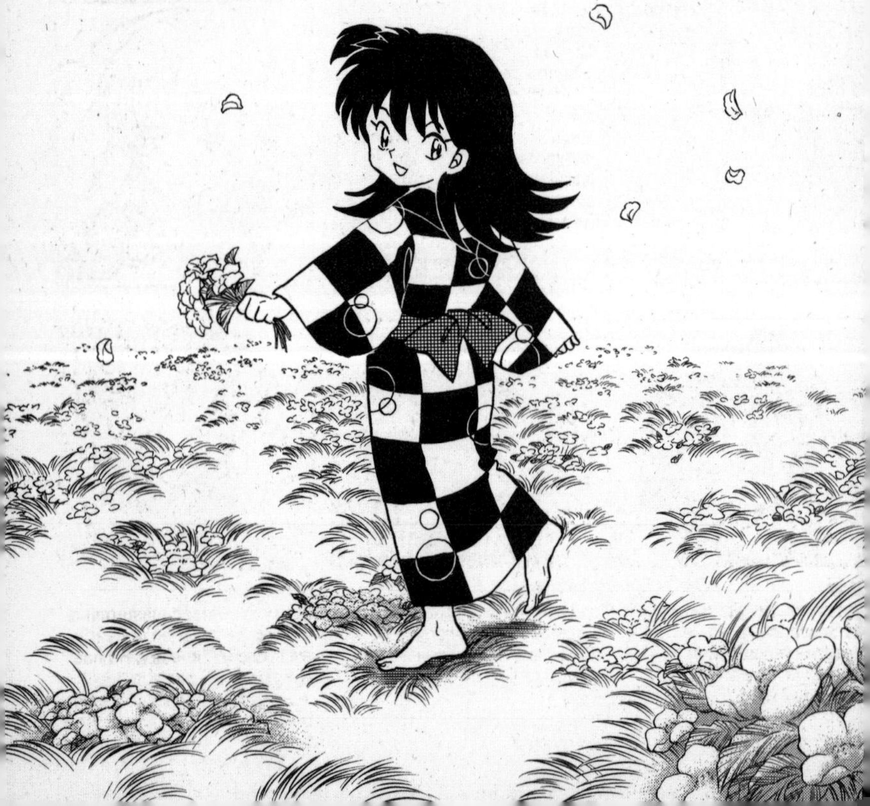

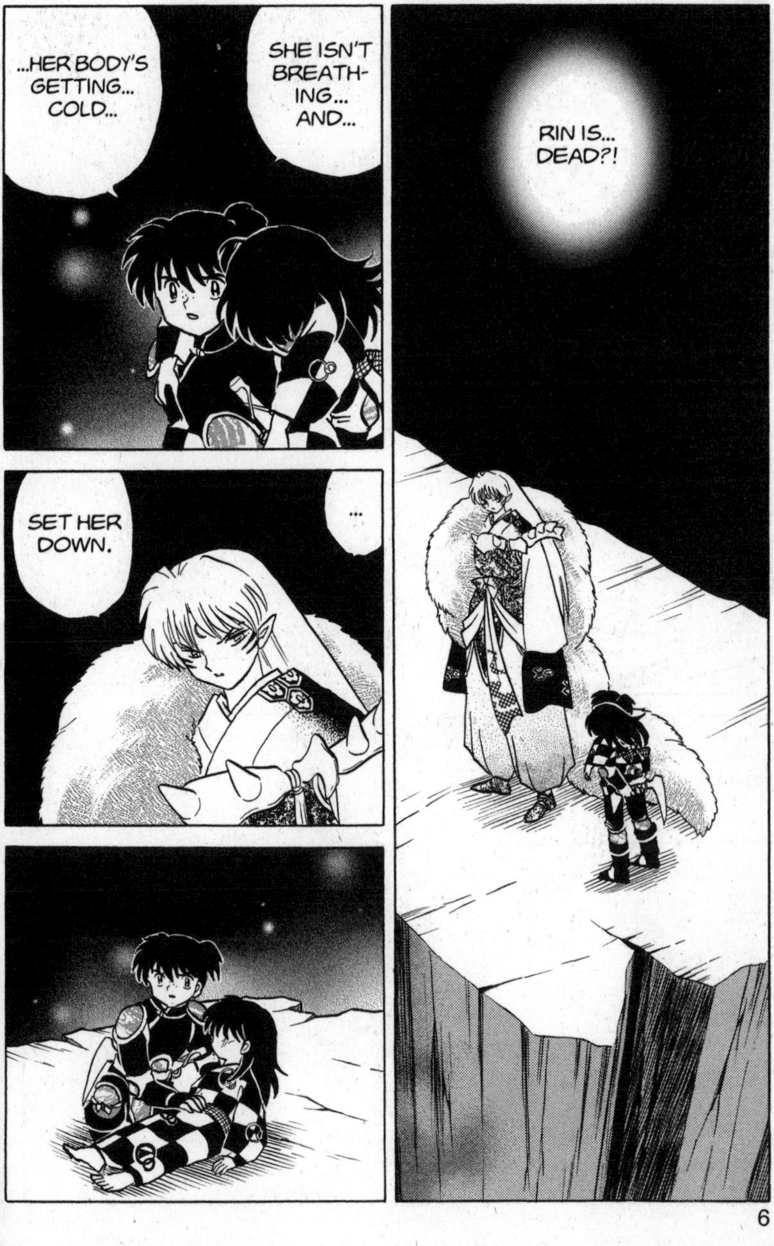
RIN IS... DEAD?!
SHE ISN'T BREATHING... AND...
...HER BODY'S GETTING... COLD...
...
SET HER DOWN.

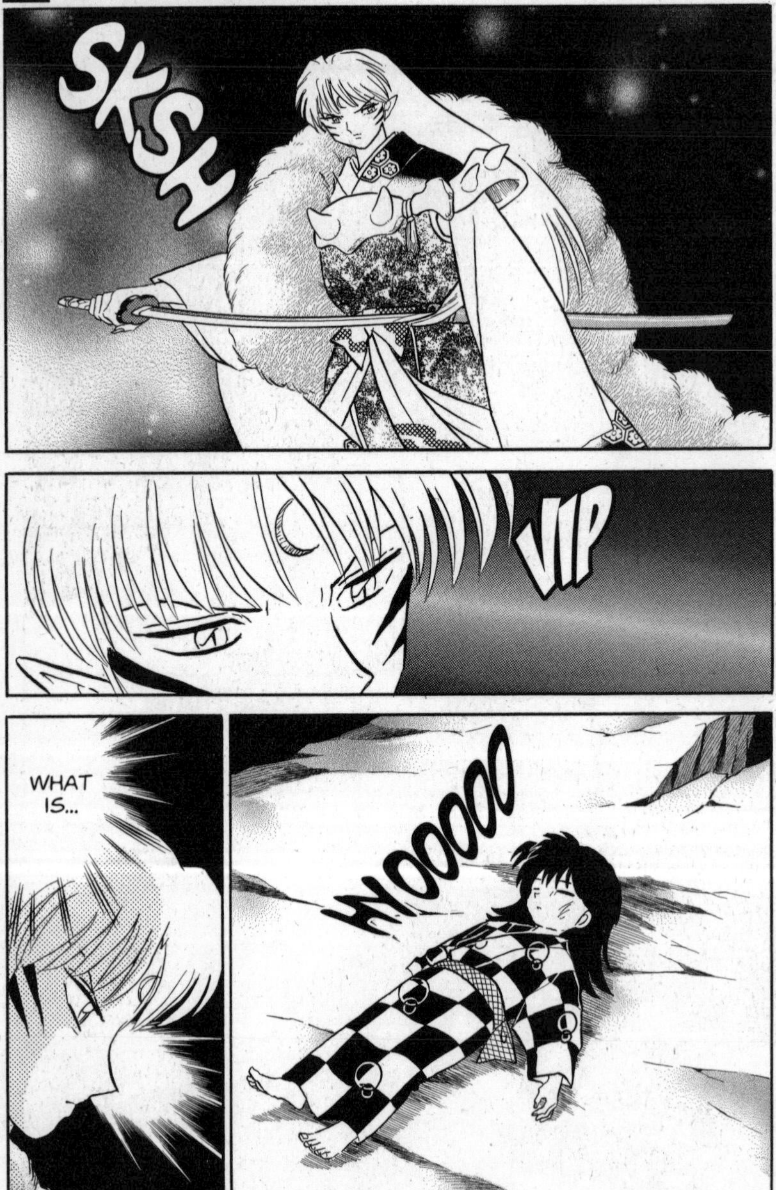
SKSH
VIP
HWOOOOO
WHAT IS...

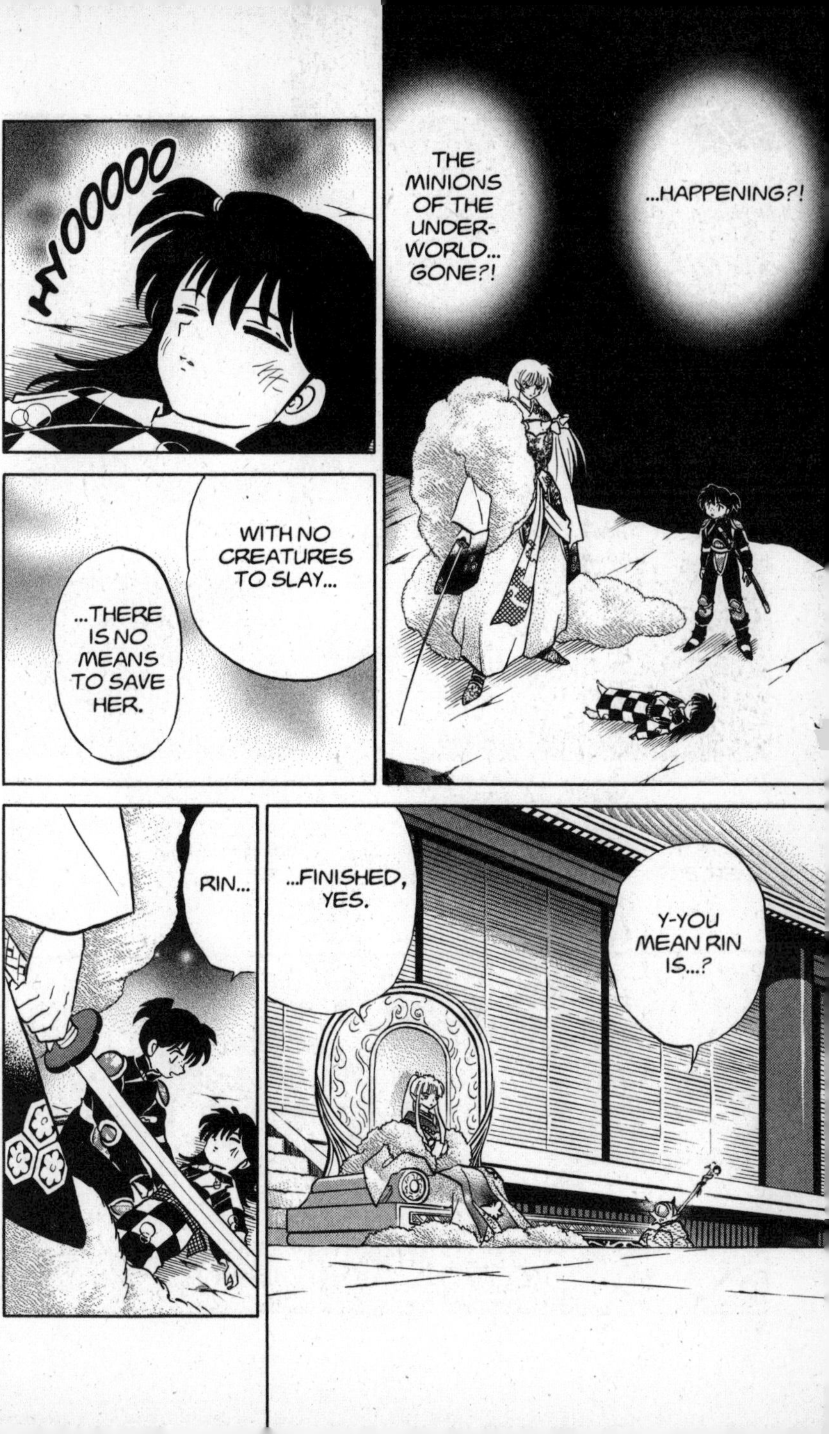
...HAPPENING?!
THE MINIONS OF THE UNDER-WORLD... GONE?!
HYOOOOO
WITH NO CREATURES TO SLAY...
...THERE IS NO MEANS TO SAVE HER.
Y-YOU MEAN RIN IS...?
...FINISHED, YES.
RIN...

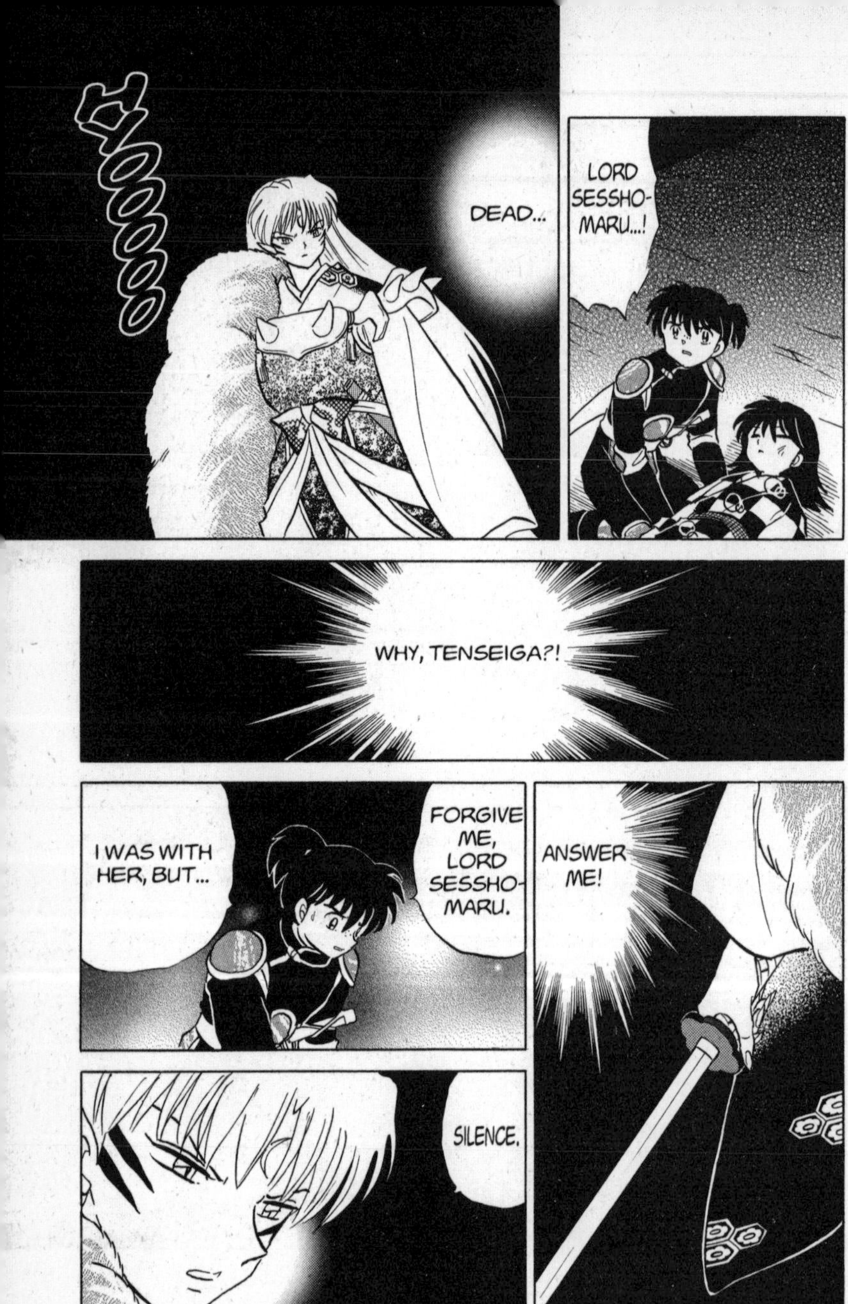
LORD SESSHOMARU...!
DEAD...
WHY, TENSEIGA?!
ANSWER ME!
FORGIVE ME, LORD SESSHOMARU.
I WAS WITH HER, BUT...
SILENCE.

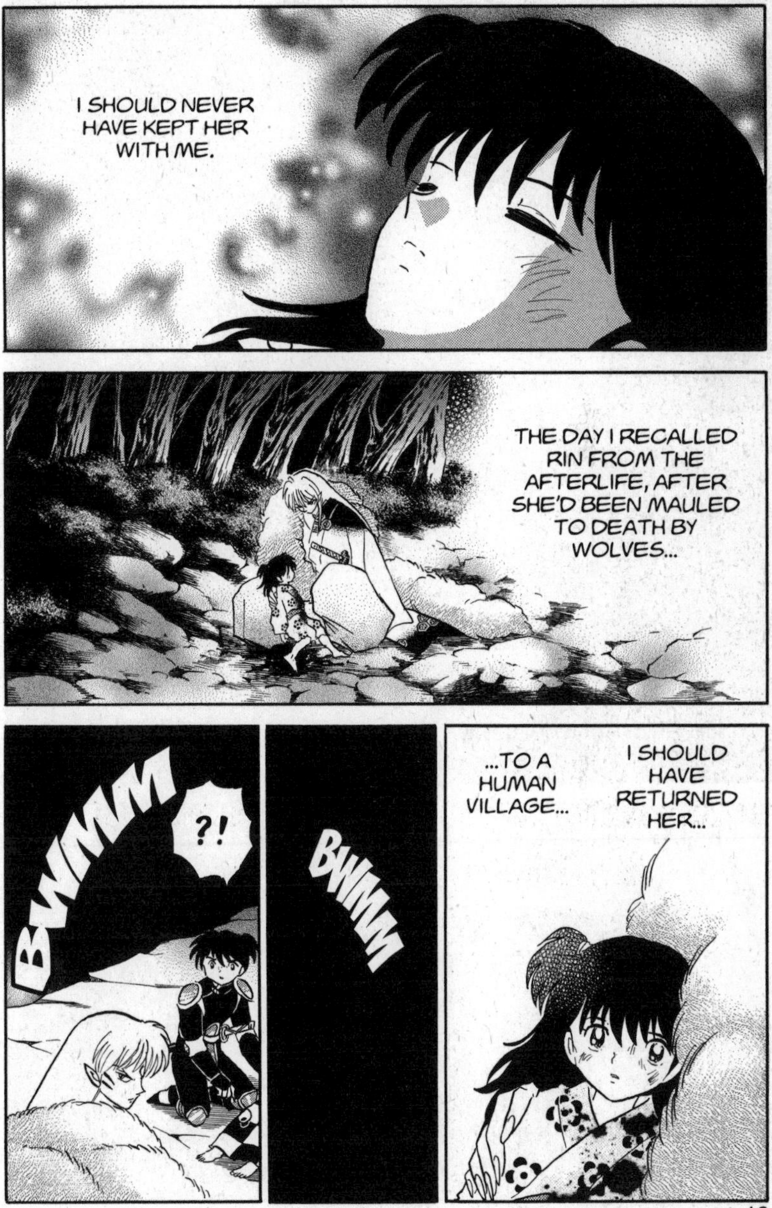
I SHOULD NEVER HAVE KEPT HER WITH ME.
THE DAY I RECALLED RIN FROM THE AFTERLIFE, AFTER SHE'D BEEN MAULED TO DEATH BY WOLVES...
I SHOULD HAVE RETURNED HER...
...TO A HUMAN VILLAGE...
BWMM
BWMM
?!

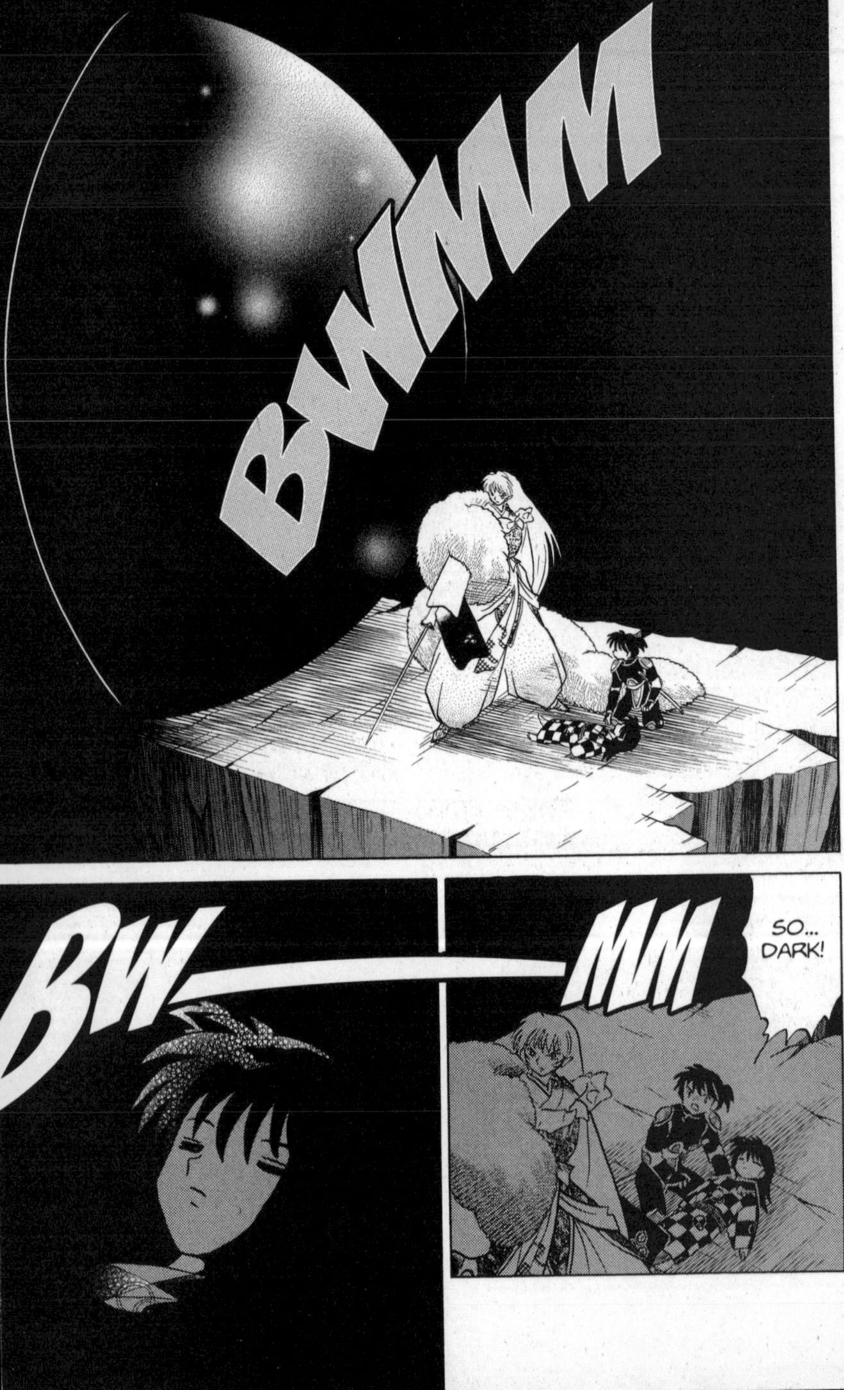
BWMMM
BW
MM
SO... DARK!

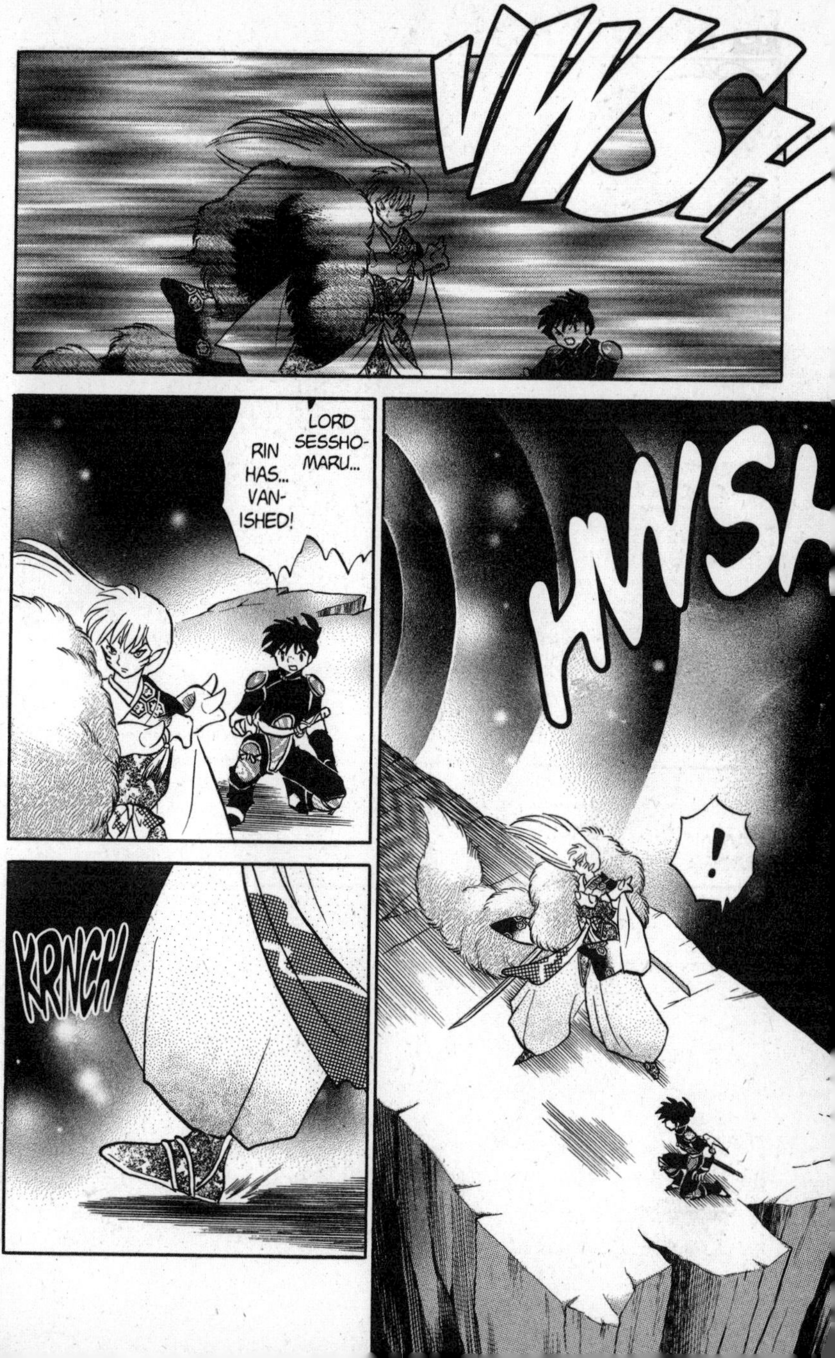
VWSH
HWSH
!
LORD SESSHO-MARU... RIN HAS... VAN-ISHED!
KRNCH

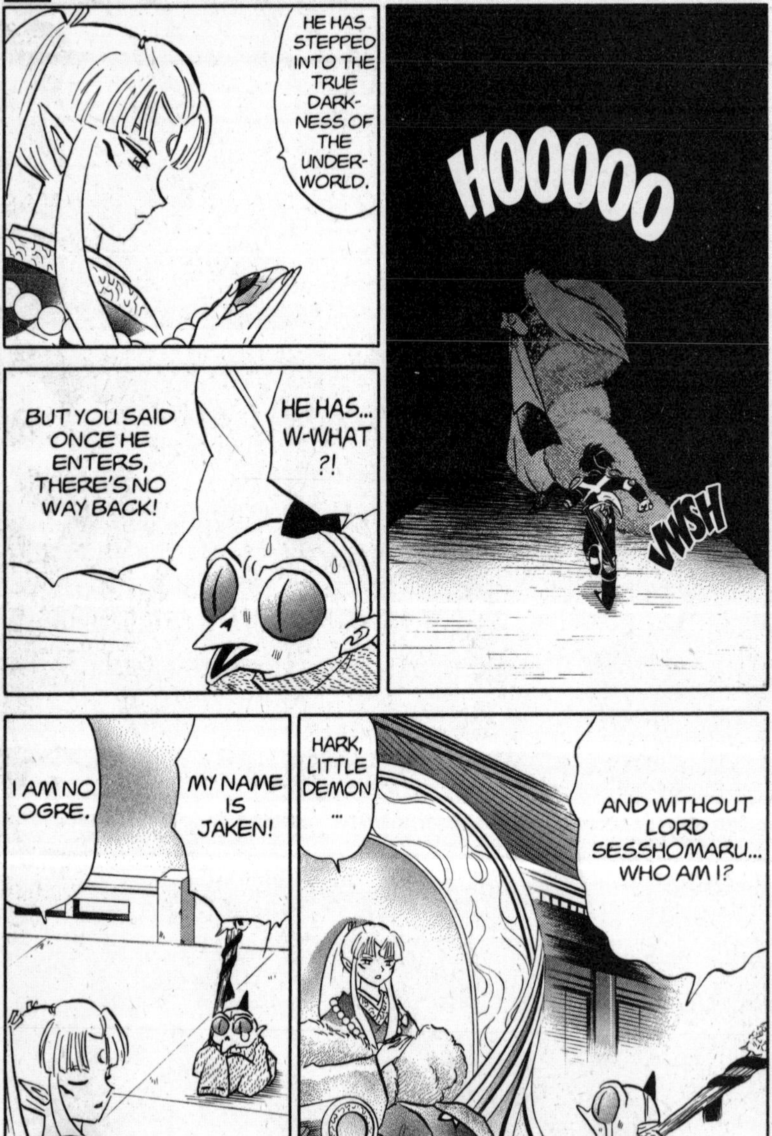
HOOOOO
VWSH
HE HAS STEPPED INTO THE TRUE DARKNESS OF THE UNDERWORLD.
HE HAS... W-WHAT?!
BUT YOU SAID ONCE HE ENTERS, THERE'S NO WAY BACK!
AND WITHOUT LORD SESSHOMARU... WHO AM I?
HARK, LITTLE DEMON...
MY NAME IS JAKEN!
I AM NO OGRE.

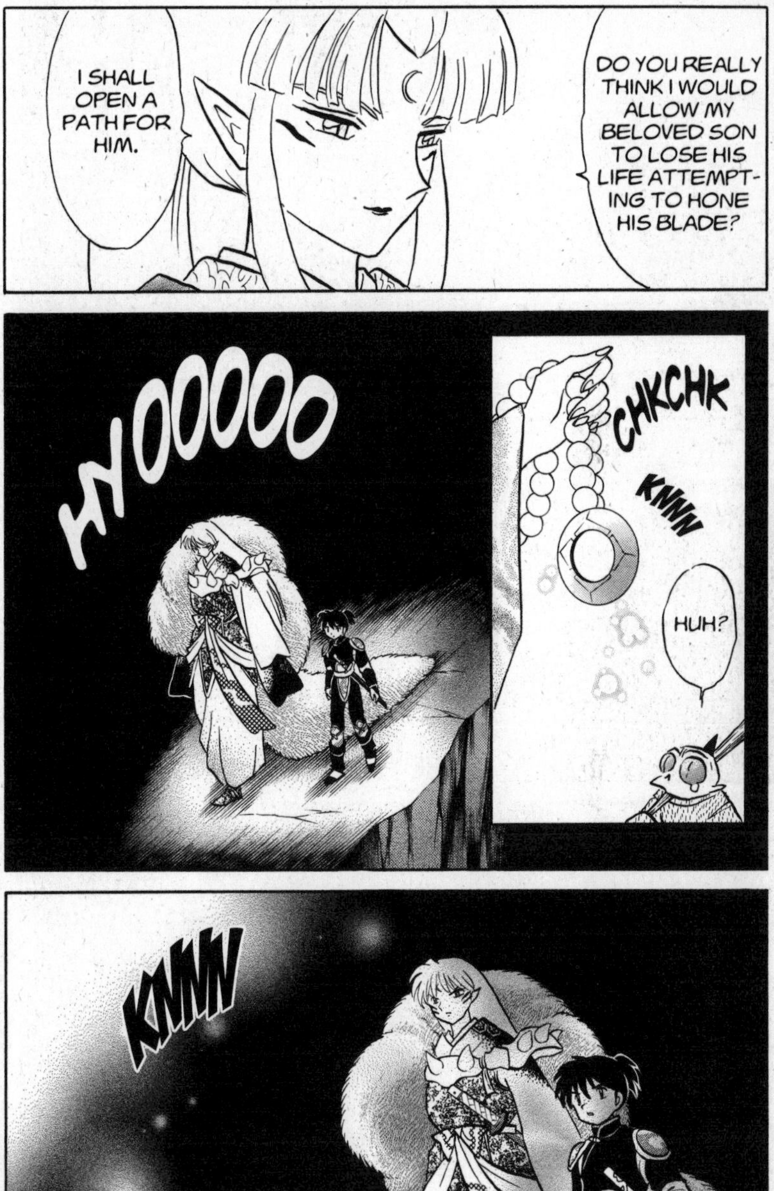
DO YOU REALLY THINK I WOULD ALLOW MY BELOVED SON TO LOSE HIS LIFE ATTEMPT-ING TO HONE HIS BLADE?
I SHALL OPEN A PATH FOR HIM.
CHKCHK
KNNN
HUH?
HYOOOOO
KNNN

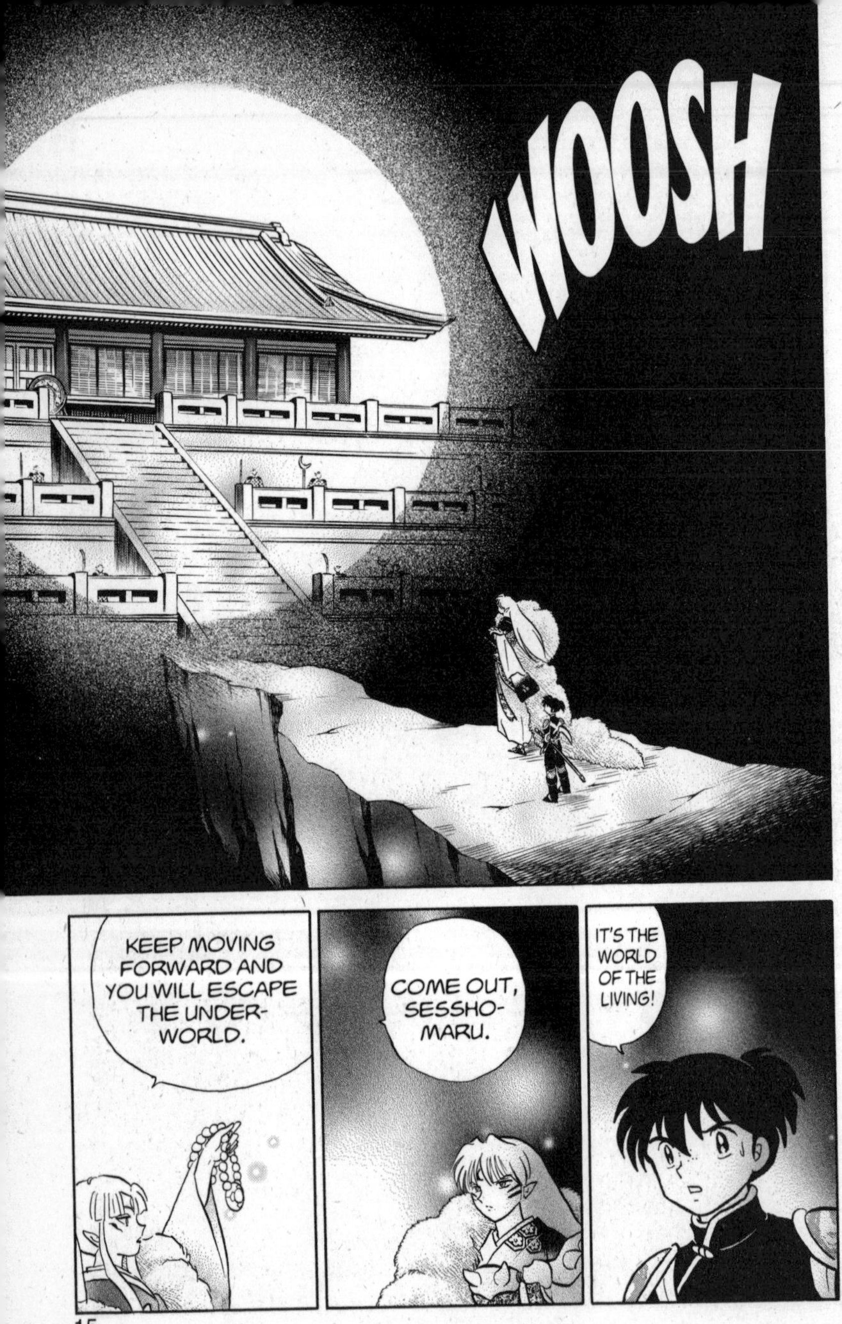
WOOSH
IT'S THE WORLD OF THE LIVING!
COME OUT, SESSHO-MARU.
KEEP MOVING FORWARD AND YOU WILL ESCAPE THE UNDER-WORLD.

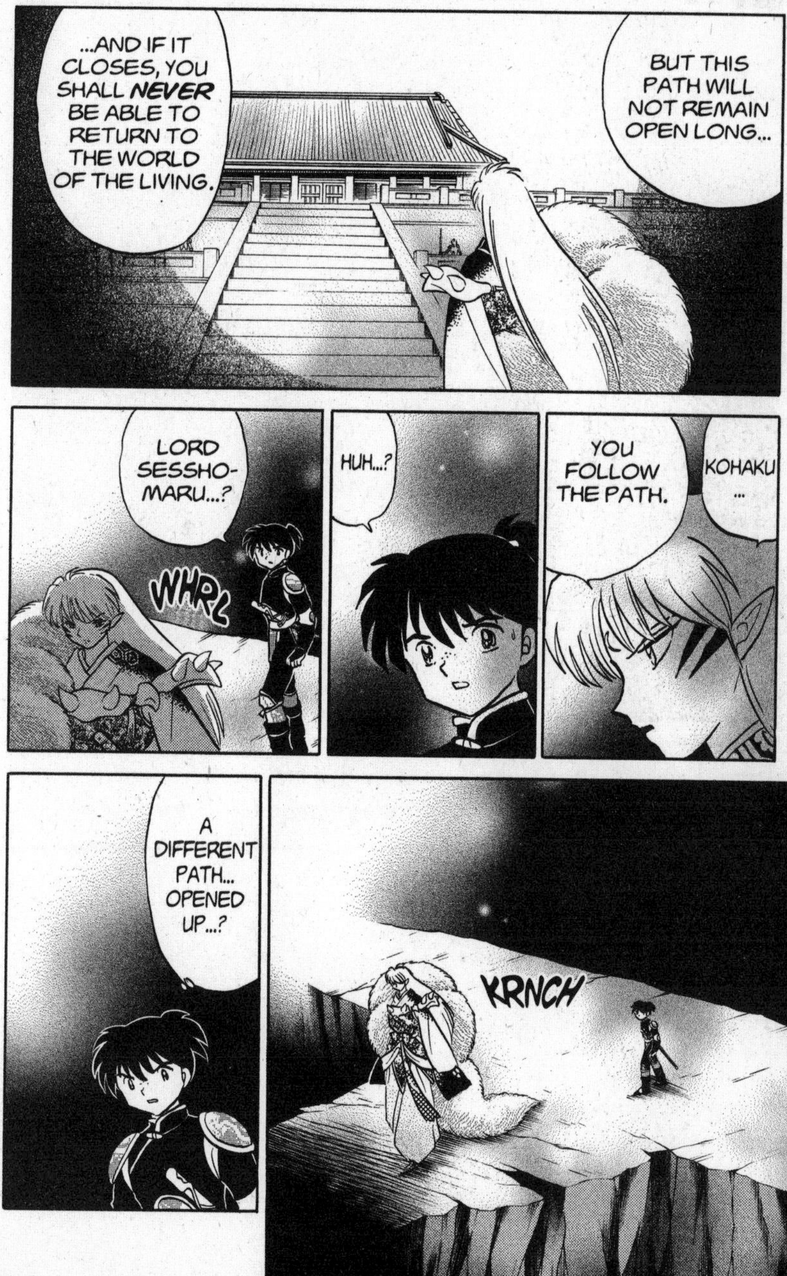
BUT THIS PATH WILL NOT REMAIN OPEN LONG...
...AND IF IT CLOSES, YOU SHALL NEVER BE ABLE TO RETURN TO THE WORLD OF THE LIVING.
KOHAKU...
YOU FOLLOW THE PATH.
HUH...?
LORD SESSHO-MARU...?
WHRL
KRNCH
A DIFFERENT PATH... OPENED UP...?

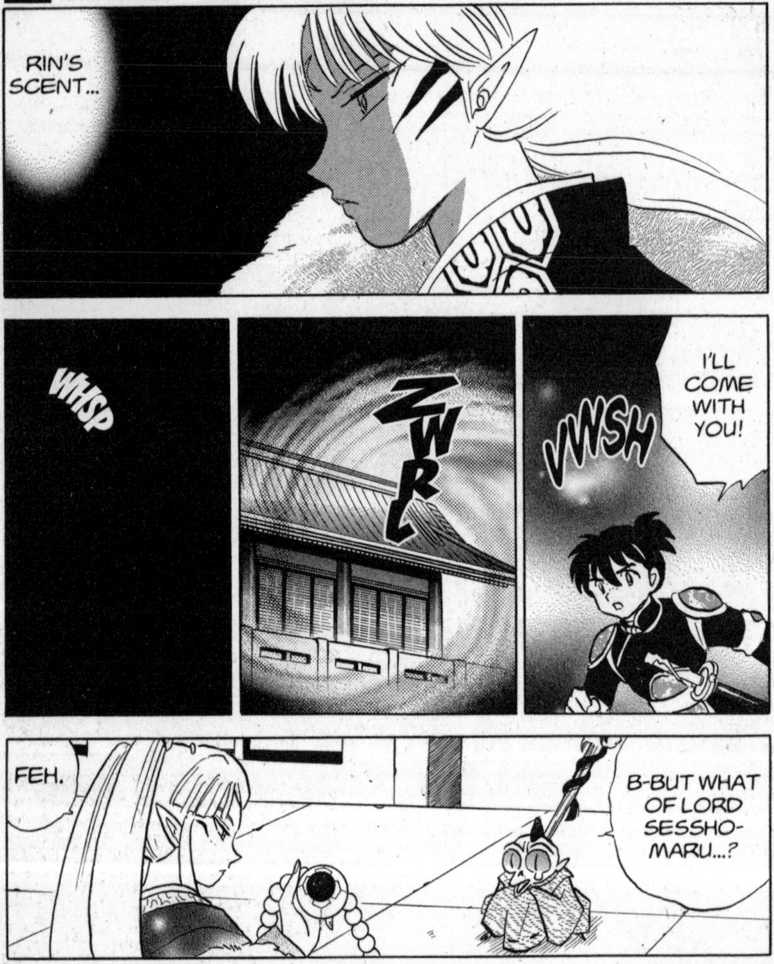
RIN'S SCENT...
I'LL COME WITH YOU!
VWSH
ZWRL
WHSP
B-BUT WHAT OF LORD SESSHO-MARU...?
FEH.
WHO CARES?
UNGRATEFUL PUP.
CHK CHK
WHAT?!

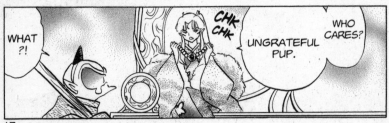

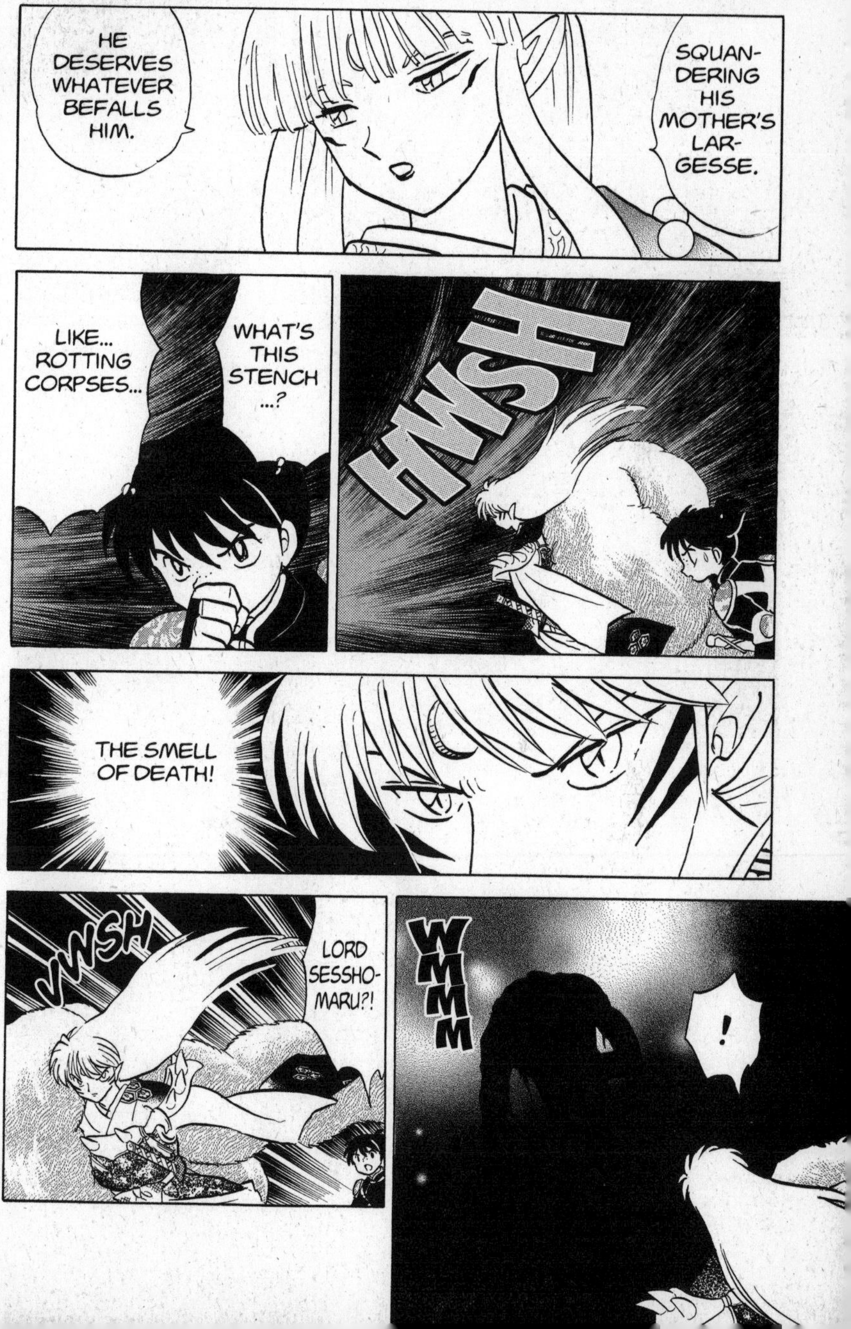
SQUANDERING HIS MOTHER'S LARGESSE.
HE DESERVES WHATEVER BEFALLS HIM.
HWSH!
WHAT'S THIS STENCH ...?
LIKE... ROTTING CORPSES...
THE SMELL OF DEATH!
WMMM
!
LORD SESSHOMARU?!
VWSH

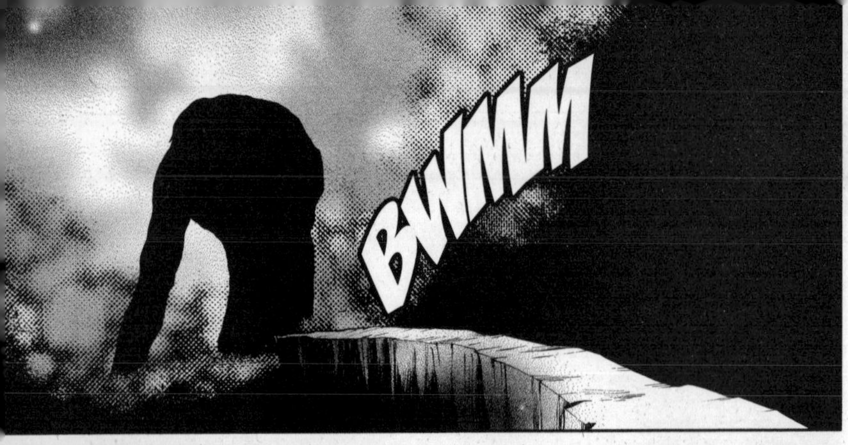
BWMM
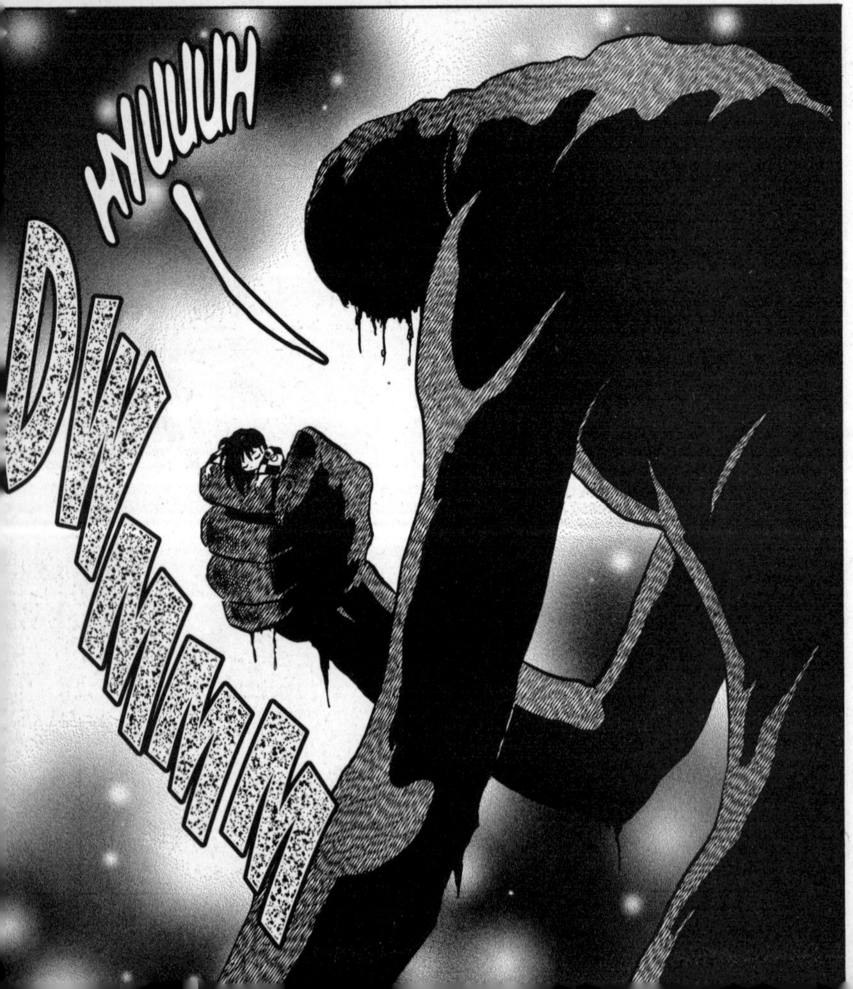
HYUUUH
DWMMMM

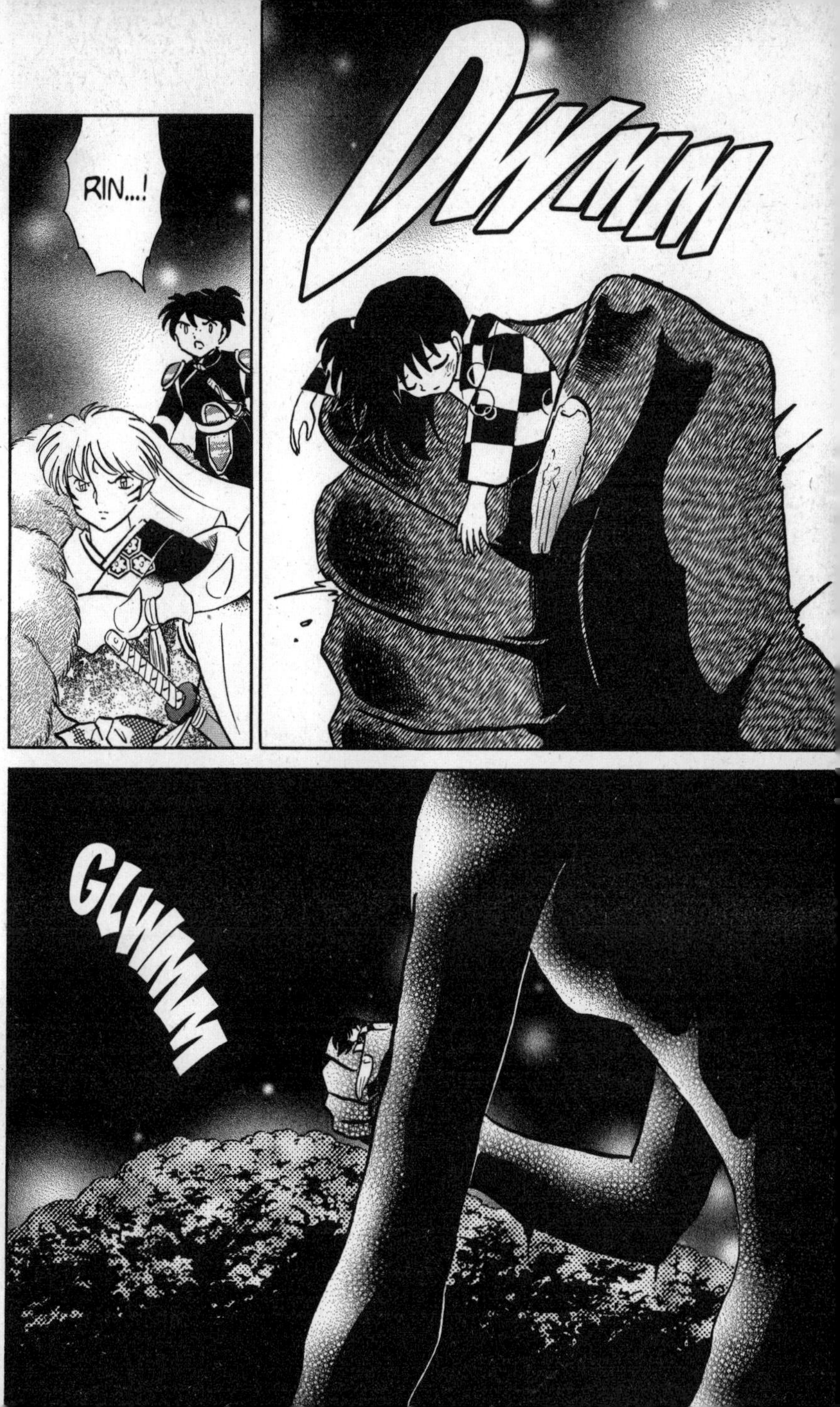
DWMM
RIN...!
GLWMMM

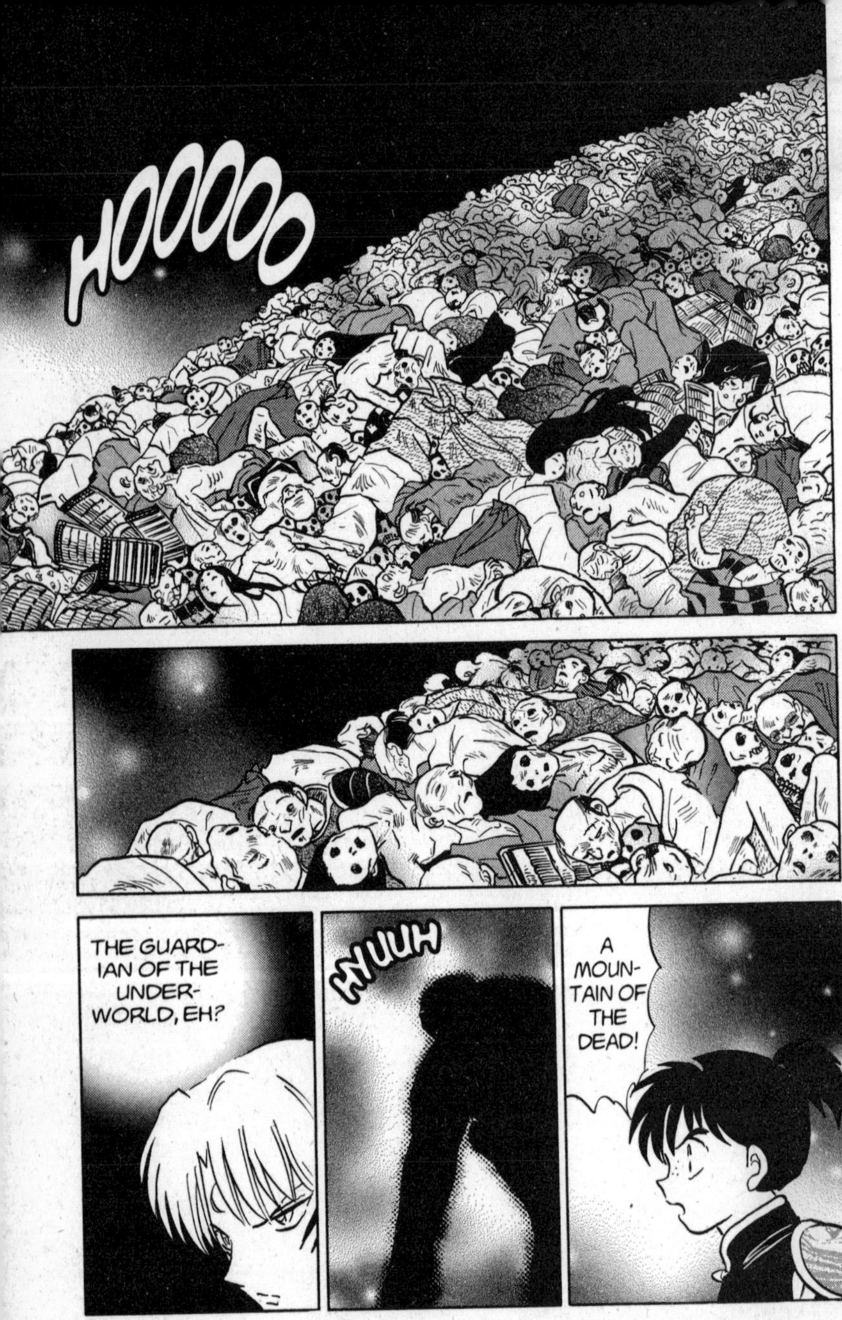
HOOOOO
A MOUN-TAIN OF THE DEAD!
HYUUH
THE GUARD-IAN OF THE UNDER-WORLD, EH?

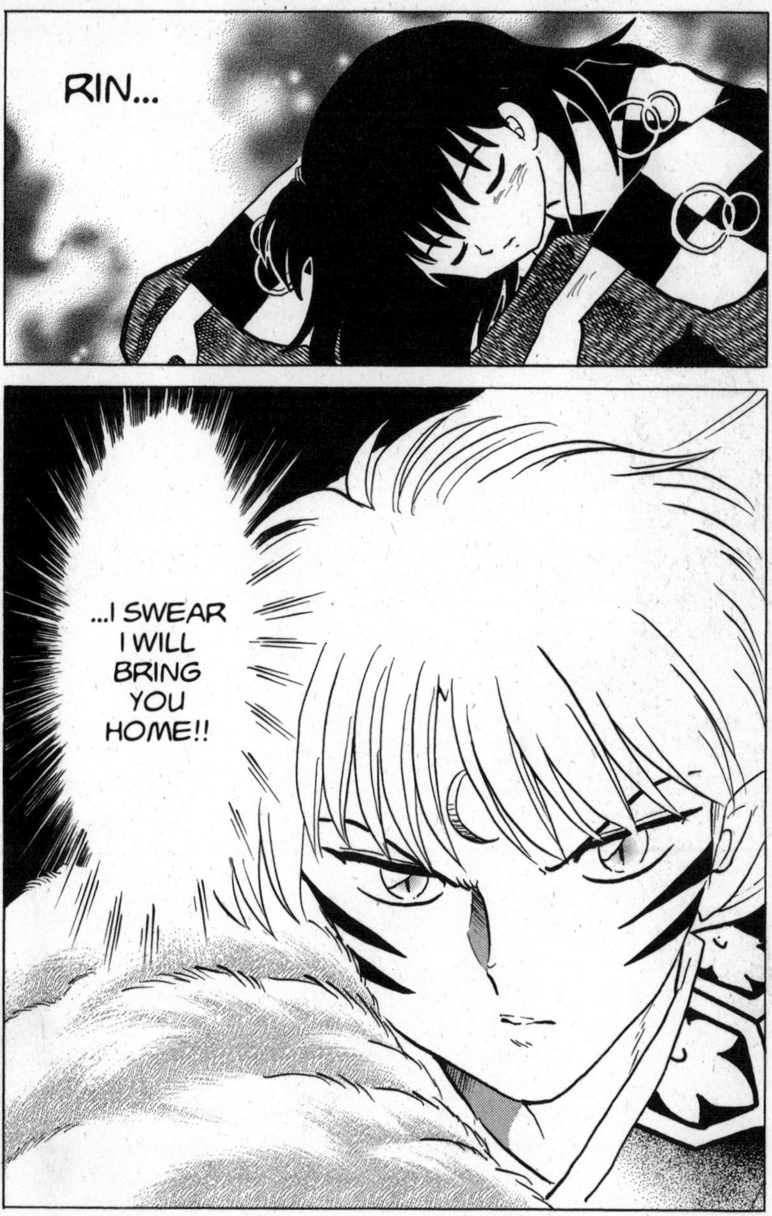
RIN...
...I SWEAR I WILL BRING YOU HOME!!

SCROLL 2

THE RETURN

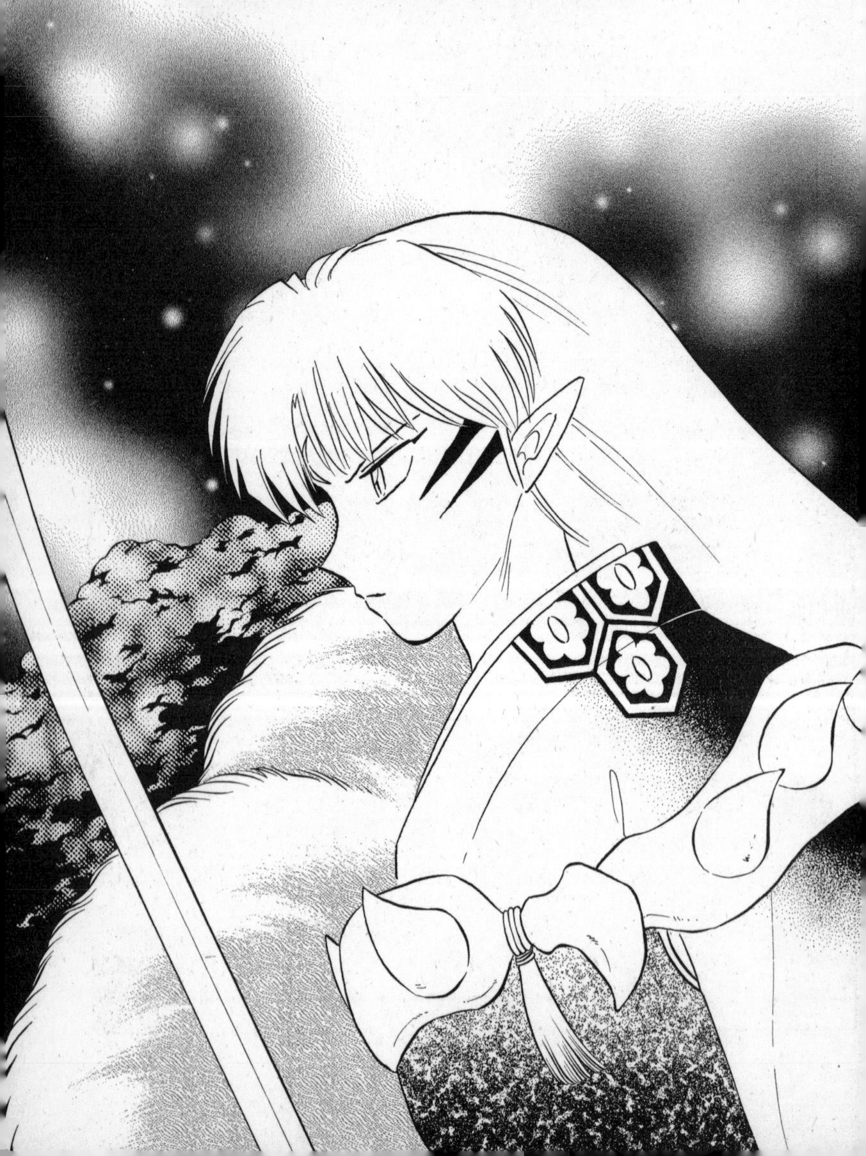

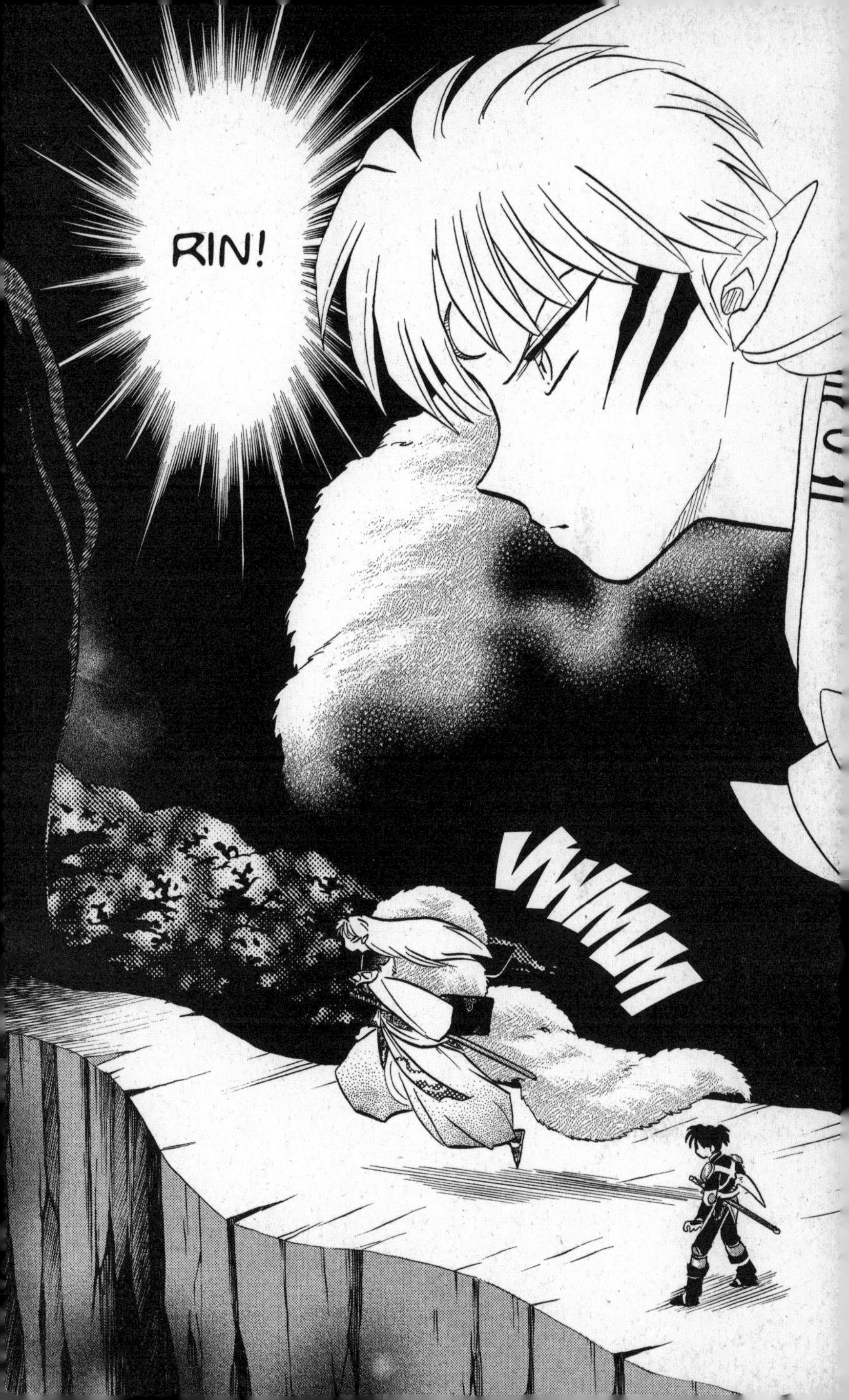
RIN!
VWMM

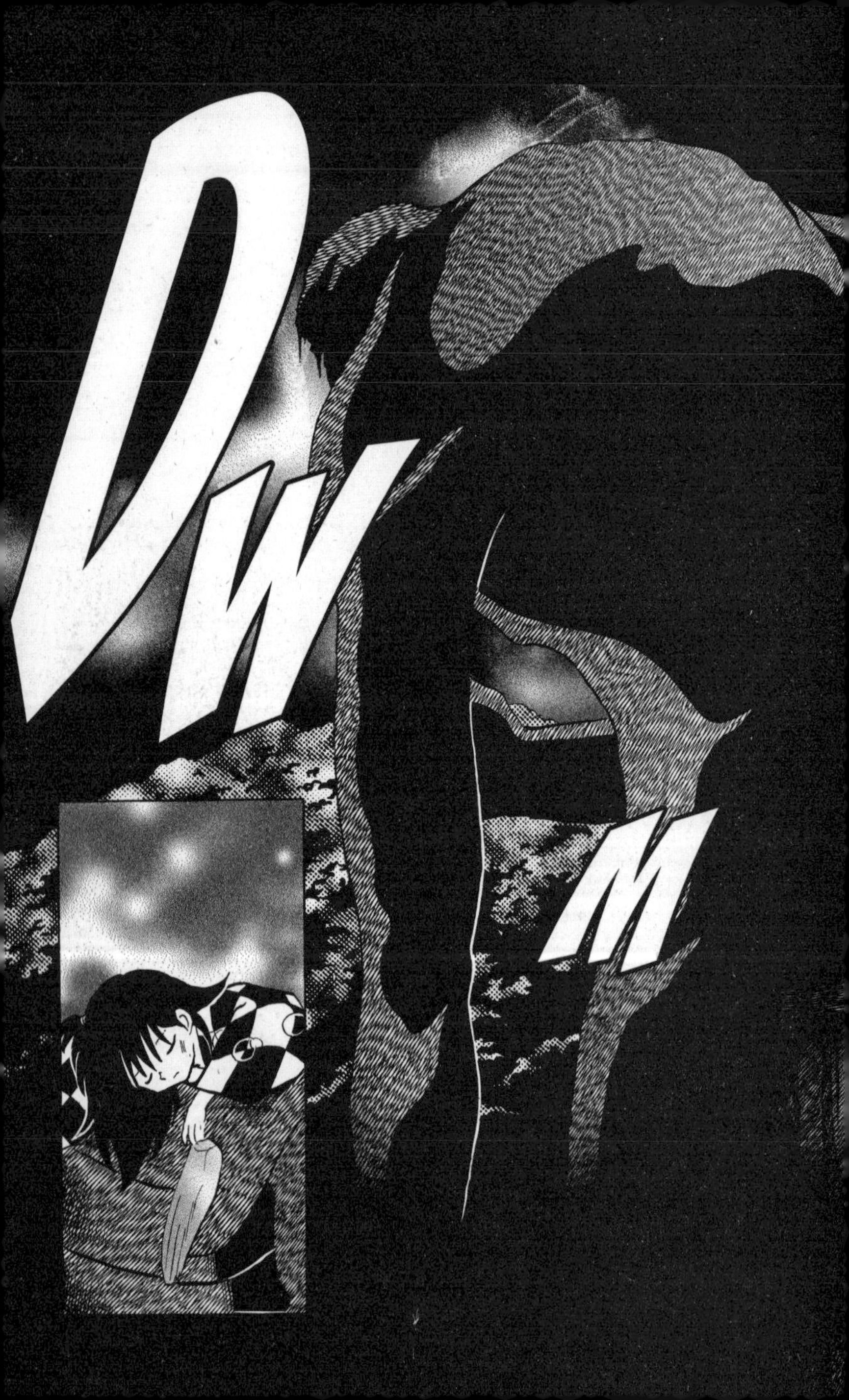
DWM

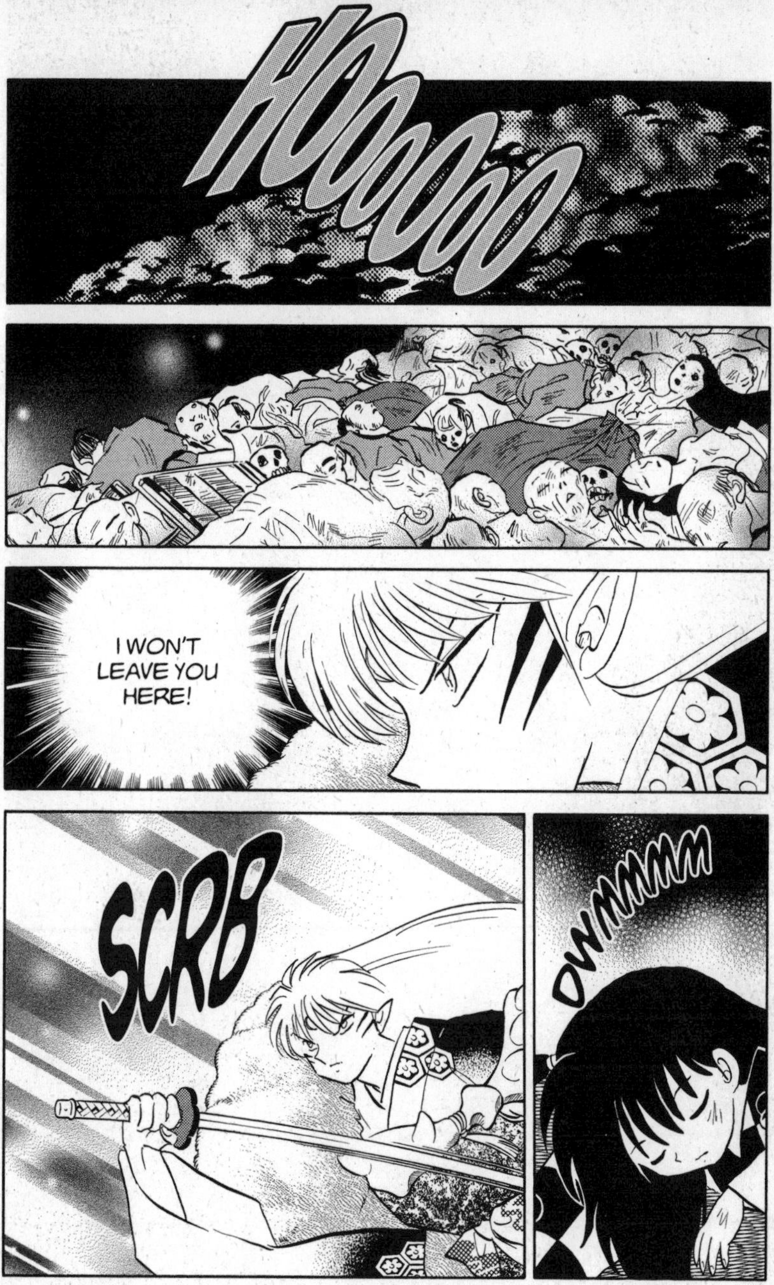
HOOOOOO
I WON'T LEAVE YOU HERE!
DWMMMMM
SCRB

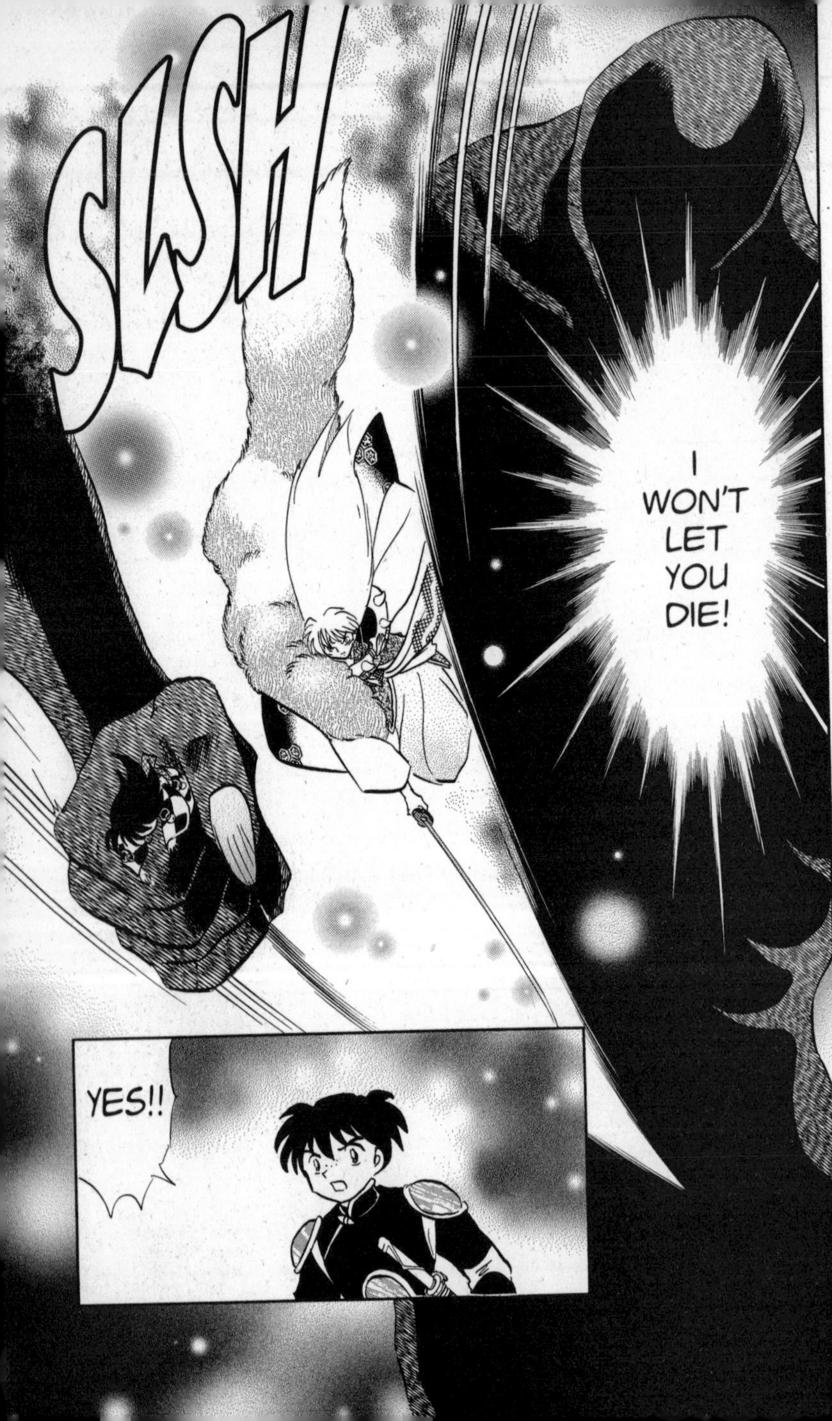
SLSH
I WON'T LET YOU DIE!
YES!!

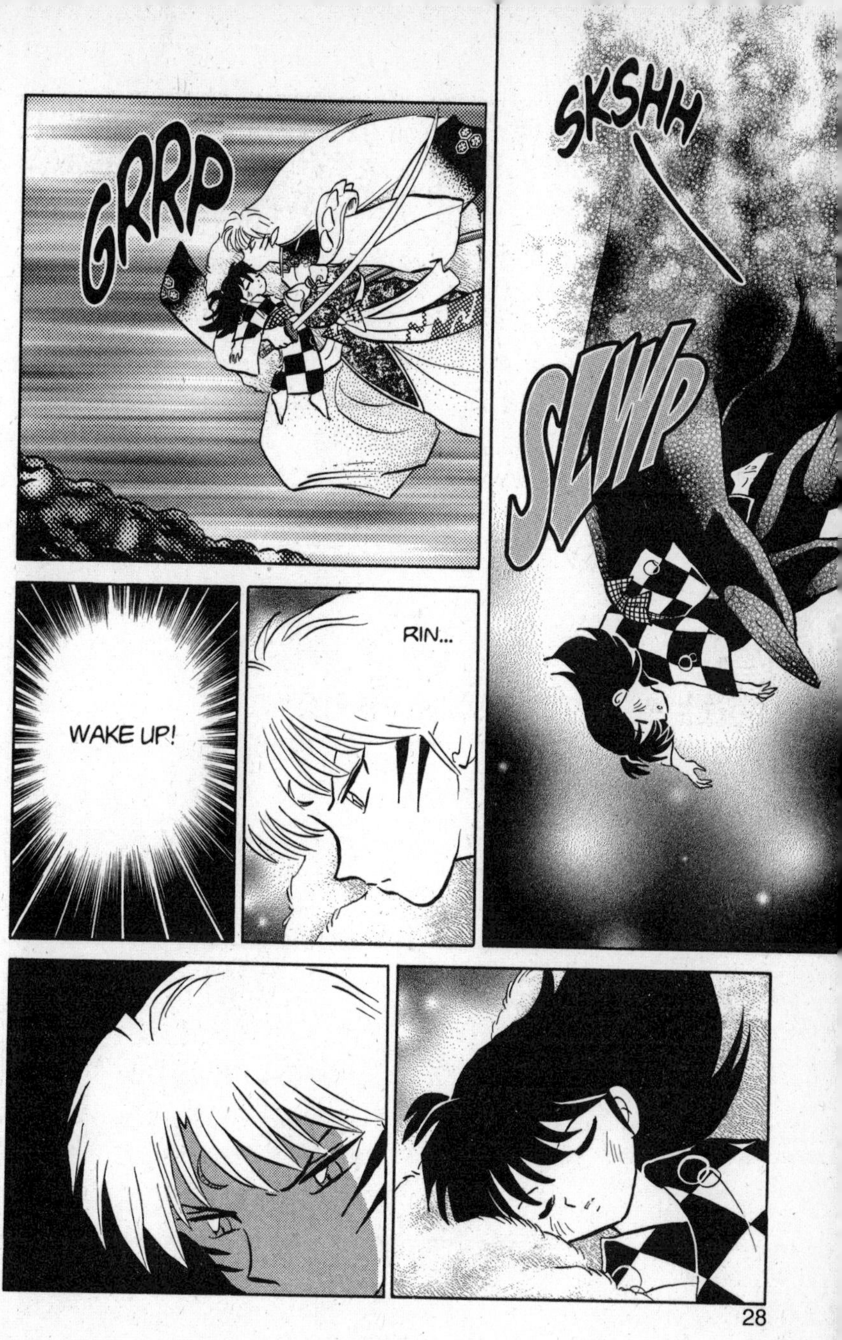
SKSHH
SLWP
GRRP
RIN...
WAKE UP!

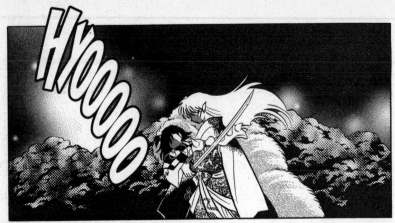

HYOOOOO
THAT'S ODD...
SESSHOMARU CUT DOWN THE GUARDIAN OF THE UNDER-WORLD... BUT THE HUMAN PUP HASN'T COME BACK TO LIFE.
LITTLE DEMON...
MY NAME IS JAKEN!
YOU REFUSE TO REMEM-BER THAT, HUH?
THAT GIRL-PUP...
...WAS SHE... BY ANY CHANCE... RESUR-RECTED BY TENSEIGA BEFORE?
EH?!
WELL... YES! WHAT OF IT?

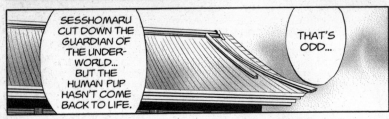

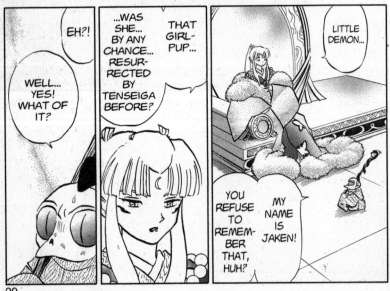

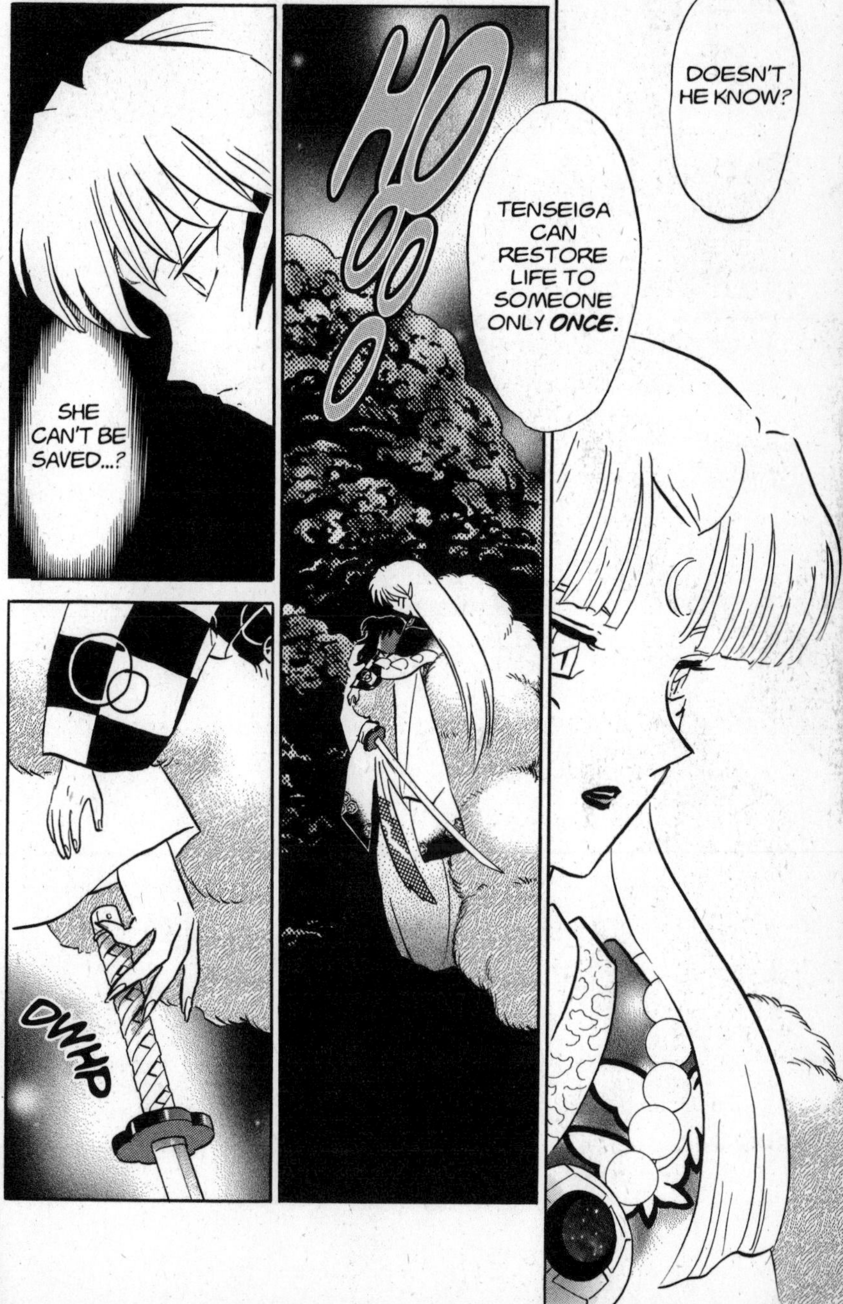
DOESN'T HE KNOW?
TENSEIGA CAN RESTORE LIFE TO SOMEONE ONLY ONCE.
SHE CAN'T BE SAVED...?
DWHP

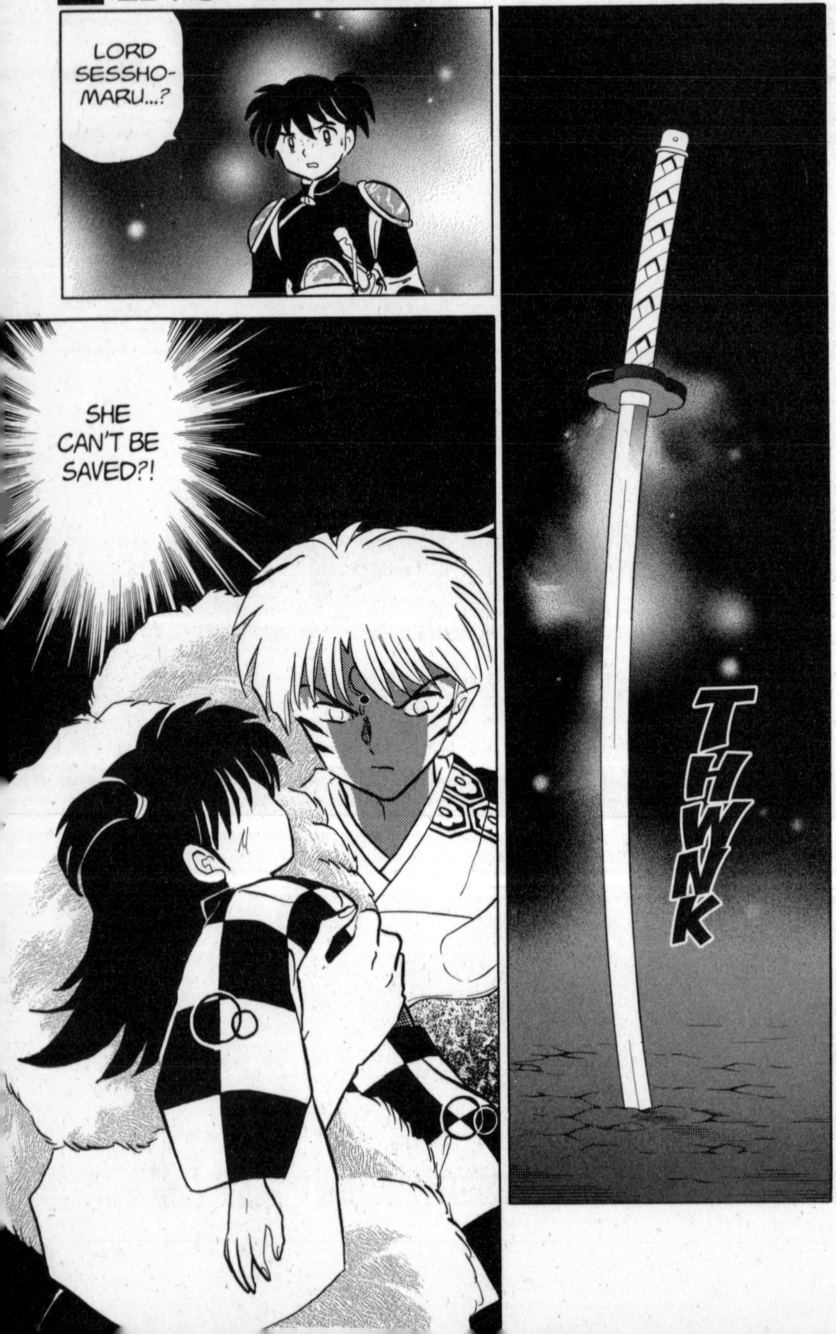
THWNK
LORD SESSHOMARU...?
SHE CAN'T BE SAVED?!

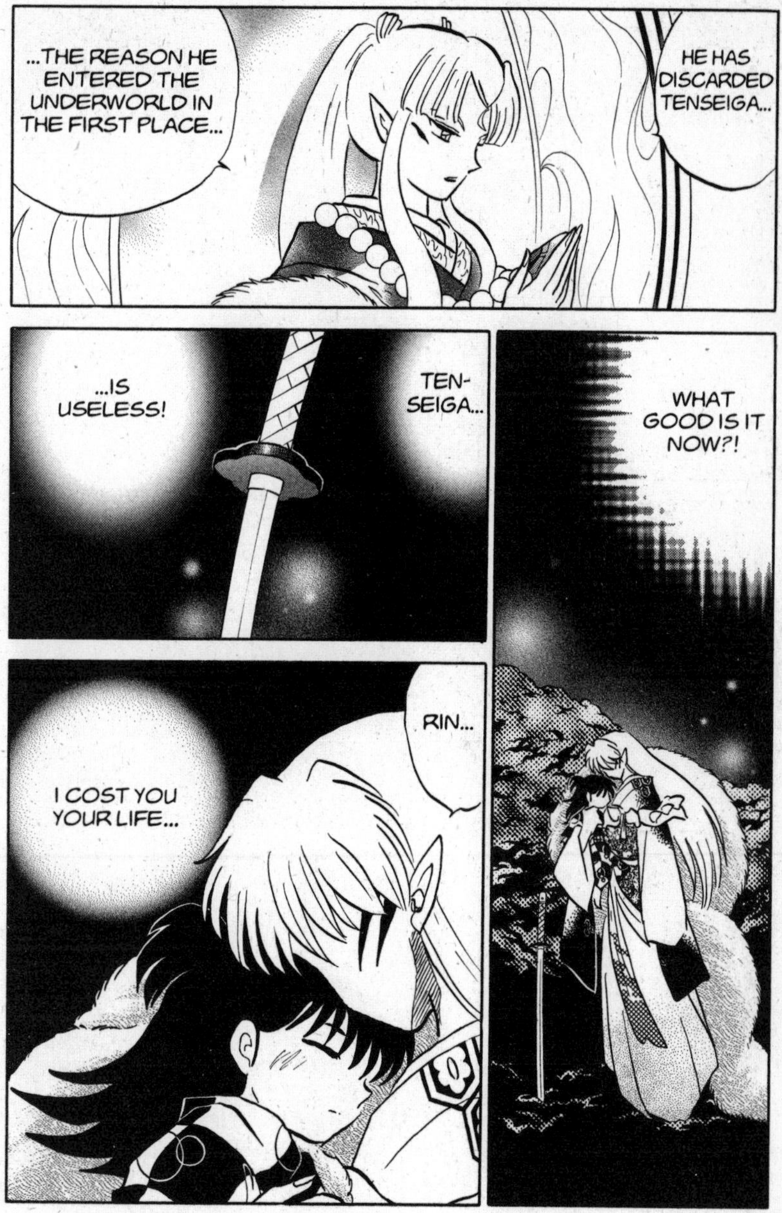
HE HAS DISCARDED TENSEIGA...
...THE REASON HE ENTERED THE UNDERWORLD IN THE FIRST PLACE...
WHAT GOOD IS IT NOW?!
TEN-SEIGA...
...IS USELESS!
RIN...
I COST YOU YOUR LIFE...

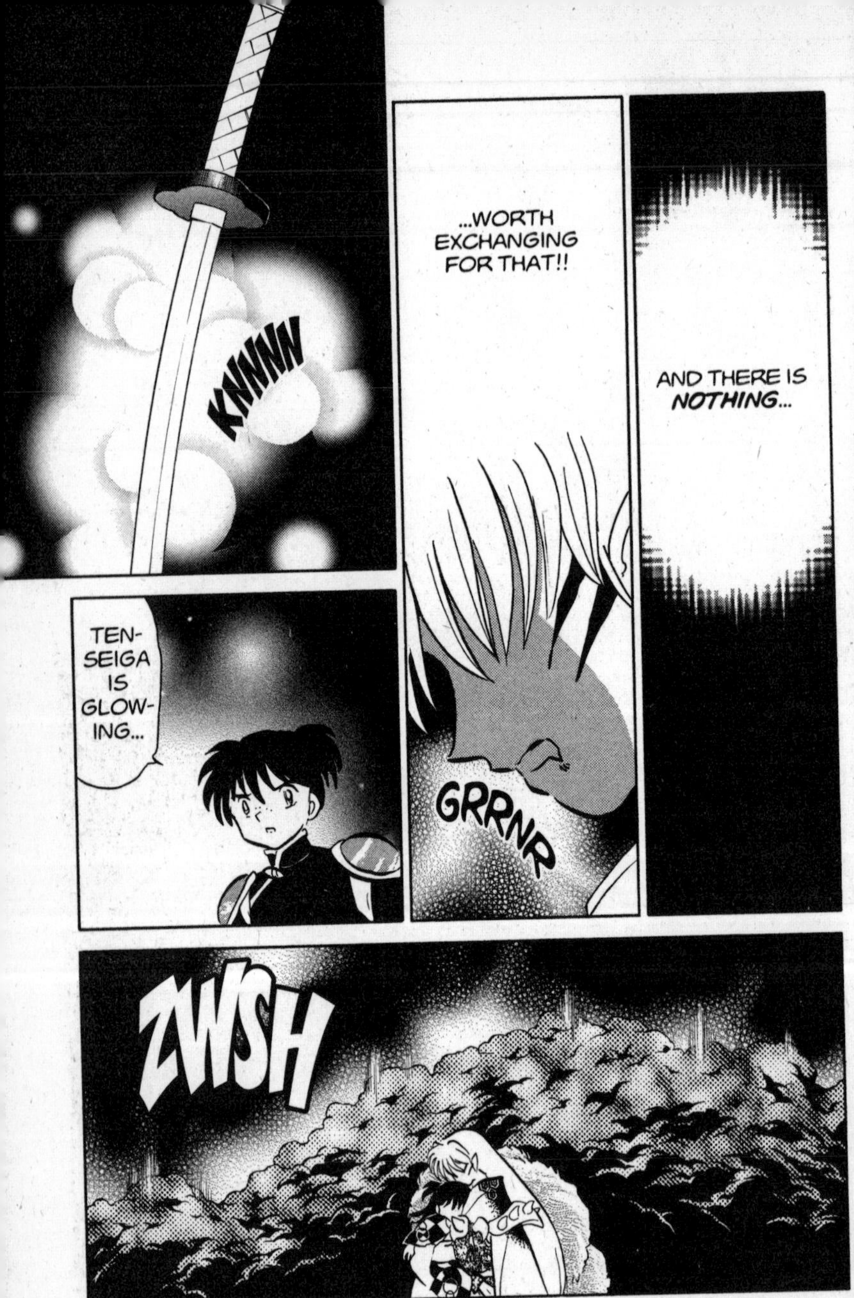
AND THERE IS *NOTHING*...
...WORTH EXCHANGING FOR THAT!!
GRRNR
KNNNN
TEN-SEIGA IS GLOWING...
ZWSH

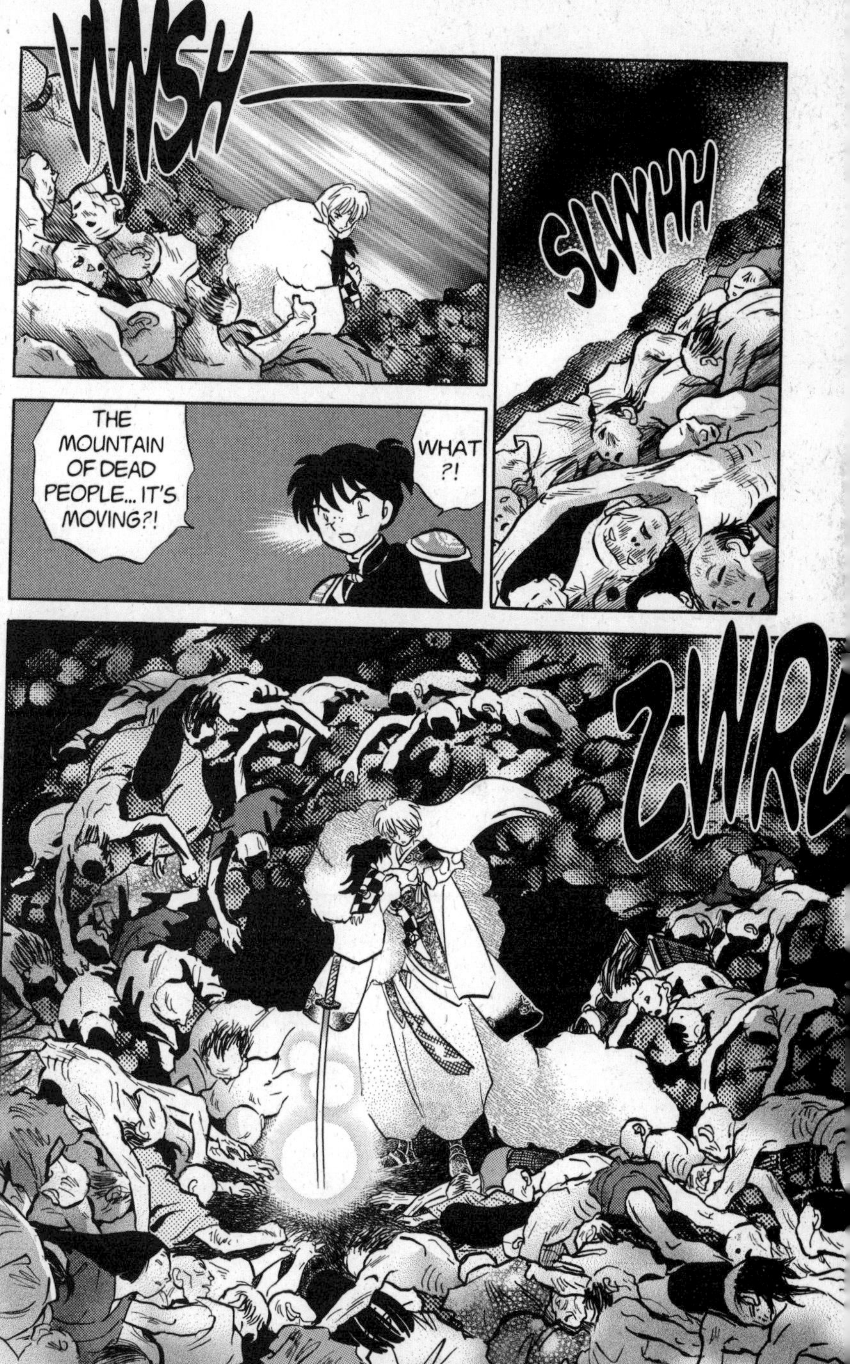
SLWHH
VWSH—
WHAT ?!
THE MOUNTAIN OF DEAD PEOPLE... IT'S MOVING?!
ZWRL

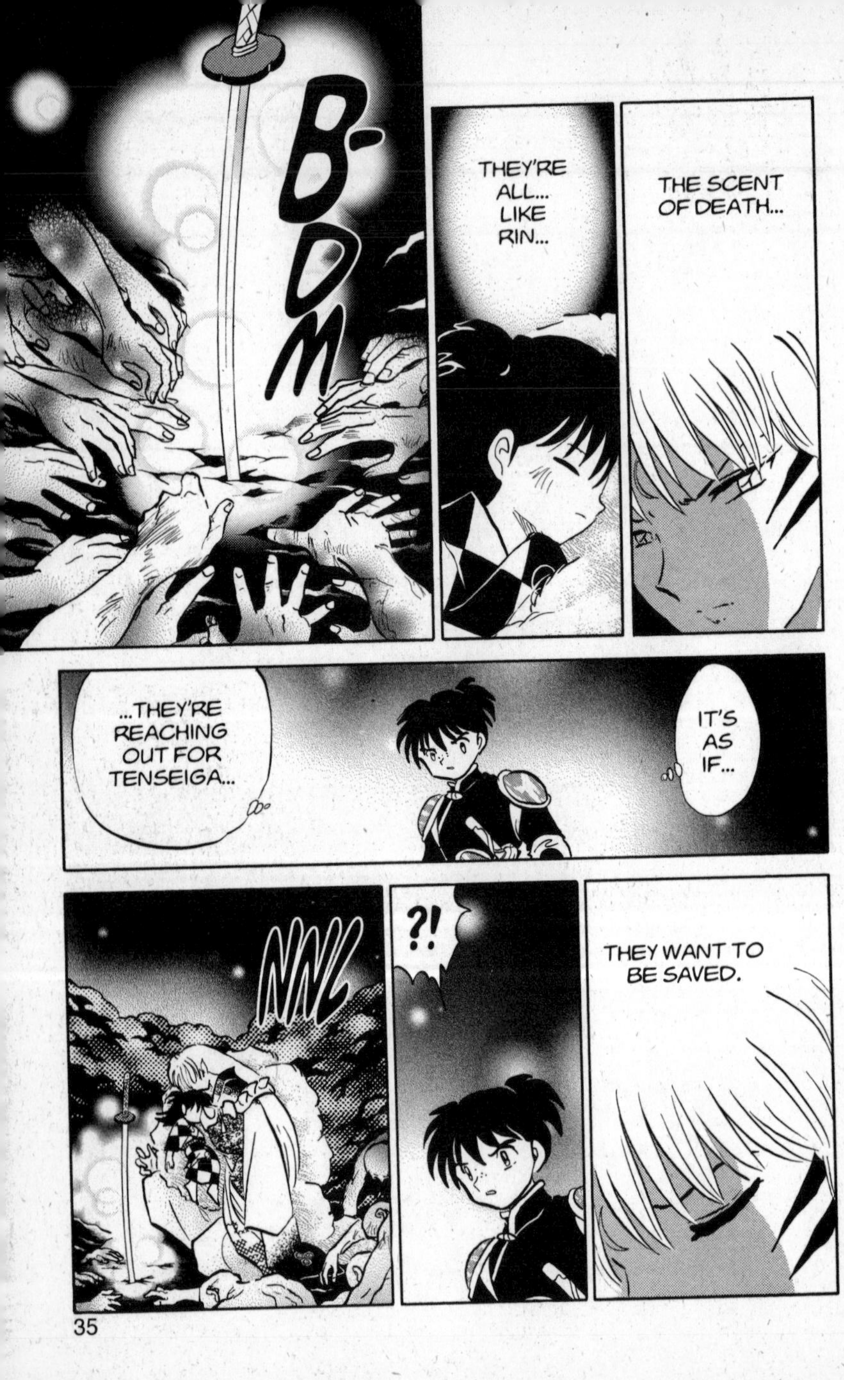
THE SCENT OF DEATH...
THEY'RE ALL... LIKE RIN...
B-DM
IT'S AS IF...
...THEY'RE REACHING OUT FOR TENSEIGA...
THEY WANT TO BE SAVED.
?!
NNL

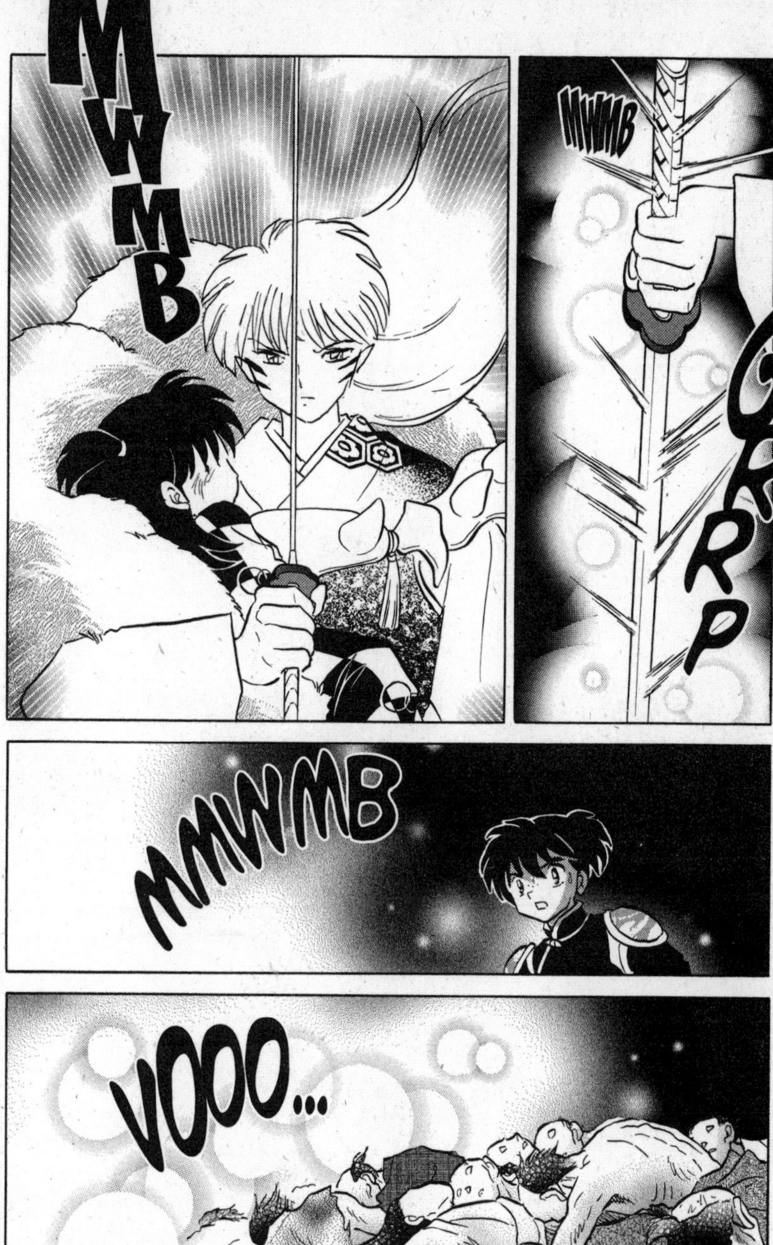
MWMB
GRRP
MWMB
MMWMB
VOOO...

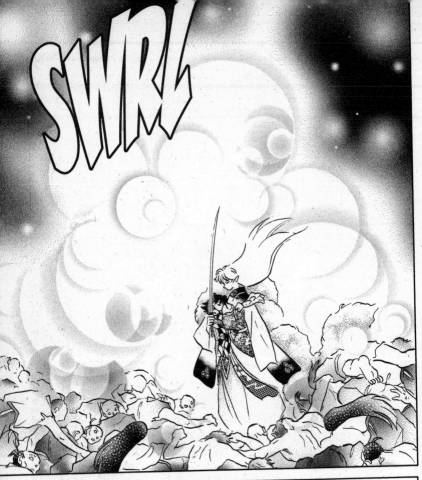

THE DEAD
OF THE
UNDER-
WORLD
ARE BEING
LAID TO
REST.

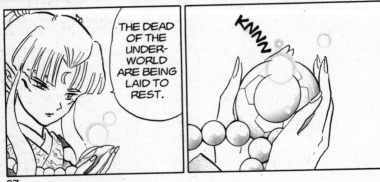

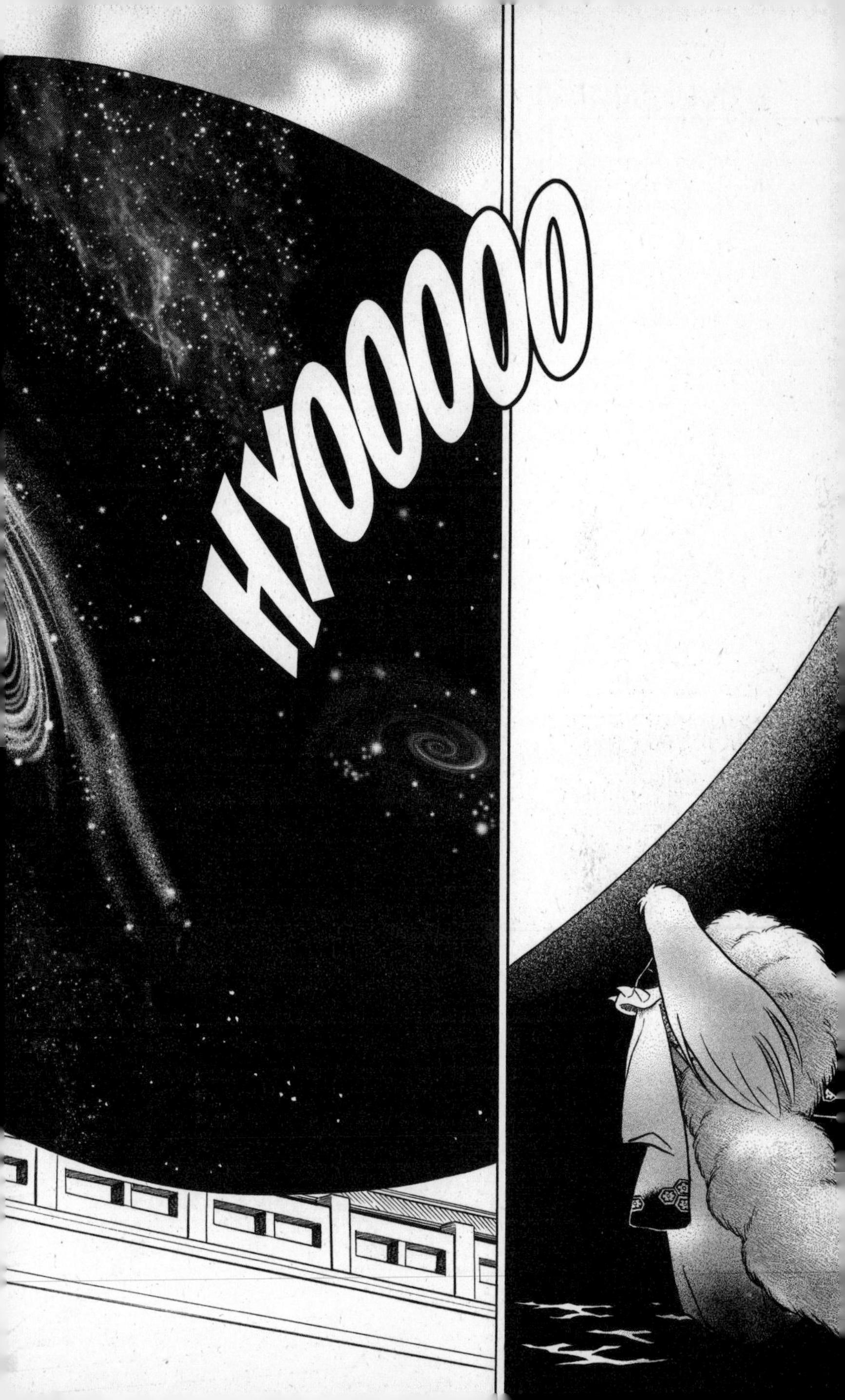
HYOOOOO

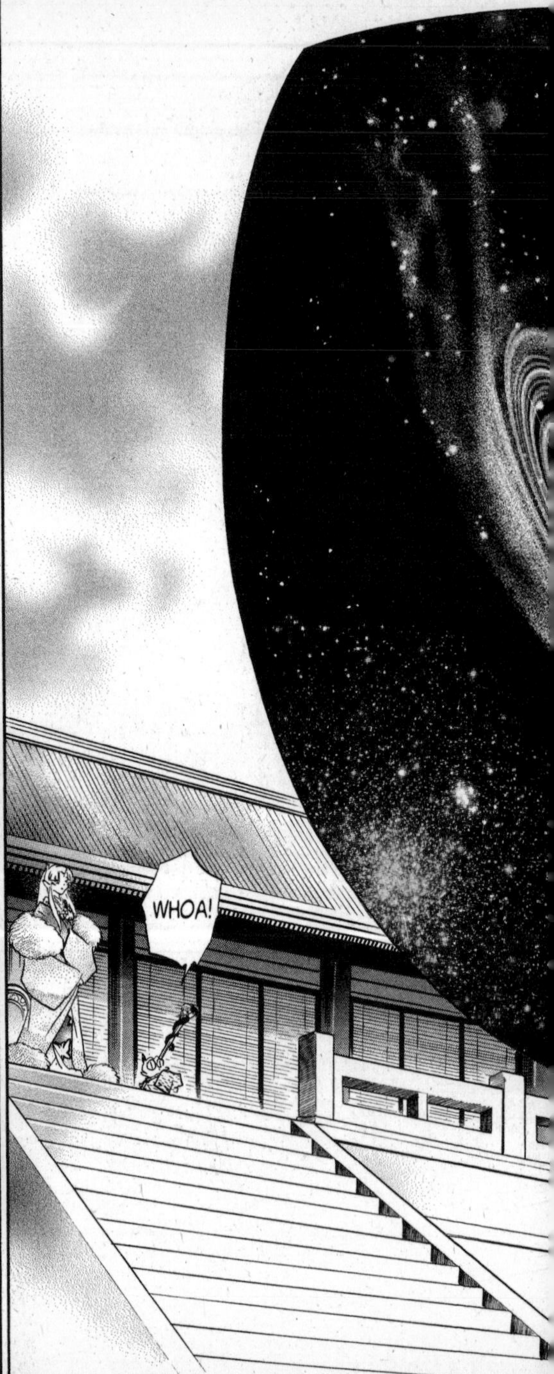
WHOA!

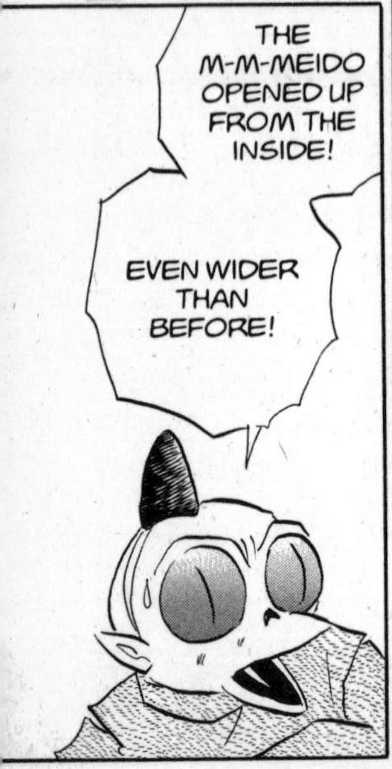
THE M-M-MEIDO OPENED UP FROM THE INSIDE!
EVEN WIDER THAN BEFORE!

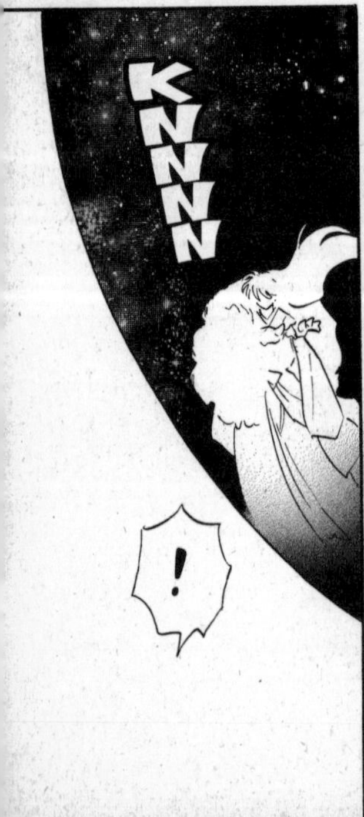
KNNNN
!

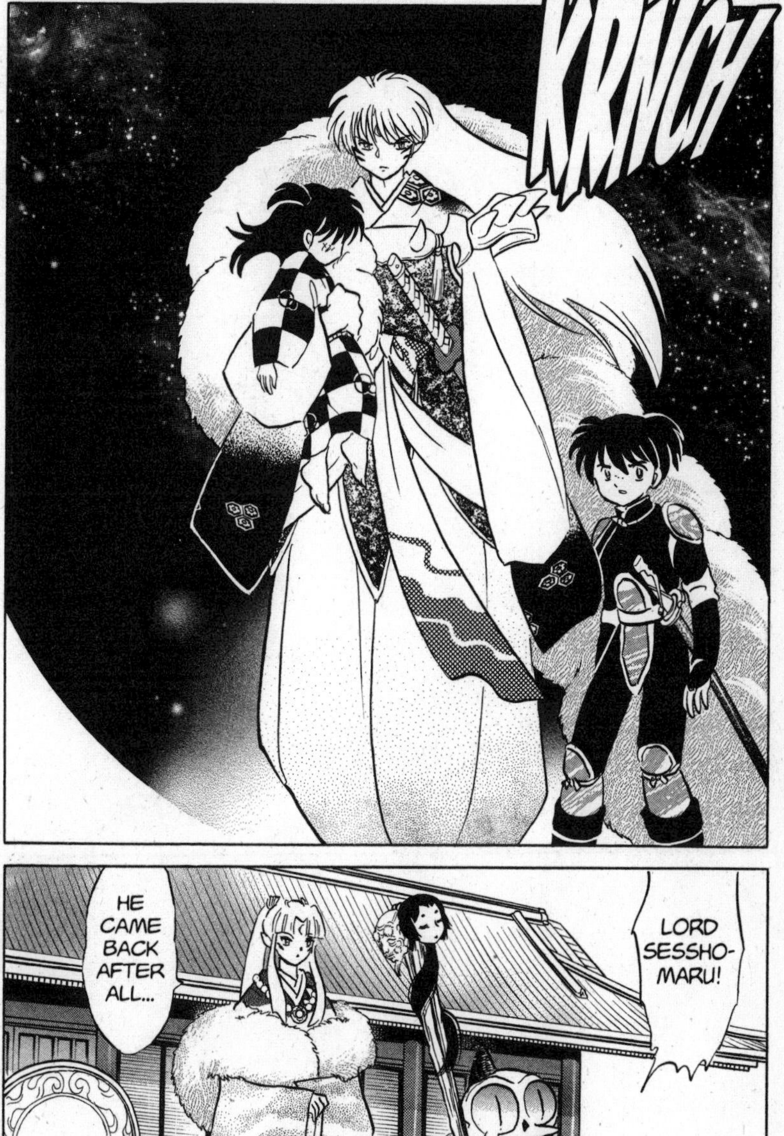
KRNCH
LORD SESSHO-MARU!
HE CAME BACK AFTER ALL...

SCROLL 3

A MERCIFUL HEART

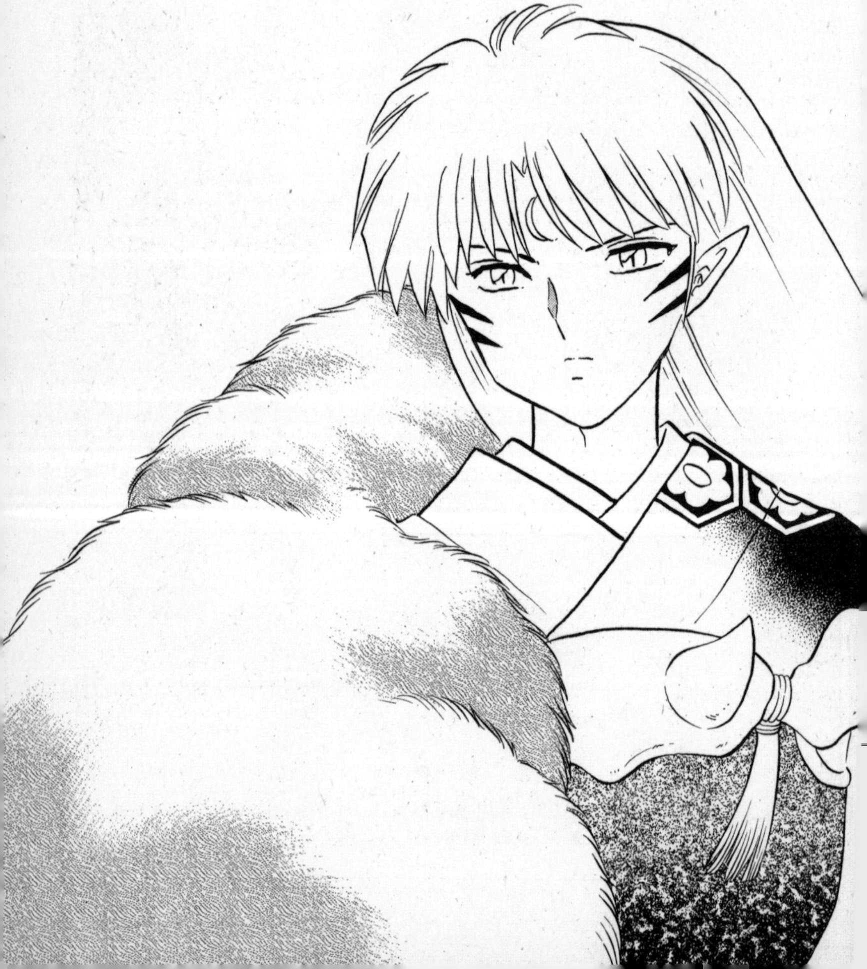

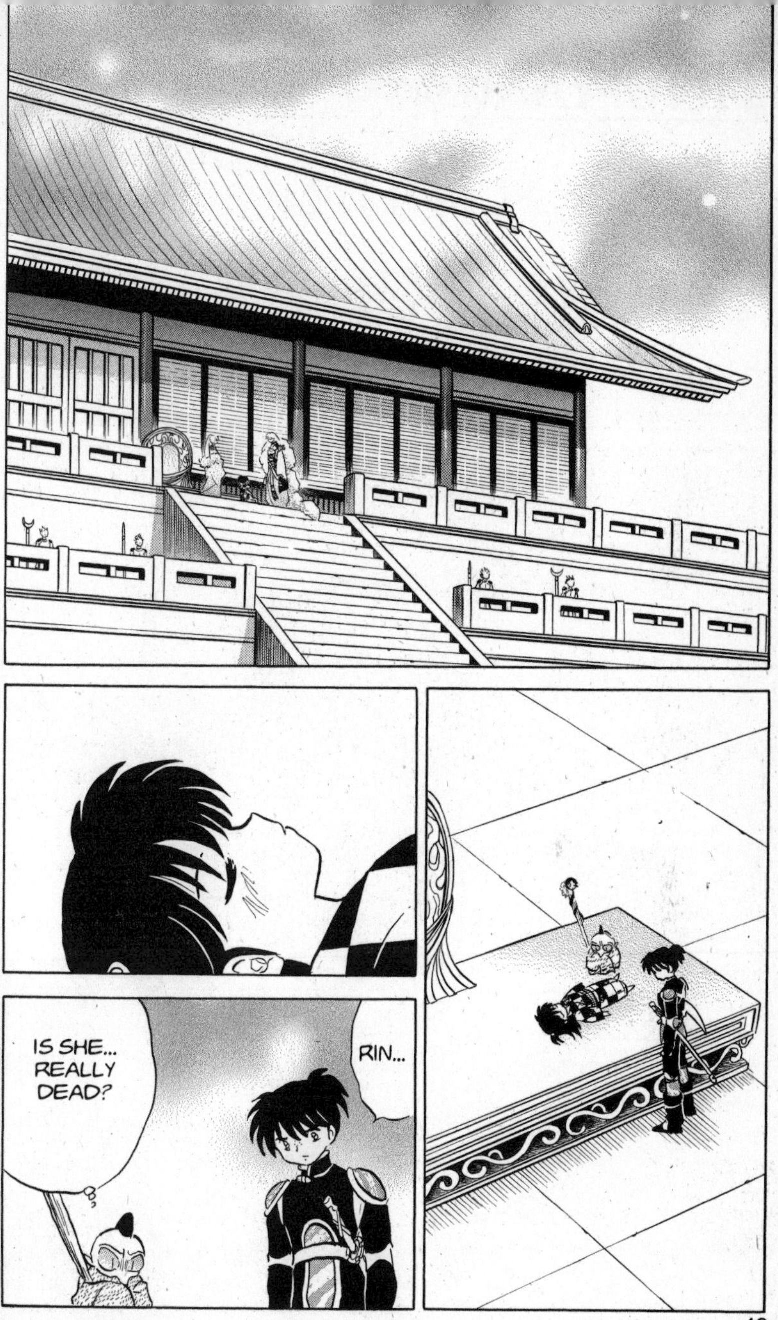
RIN...
IS SHE... REALLY DEAD?

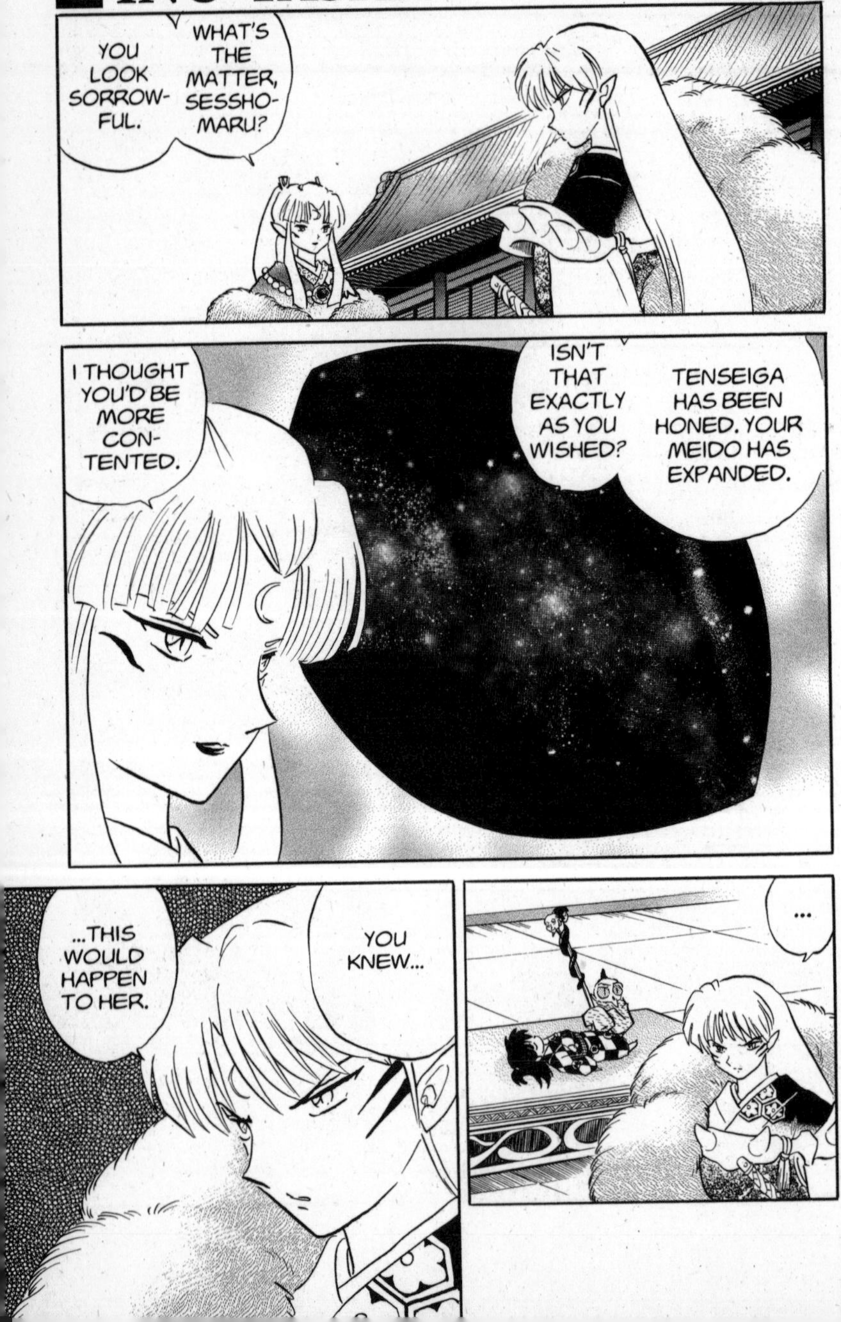
WHAT'S THE MATTER, SESSHO-MARU?
YOU LOOK SORROW-FUL.
TENSEIGA HAS BEEN HONED. YOUR MEIDO HAS EXPANDED.
ISN'T THAT EXACTLY AS YOU WISHED?
I THOUGHT YOU'D BE MORE CON-TENTED.
...
YOU KNEW...
...THIS WOULD HAPPEN TO HER.

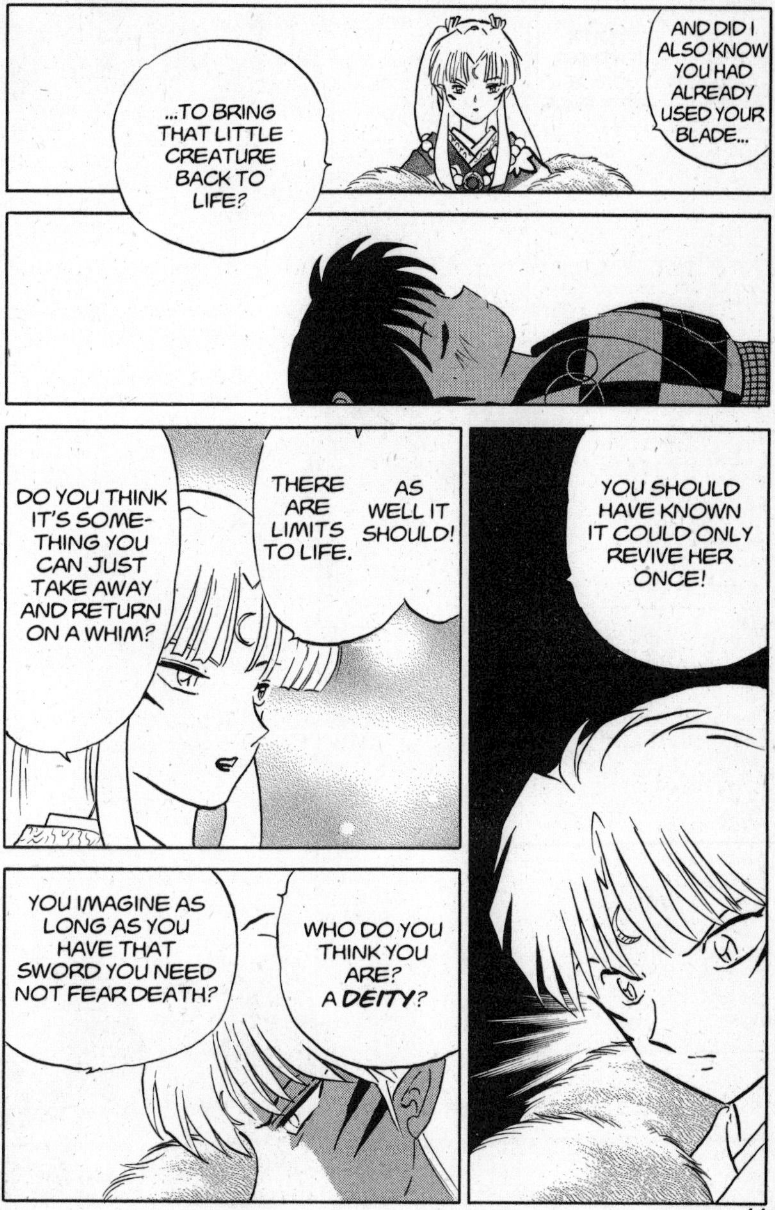
AND DID I ALSO KNOW YOU HAD ALREADY USED YOUR BLADE...
...TO BRING THAT LITTLE CREATURE BACK TO LIFE?
YOU SHOULD HAVE KNOWN IT COULD ONLY REVIVE HER ONCE!
AS WELL IT SHOULD!
THERE ARE LIMITS TO LIFE.
DO YOU THINK IT'S SOME-THING YOU CAN JUST TAKE AWAY AND RETURN ON A WHIM?
WHO DO YOU THINK YOU ARE? A **DEITY**?
YOU IMAGINE AS LONG AS YOU HAVE THAT SWORD YOU NEED NOT FEAR DEATH?

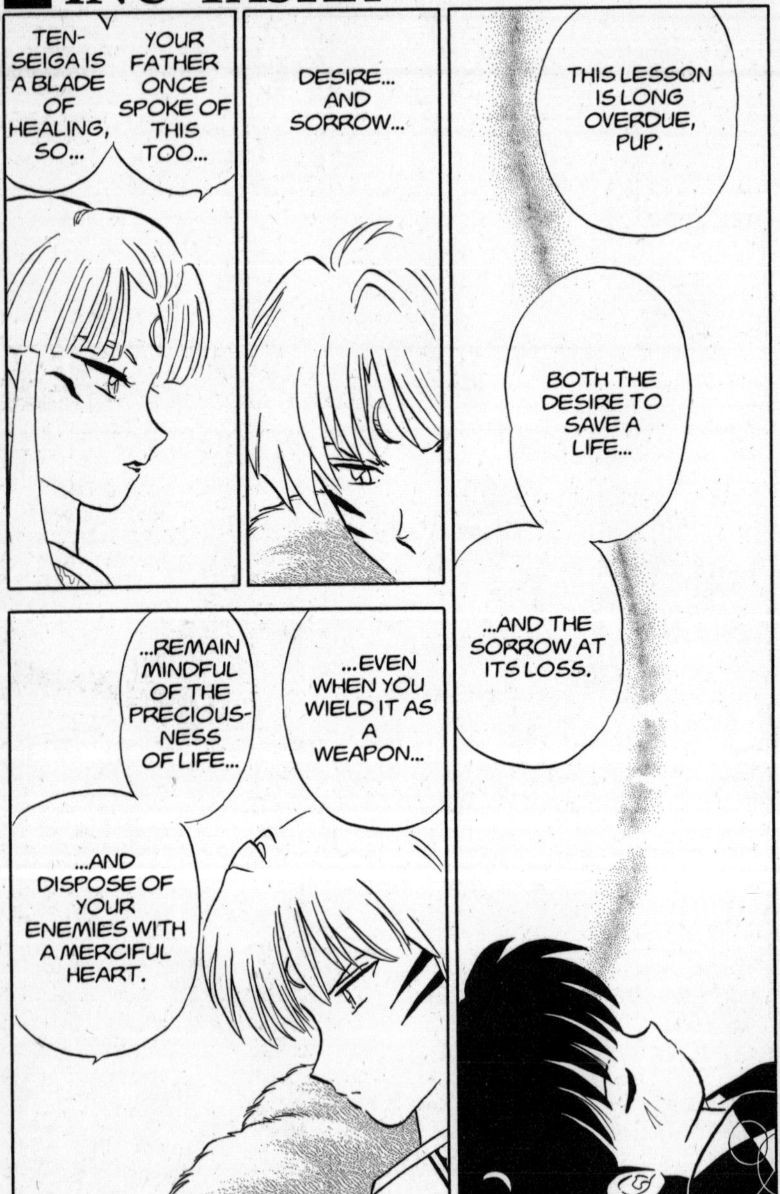
THIS LESSON IS LONG OVERDUE, PUP.
BOTH THE DESIRE TO SAVE A LIFE...
...AND THE SORROW AT ITS LOSS.
DESIRE... AND SORROW...
YOUR FATHER ONCE SPOKE OF THIS TOO...
TEN-SEIGA IS A BLADE OF HEALING, SO...
...EVEN WHEN YOU WIELD IT AS A WEAPON...
...REMAIN MINDFUL OF THE PRECIOUS-NESS OF LIFE...
...AND DISPOSE OF YOUR ENEMIES WITH A MERCIFUL HEART.

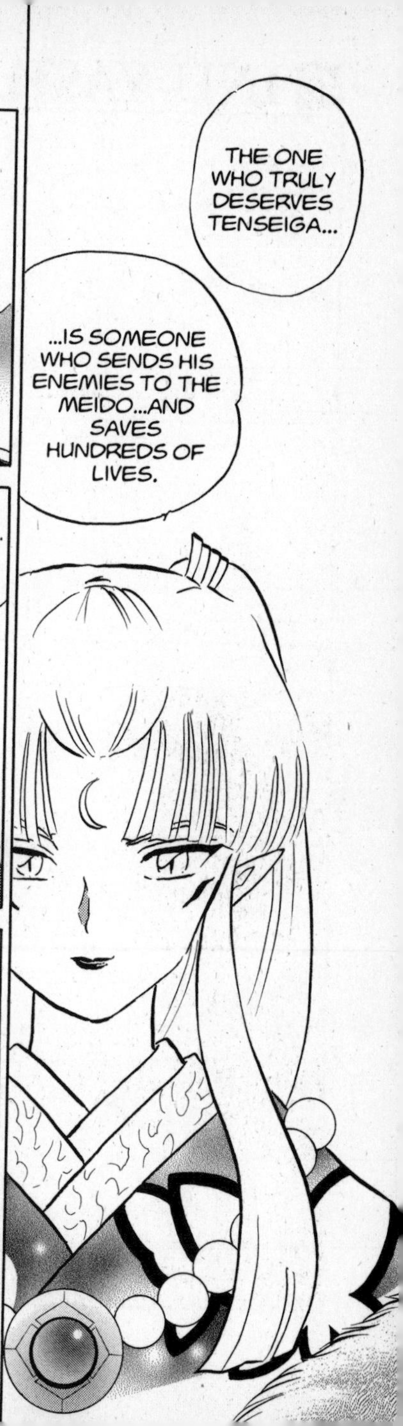
THE ONE WHO TRULY DESERVES TENSEIGA...
...IS SOMEONE WHO SENDS HIS ENEMIES TO THE MEIDO...AND SAVES HUNDREDS OF LIVES.

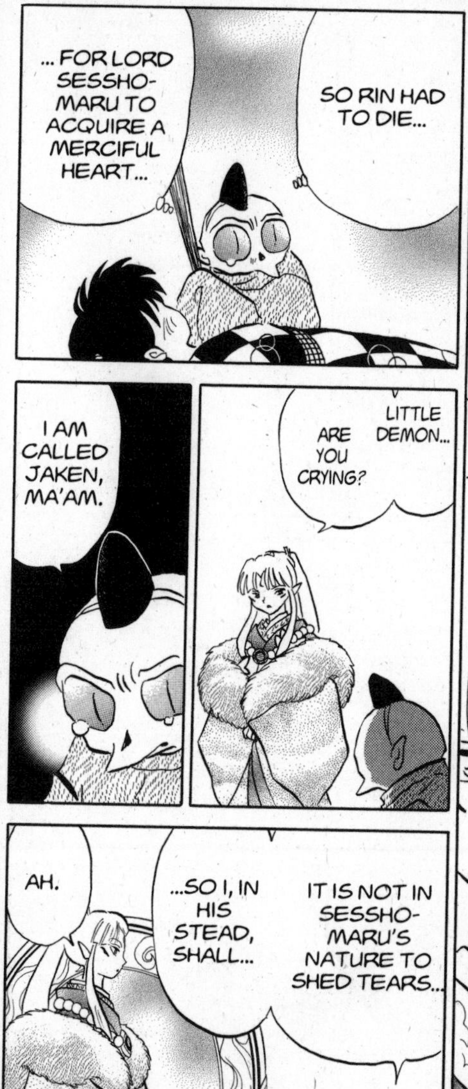
SO RIN HAD TO DIE...
... FOR LORD SESSHO-MARU TO ACQUIRE A MERCIFUL HEART...
LITTLE DEMON...
ARE YOU CRYING?
I AM CALLED JAKEN, MA'AM.
IT IS NOT IN SESSHO-MARU'S NATURE TO SHED TEARS...
...SO I, IN HIS STEAD, SHALL...
AH.

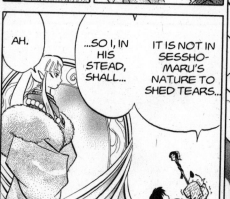

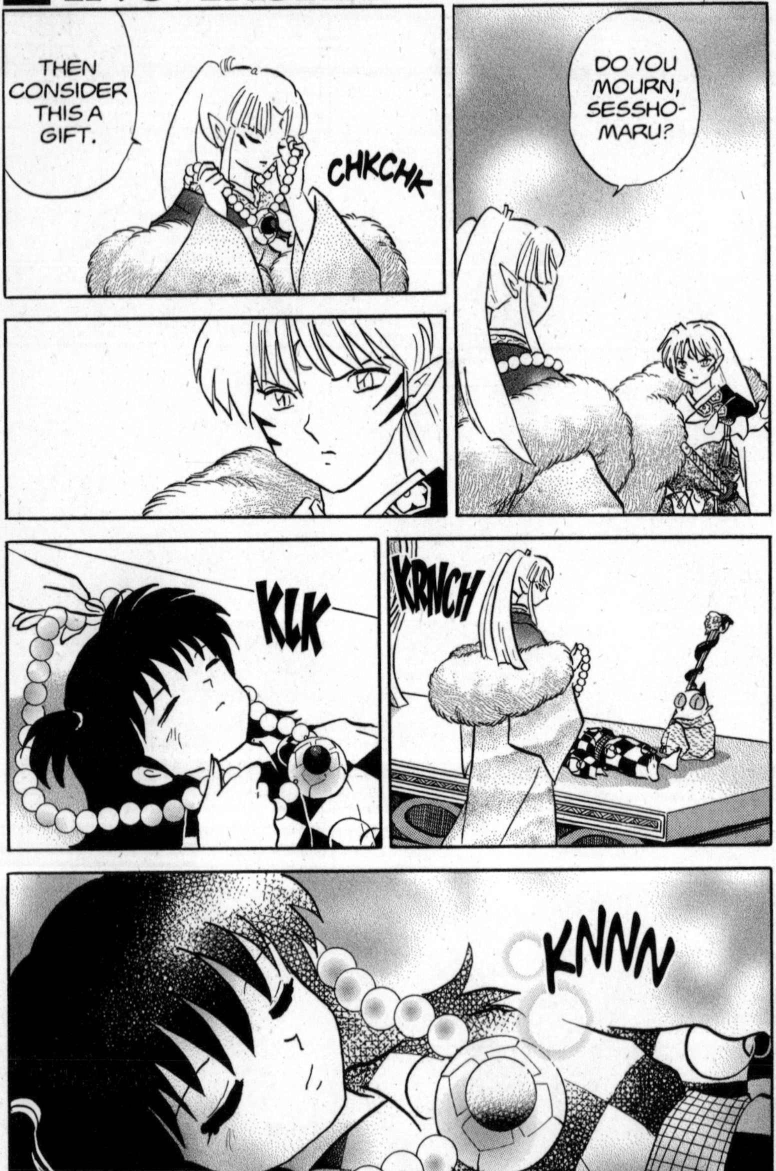
DO YOU MOURN, SESSHO-MARU?
THEN CONSIDER THIS A GIFT.
CHKCHK
KRNCH
KLK
KNNN

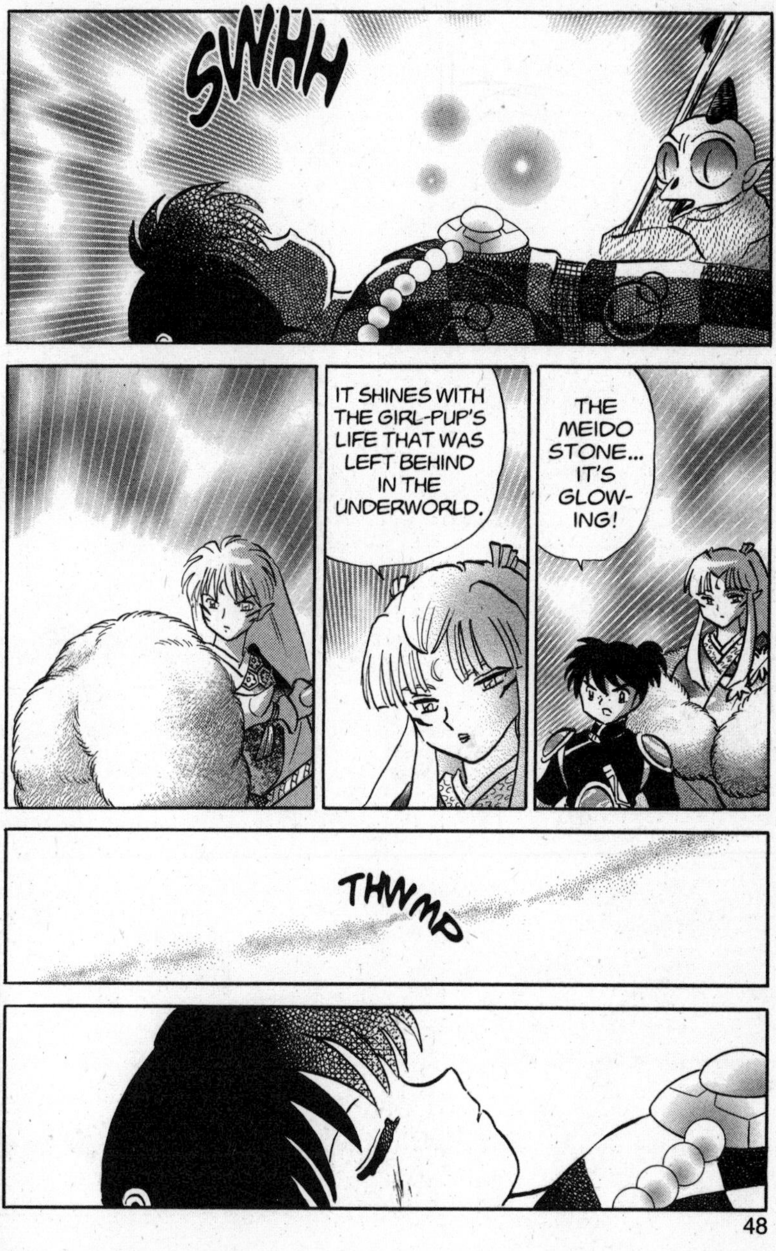
SWHH
THE MEIDO STONE... IT'S GLOWING!
IT SHINES WITH THE GIRL-PUP'S LIFE THAT WAS LEFT BEHIND IN THE UNDERWORLD.
THWMP

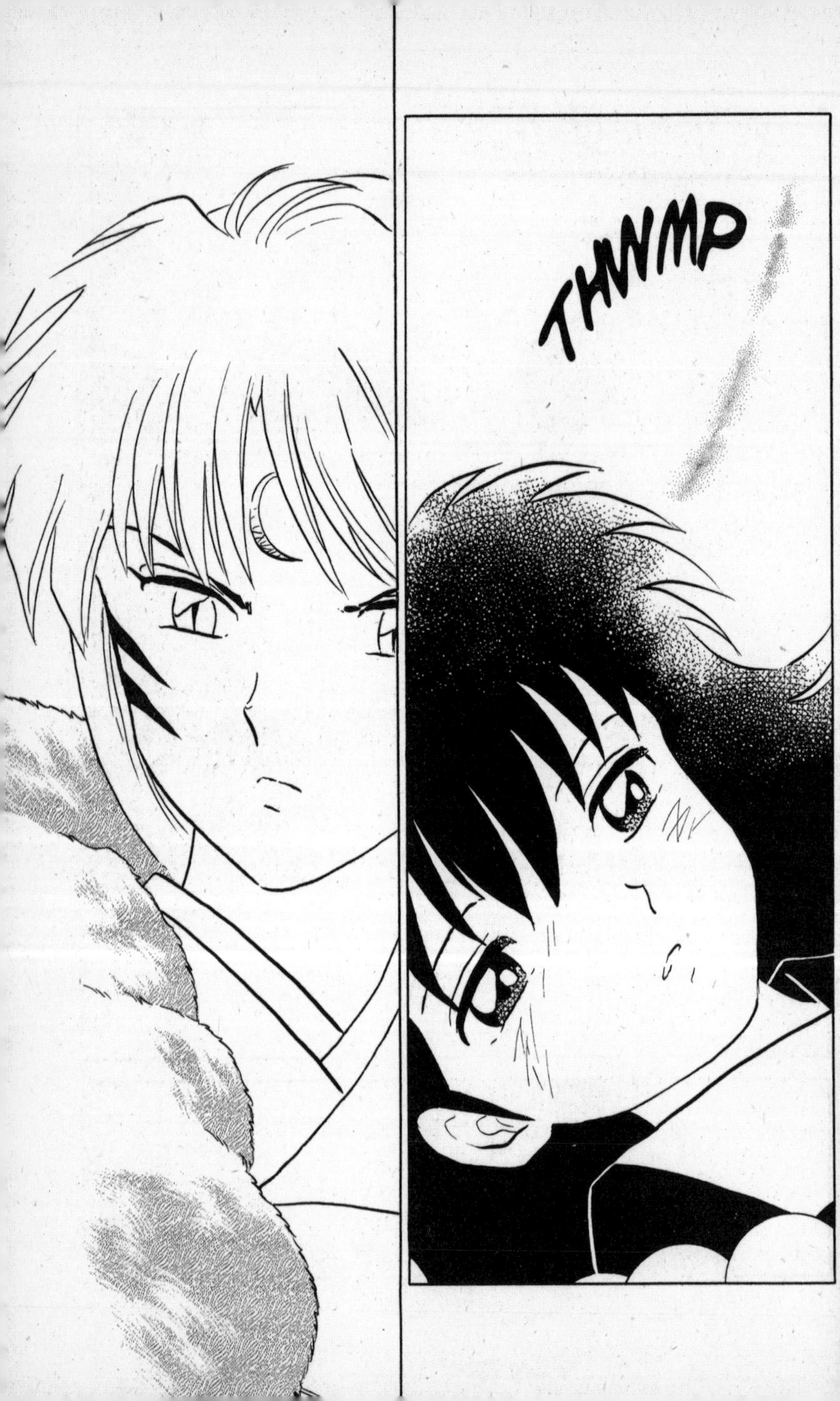
THWMP

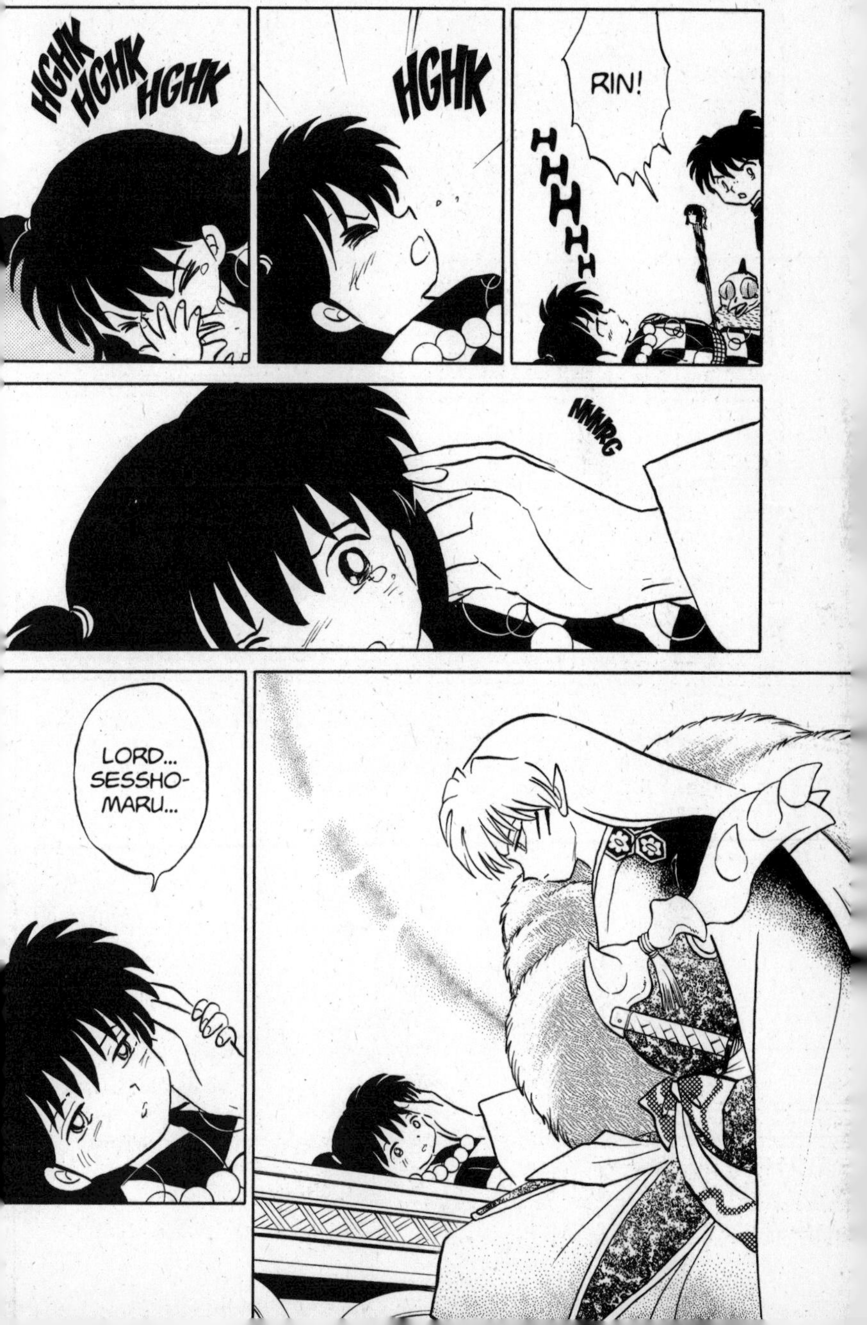
RIN!
HHHHH
HGHK
HGHK HGHK HGHK
MNRG
LORD... SESSHO-MARU...

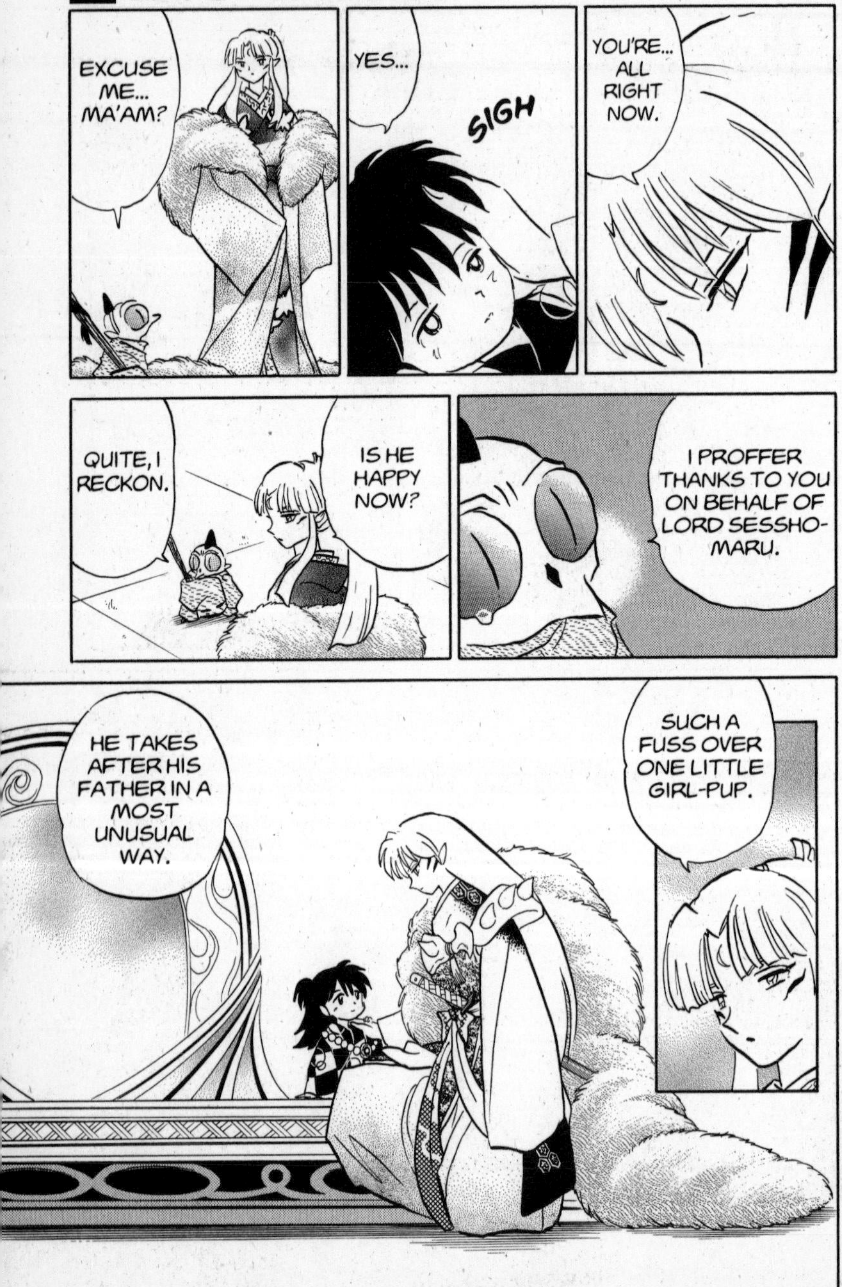
YOU'RE... ALL RIGHT NOW.
YES...
SIGH
EXCUSE ME... MA'AM?
I PROFFER THANKS TO YOU ON BEHALF OF LORD SESSHO-MARU.
IS HE HAPPY NOW?
QUITE, I RECKON.
SUCH A FUSS OVER ONE LITTLE GIRL-PUP.
HE TAKES AFTER HIS FATHER IN A MOST UNUSUAL WAY.

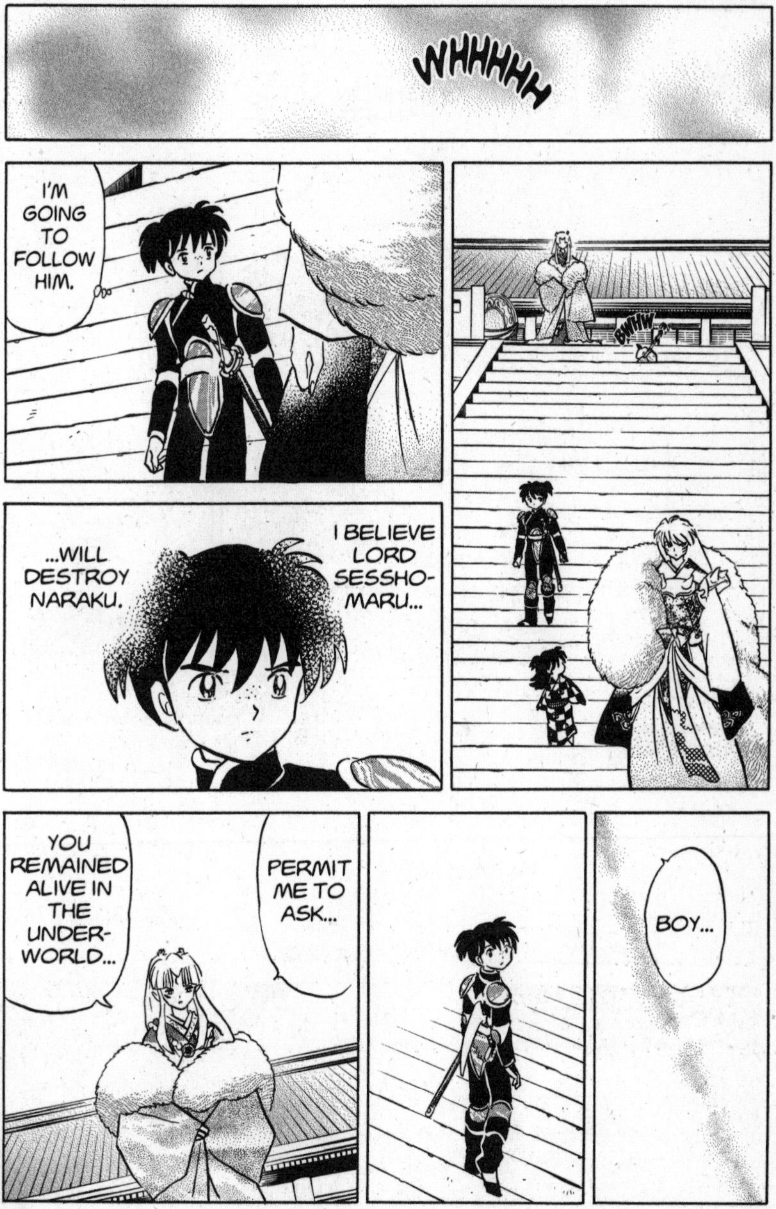

WHHHHH
BWHW
I'M GOING TO FOLLOW HIM.
I BELIEVE LORD SESSHOMARU...
...WILL DESTROY NARAKU.
BOY...
PERMIT ME TO ASK...
YOU REMAINED ALIVE IN THE UNDERWORLD...

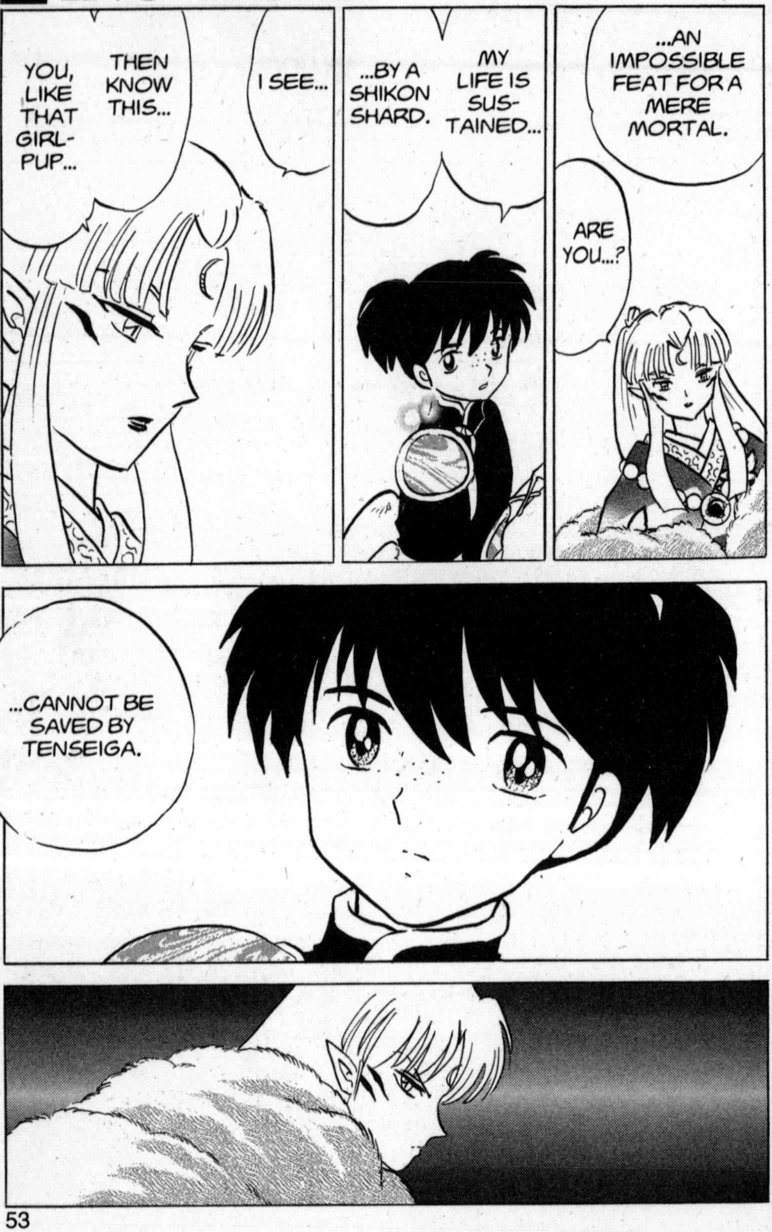
...AN IMPOSSIBLE FEAT FOR A MERE MORTAL.
ARE YOU...?
MY LIFE IS SUSTAINED...
...BY A SHIKON SHARD.
I SEE...
THEN KNOW THIS...
YOU, LIKE THAT GIRL-PUP...
...CANNOT BE SAVED BY TENSEIGA.

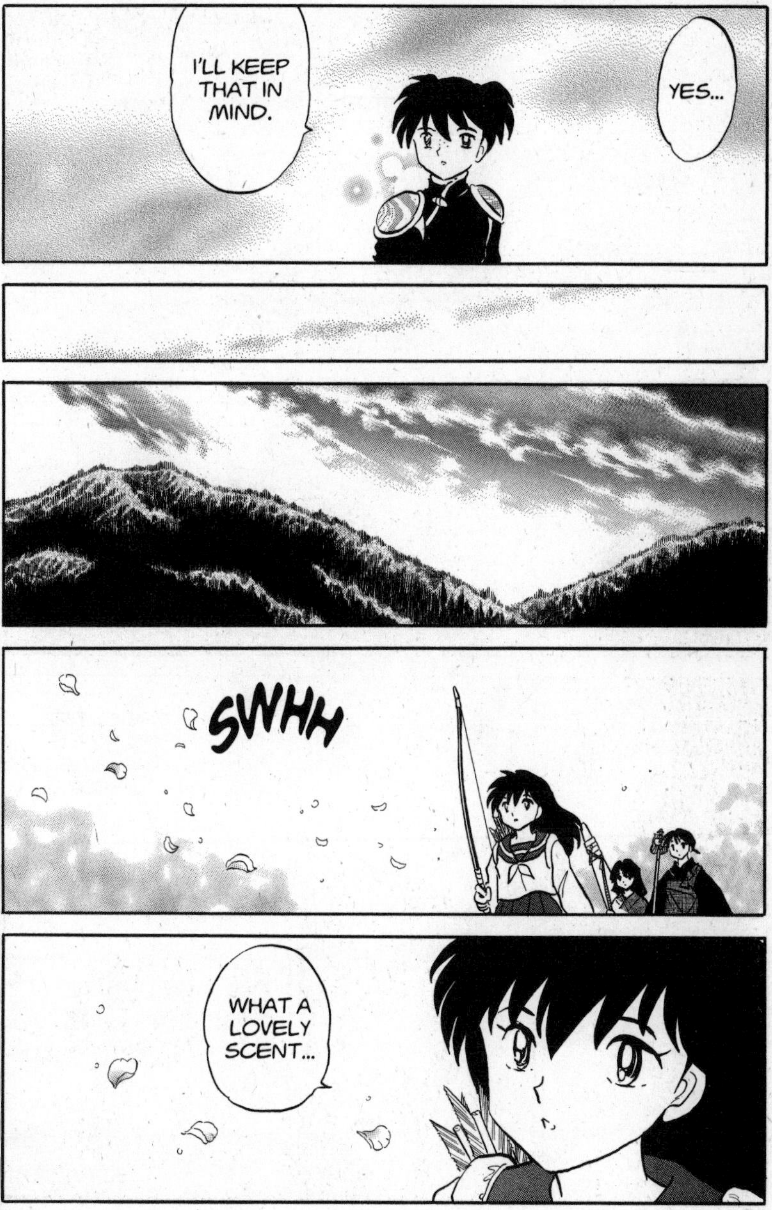
YES...
I'LL KEEP THAT IN MIND.
SWHH
WHAT A LOVELY SCENT...

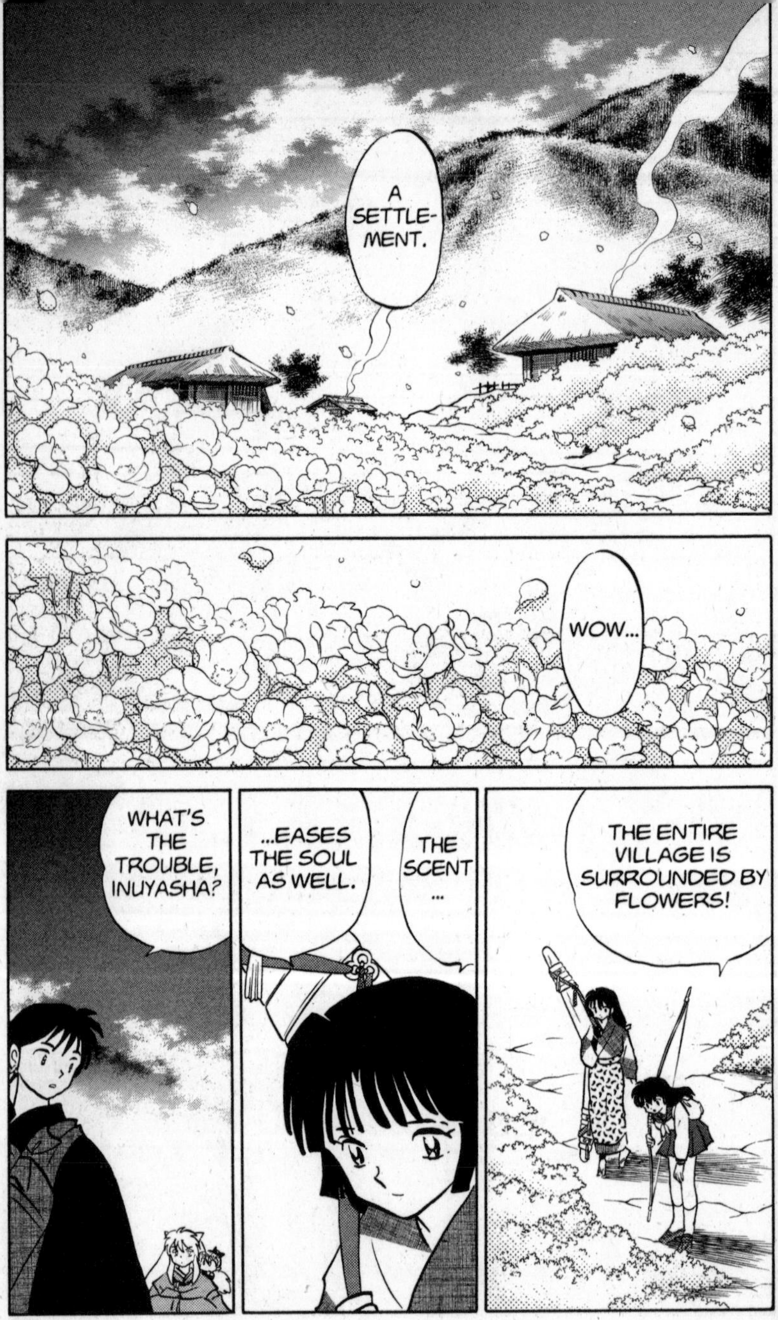
A SETTLE-MENT.
WOW...
THE ENTIRE VILLAGE IS SURROUNDED BY FLOWERS!
THE SCENT ...
...EASES THE SOUL AS WELL.
WHAT'S THE TROUBLE, INUYASHA?

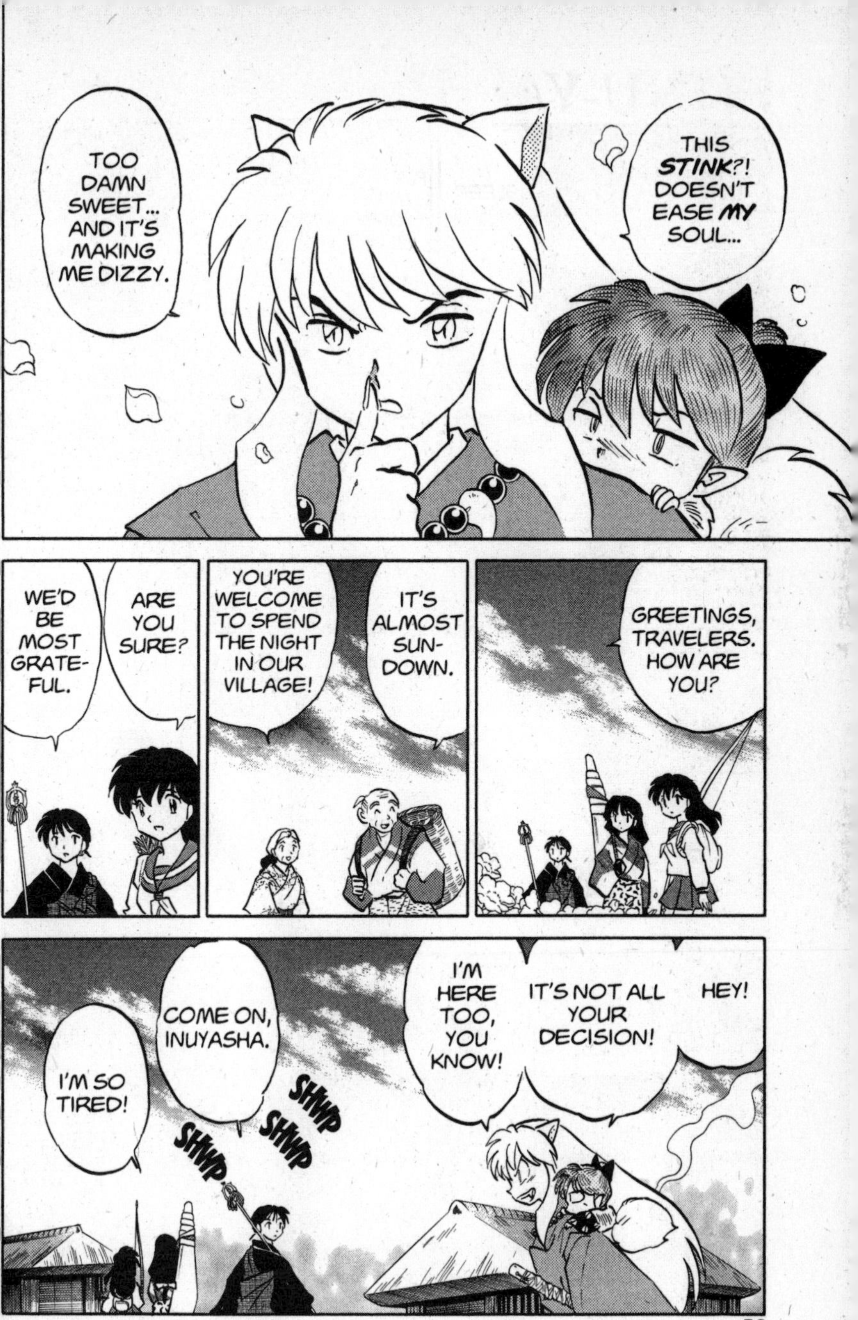
THIS STINK?! DOESN'T EASE MY SOUL...
TOO DAMN SWEET... AND IT'S MAKING ME DIZZY.
GREETINGS, TRAVELERS. HOW ARE YOU?
IT'S ALMOST SUN-DOWN.
YOU'RE WELCOME TO SPEND THE NIGHT IN OUR VILLAGE!
ARE YOU SURE?
WE'D BE MOST GRATE-FUL.
HEY!
IT'S NOT ALL YOUR DECISION!
I'M HERE TOO, YOU KNOW!
COME ON, INUYASHA.
SHWP
SHWP
SHWP
I'M SO TIRED!

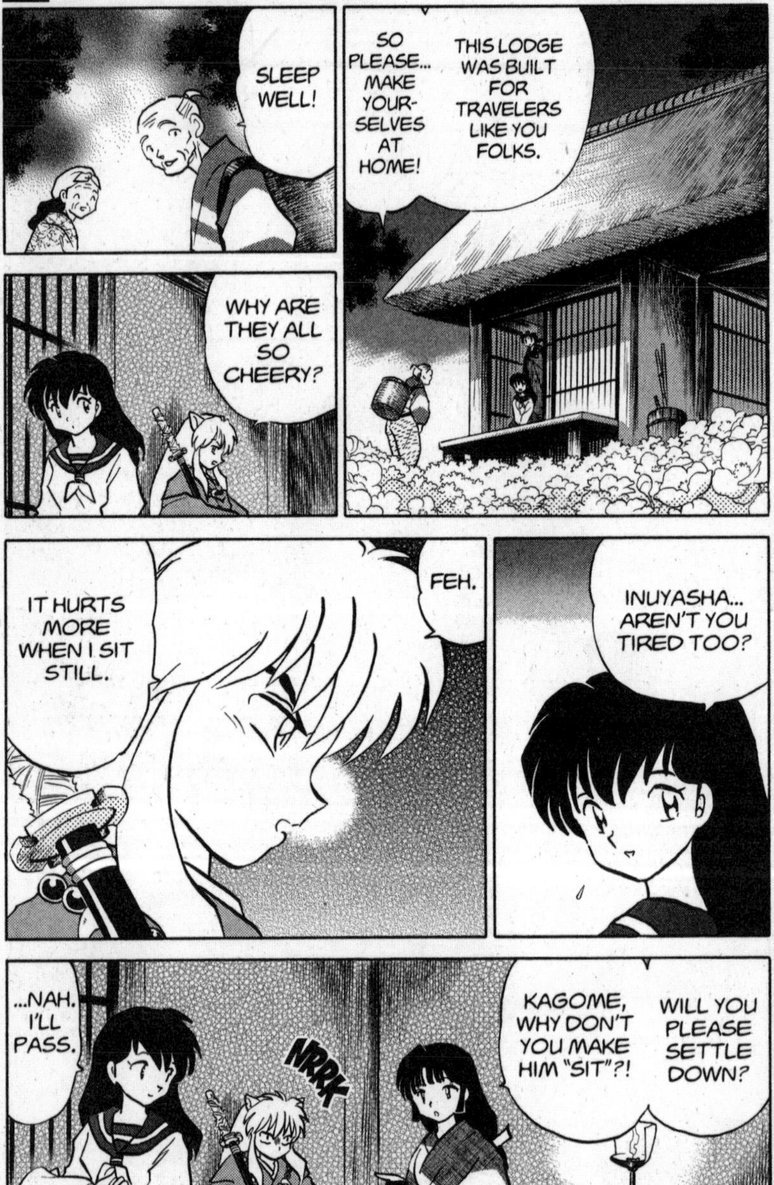
THIS LODGE WAS BUILT FOR TRAVELERS LIKE YOU FOLKS.
SO PLEASE... MAKE YOURSELVES AT HOME!
SLEEP WELL!
WHY ARE THEY ALL SO CHEERY?
INUYASHA... AREN'T YOU TIRED TOO?
FEH.
IT HURTS MORE WHEN I SIT STILL.
WILL YOU PLEASE SETTLE DOWN?
KAGOME, WHY DON'T YOU MAKE HIM "SIT"?!
NRRK
...NAH. I'LL PASS.

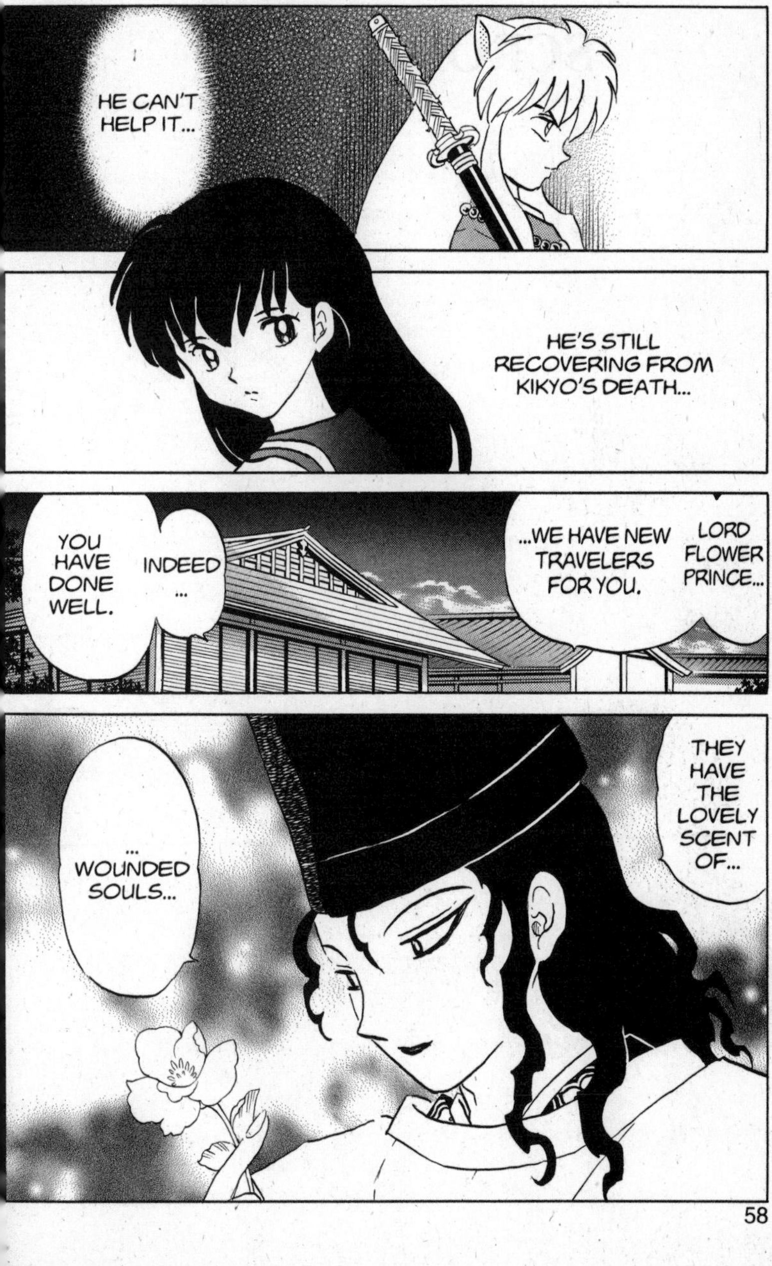
HE CAN'T HELP IT...
HE'S STILL RECOVERING FROM KIKYO'S DEATH...
LORD FLOWER PRINCE...
...WE HAVE NEW TRAVELERS FOR YOU.
INDEED...
YOU HAVE DONE WELL.
THEY HAVE THE LOVELY SCENT OF...
...WOUNDED SOULS...

SCROLL 4

THE FLOWER PRINCE

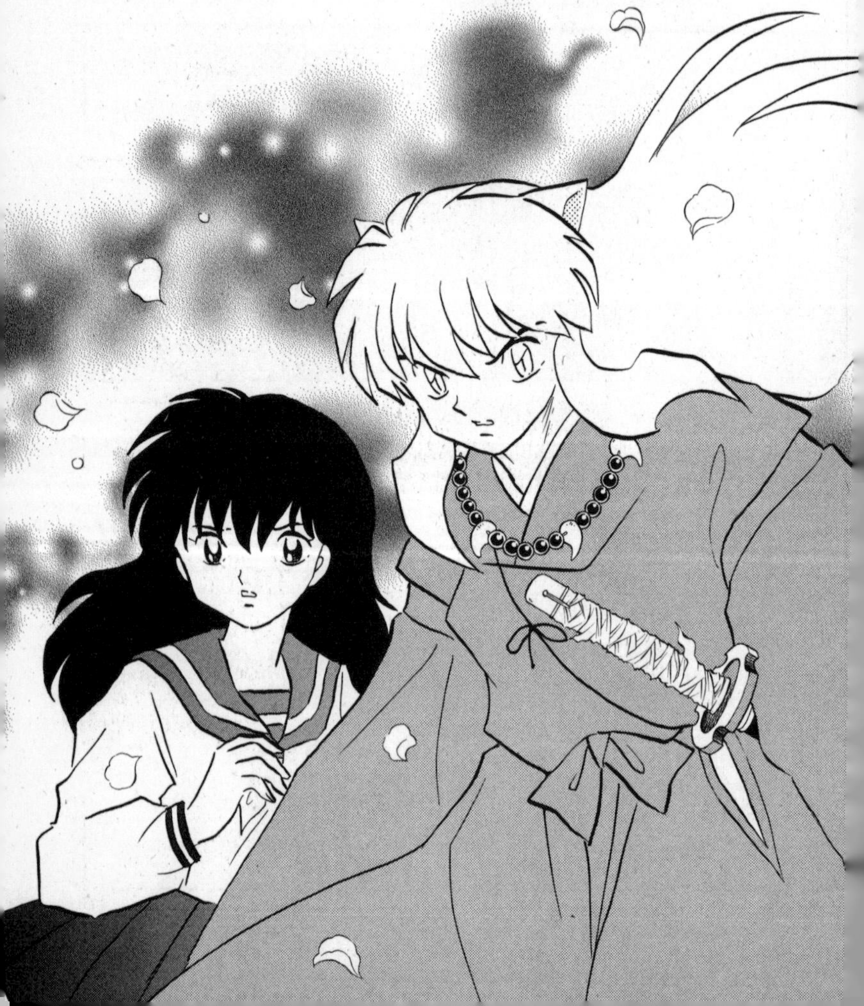

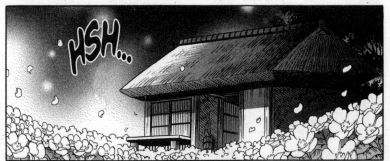

HSH...

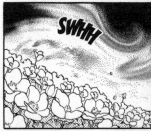

SWHH

THE STENCH
OF THOSE
FLOWERS IS
GETTING
STRONGER...

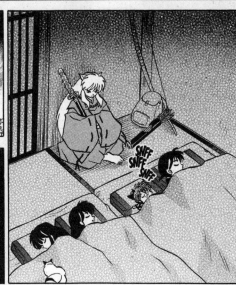

SNIFF
SNIFF
SNIFF

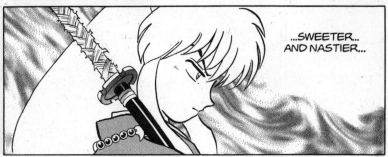

...SWEETER...
AND NASTIER...

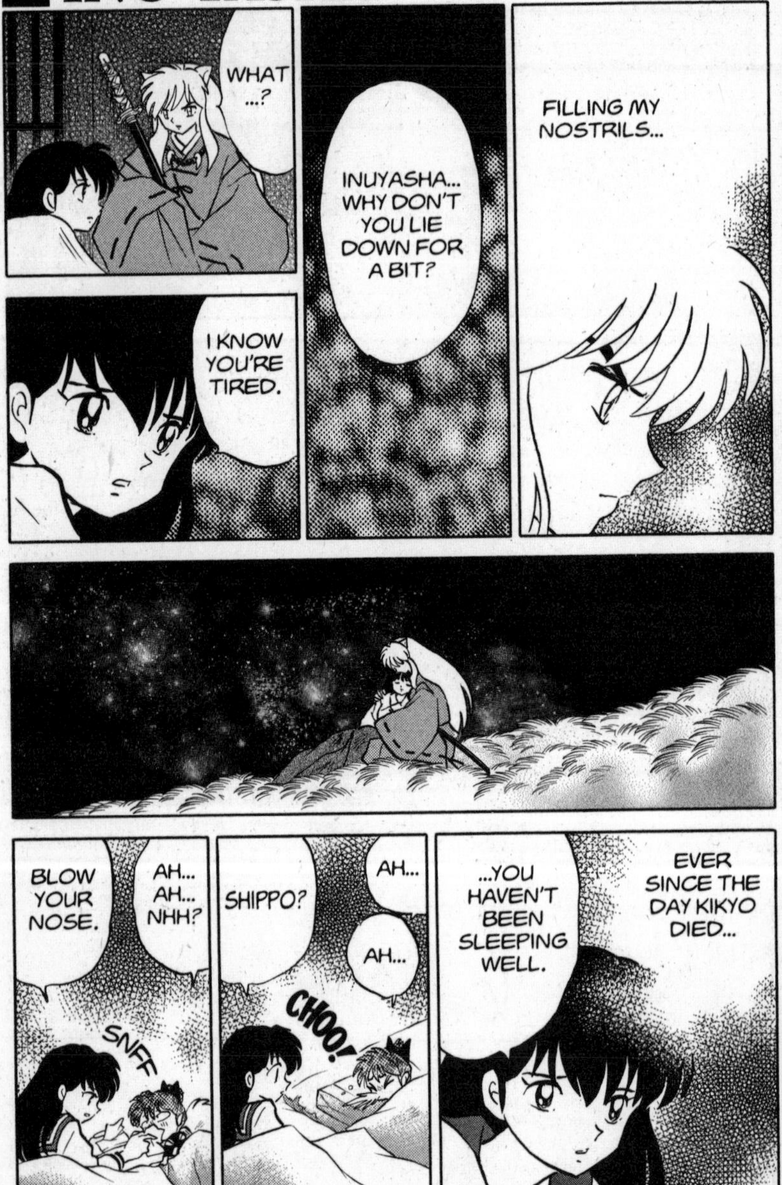
FILLING MY NOSTRILS...
INUYASHA... WHY DON'T YOU LIE DOWN FOR A BIT?
WHAT ...?
I KNOW YOU'RE TIRED.
EVER SINCE THE DAY KIKYO DIED...
...YOU HAVEN'T BEEN SLEEPING WELL.
AH...
SHIPPO?
AH...
CHOO!
AH... AH... NHH?
BLOW YOUR NOSE.
SNFF

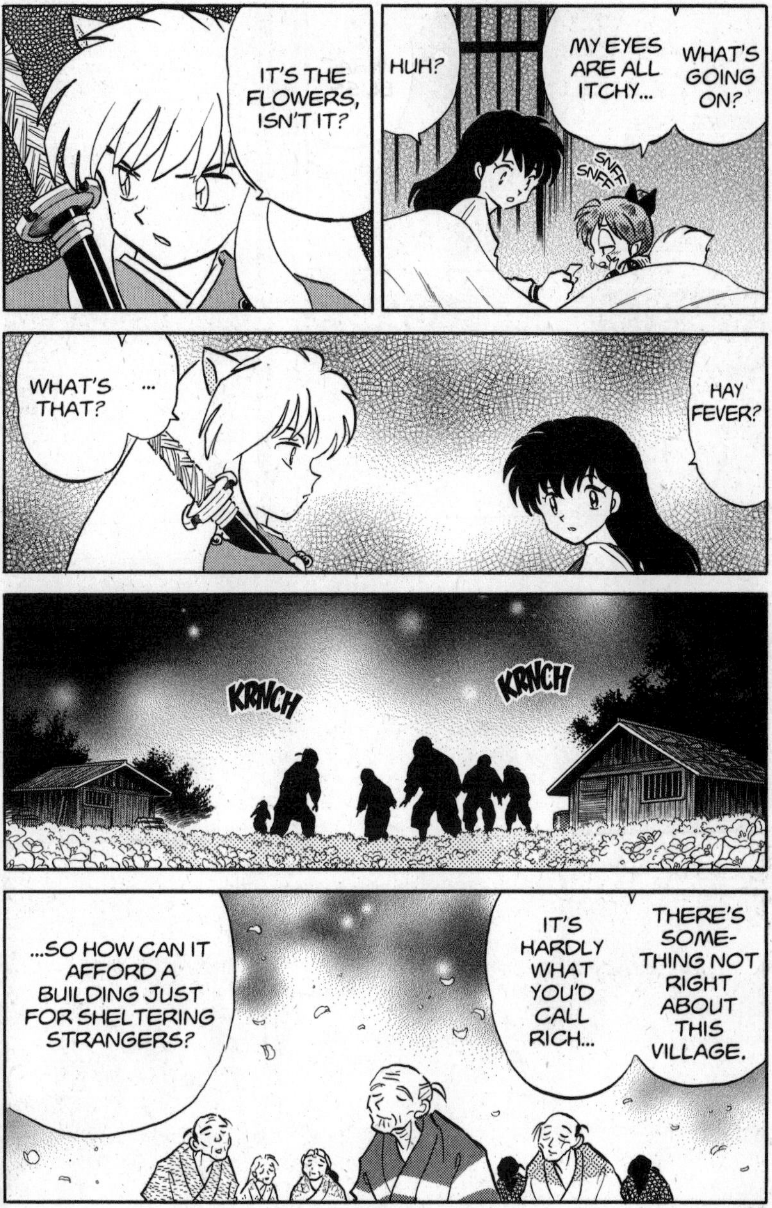
WHAT'S GOING ON?
MY EYES ARE ALL ITCHY...
SNFF SNFF
HUH?
IT'S THE FLOWERS, ISN'T IT?
HAY FEVER?
...
WHAT'S THAT?
KRNCH
KRNCH
THERE'S SOME-THING NOT RIGHT ABOUT THIS VILLAGE.
IT'S HARDLY WHAT YOU'D CALL RICH...
...SO HOW CAN IT AFFORD A BUILDING JUST FOR SHELTERING STRANGERS?

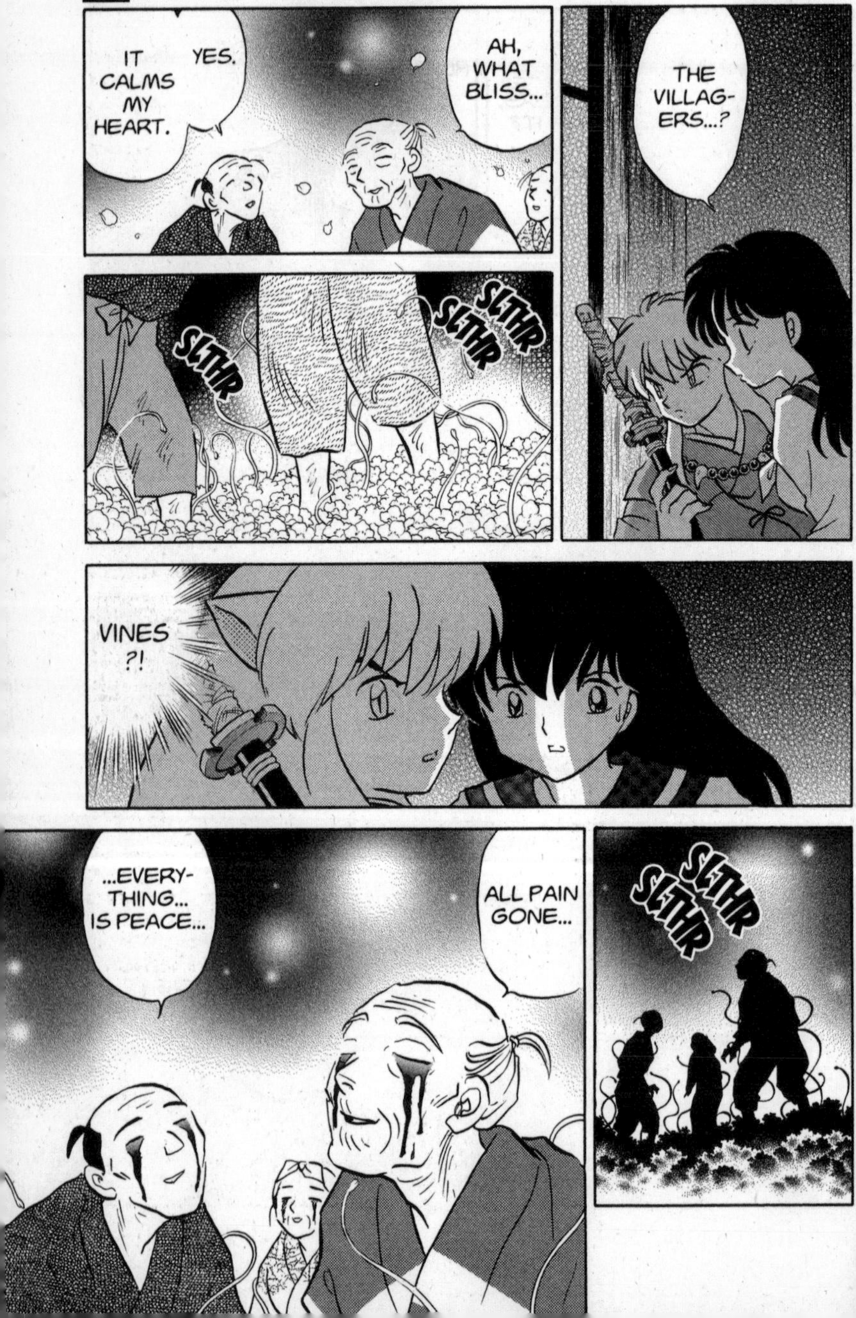
THE VILLAG-ERS...?
AH, WHAT BLISS...
YES.
IT CALMS MY HEART.
SLTHR SLTHR
SLTHR
VINES ?!
SLTHR SLTHR
ALL PAIN GONE...
...EVERY-THING... IS PEACE...

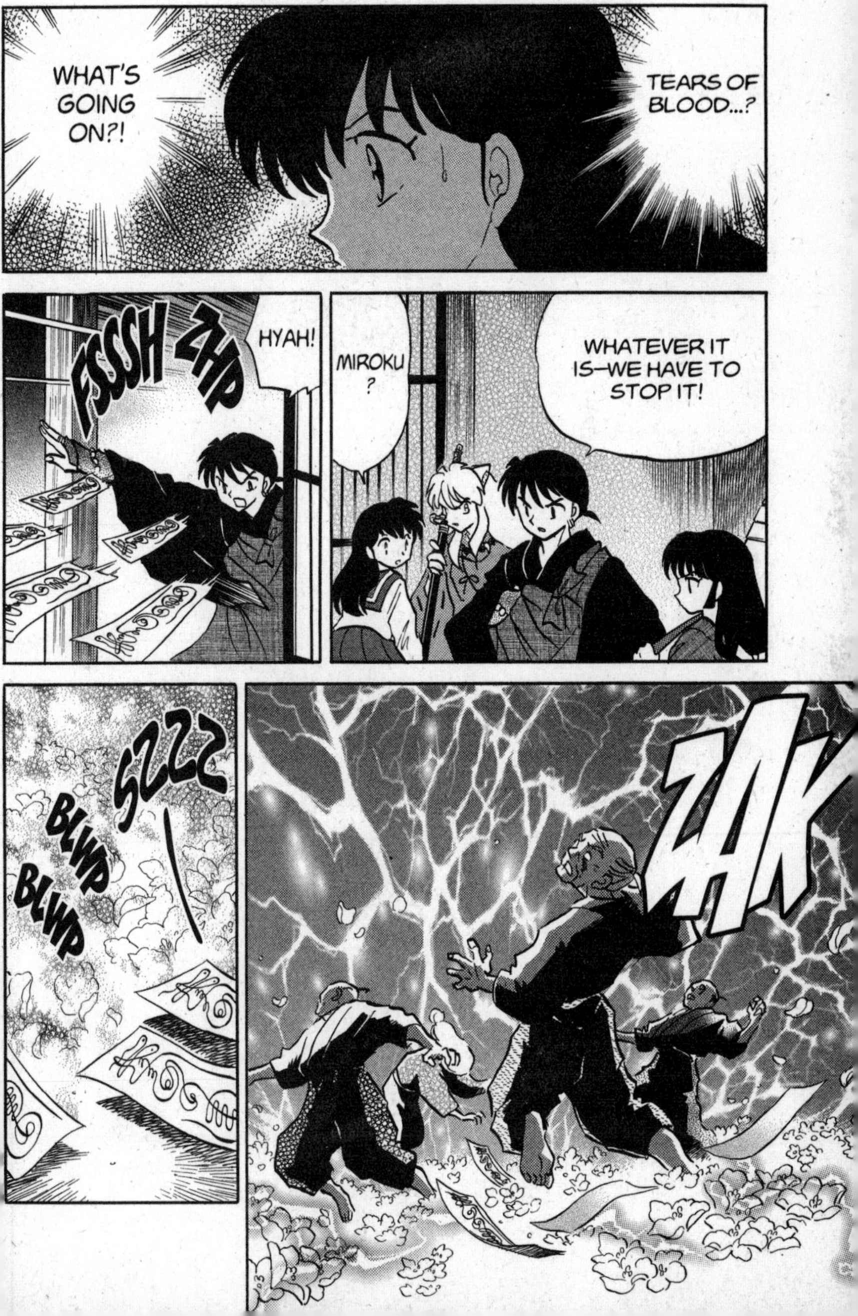
TEARS OF BLOOD...?
WHAT'S GOING ON?!
WHATEVER IT IS—WE HAVE TO STOP IT!
MIROKU?
HYAH!
FSSSH ZHIP
ZAK
SZZZ
BLWP BLWP

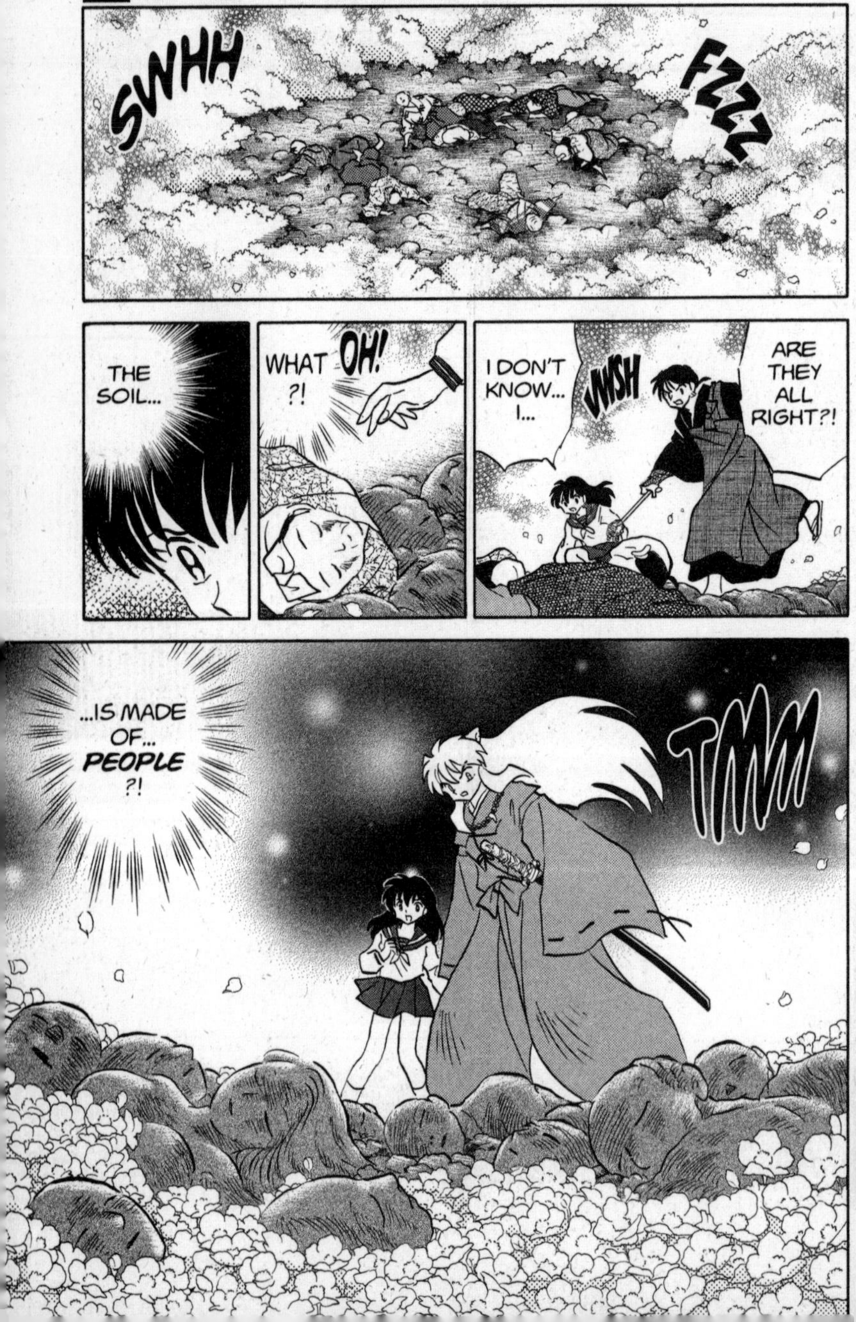
FZZZ
SWHH
ARE THEY ALL RIGHT?!
WSH
I DON'T KNOW... I...
OH!
WHAT ?!
THE SOIL...
TMM
...IS MADE OF... PEOPLE ?!

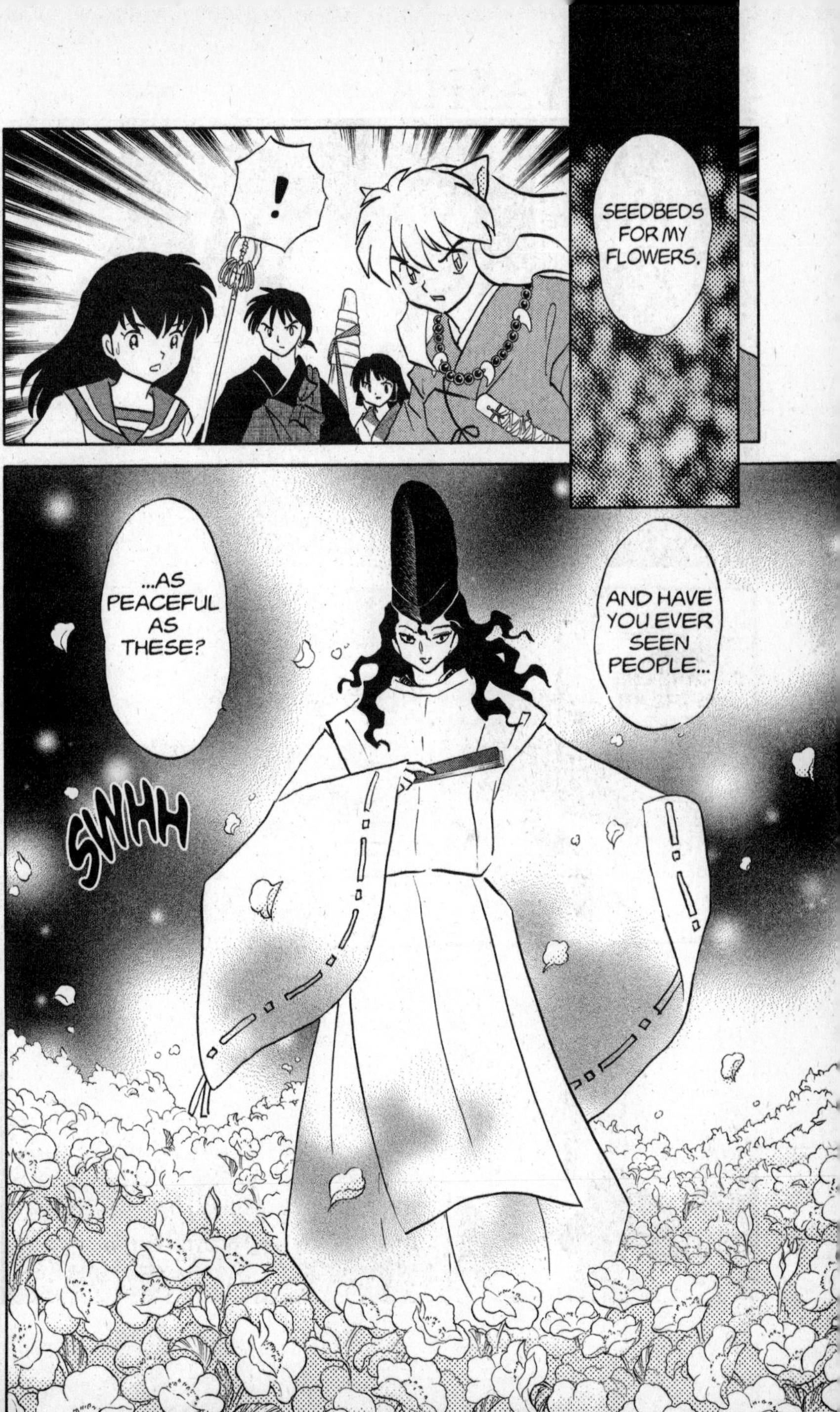
SEEDBEDS FOR MY FLOWERS.
!
AND HAVE YOU EVER SEEN PEOPLE...
...AS PEACEFUL AS THESE?
SWHH

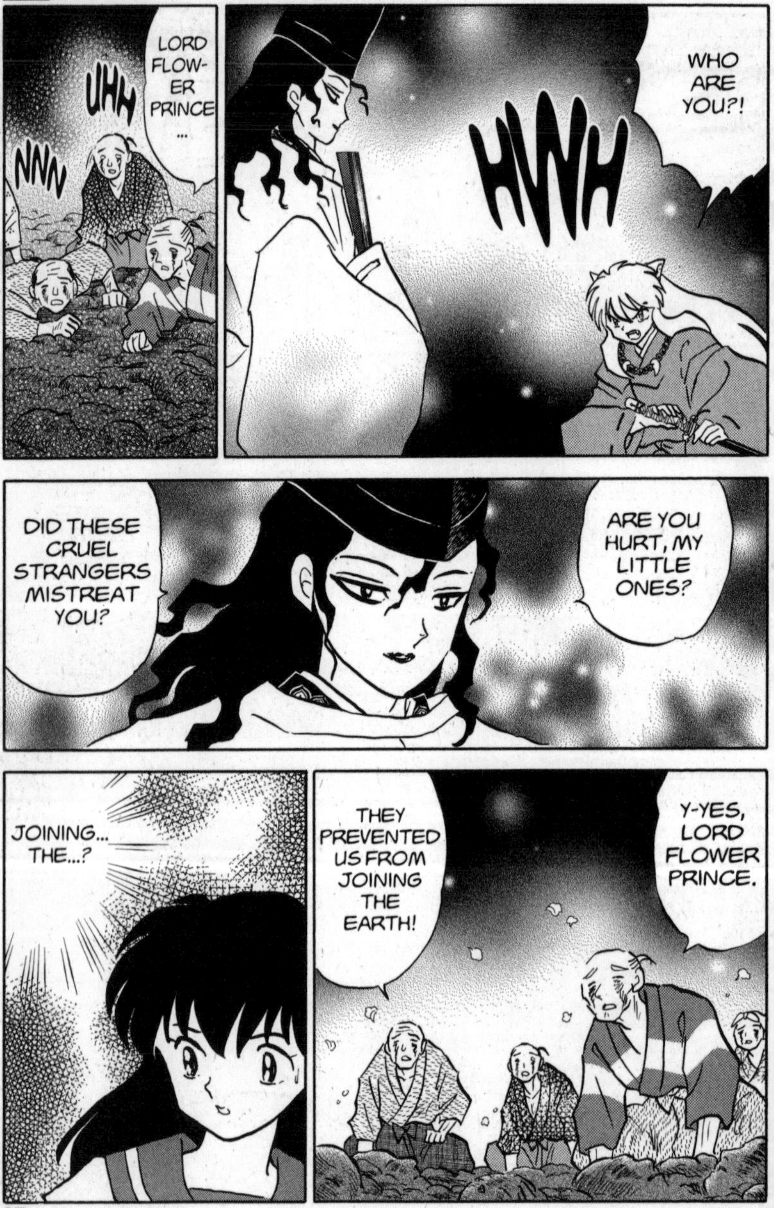
WHO ARE YOU?!
HNNH
LORD FLOW-ER PRINCE ...
UHH
NNN
ARE YOU HURT, MY LITTLE ONES?
DID THESE CRUEL STRANGERS MISTREAT YOU?
Y-YES, LORD FLOWER PRINCE.
THEY PREVENTED US FROM JOINING THE EARTH!
JOINING... THE...?

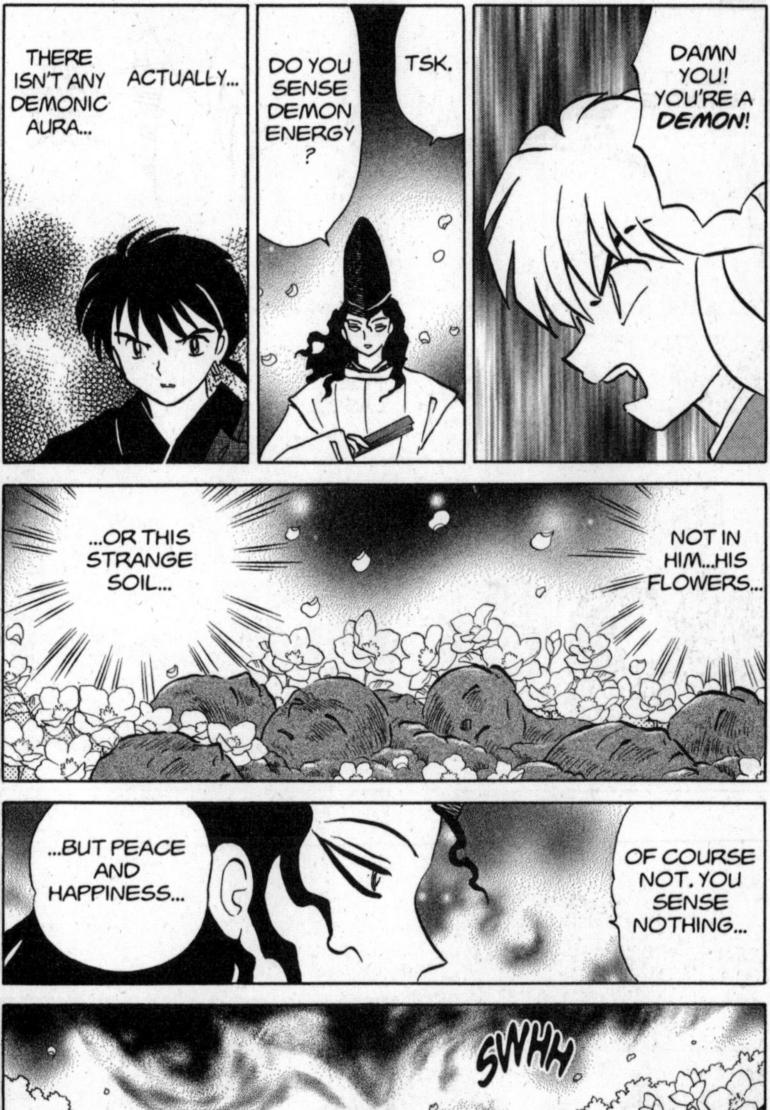
DAMN YOU! YOU'RE A **DEMON**!
TSK.
DO YOU SENSE DEMON ENERGY?
ACTUALLY...
THERE ISN'T ANY DEMONIC AURA...
NOT IN HIM...HIS FLOWERS...
...OR THIS STRANGE SOIL...
OF COURSE NOT. YOU SENSE NOTHING...
...BUT PEACE AND HAPPINESS...
SWHH

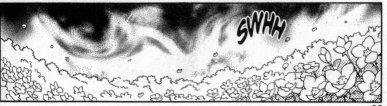

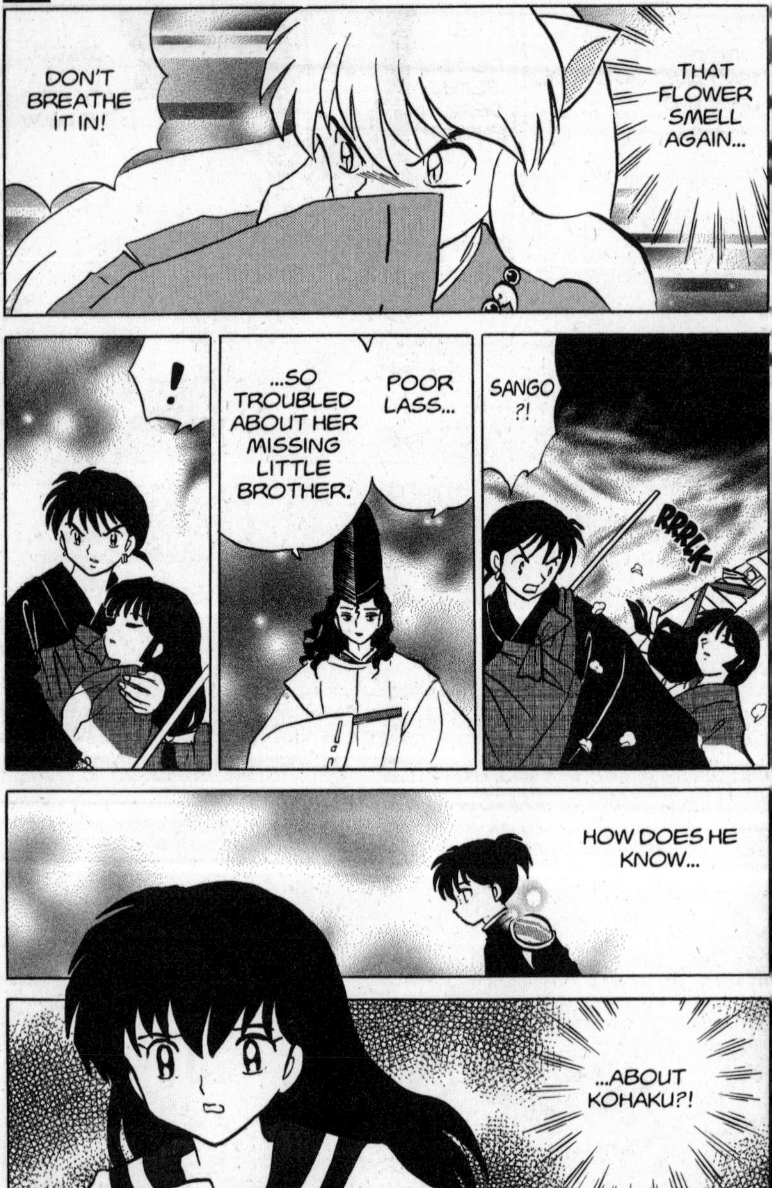
THAT FLOWER SMELL AGAIN...
DON'T BREATHE IT IN!
SANGO ?!
RRRLK
POOR LASS...
...SO TROUBLED ABOUT HER MISSING LITTLE BROTHER.
!
HOW DOES HE KNOW...
...ABOUT KOHAKU?!

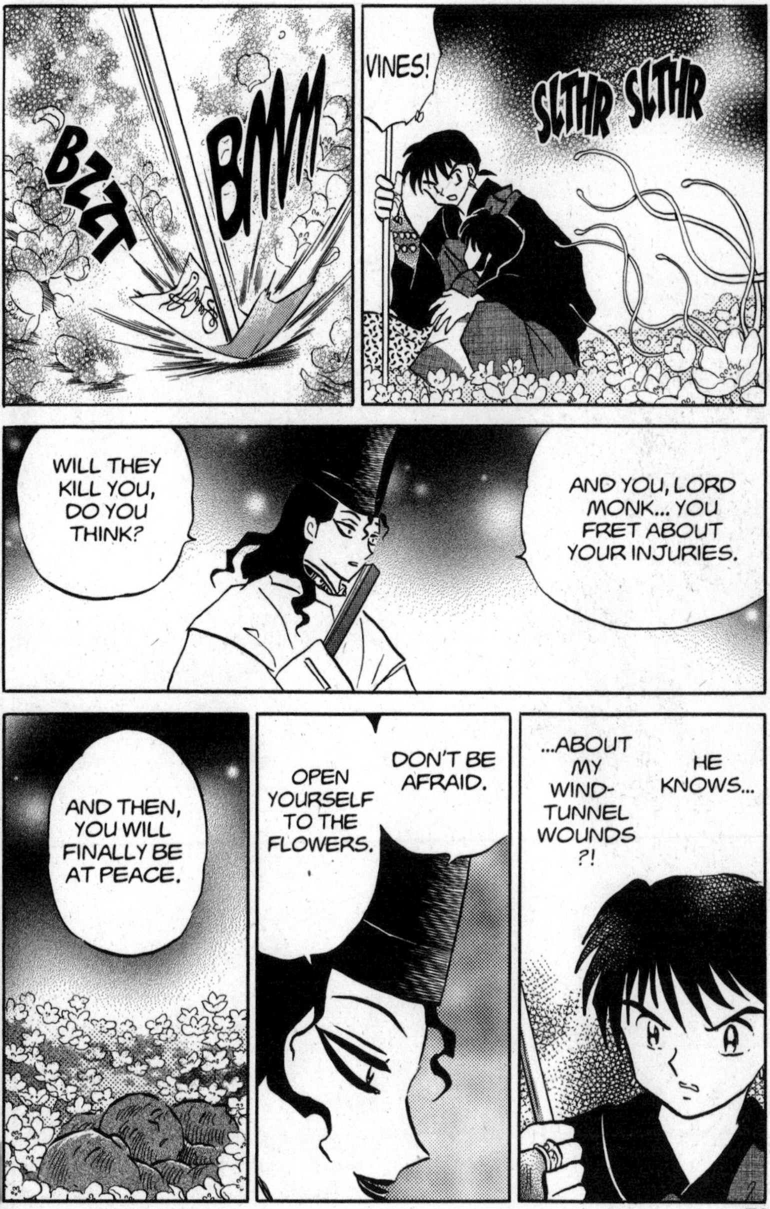
VINES!
SLTHR SLTHR
BZZT
BMM
AND YOU, LORD MONK... YOU FRET ABOUT YOUR INJURIES.
WILL THEY KILL YOU, DO YOU THINK?
HE KNOWS...
...ABOUT MY WIND-TUNNEL WOUNDS?!
DON'T BE AFRAID.
OPEN YOURSELF TO THE FLOWERS.
AND THEN, YOU WILL FINALLY BE AT PEACE.

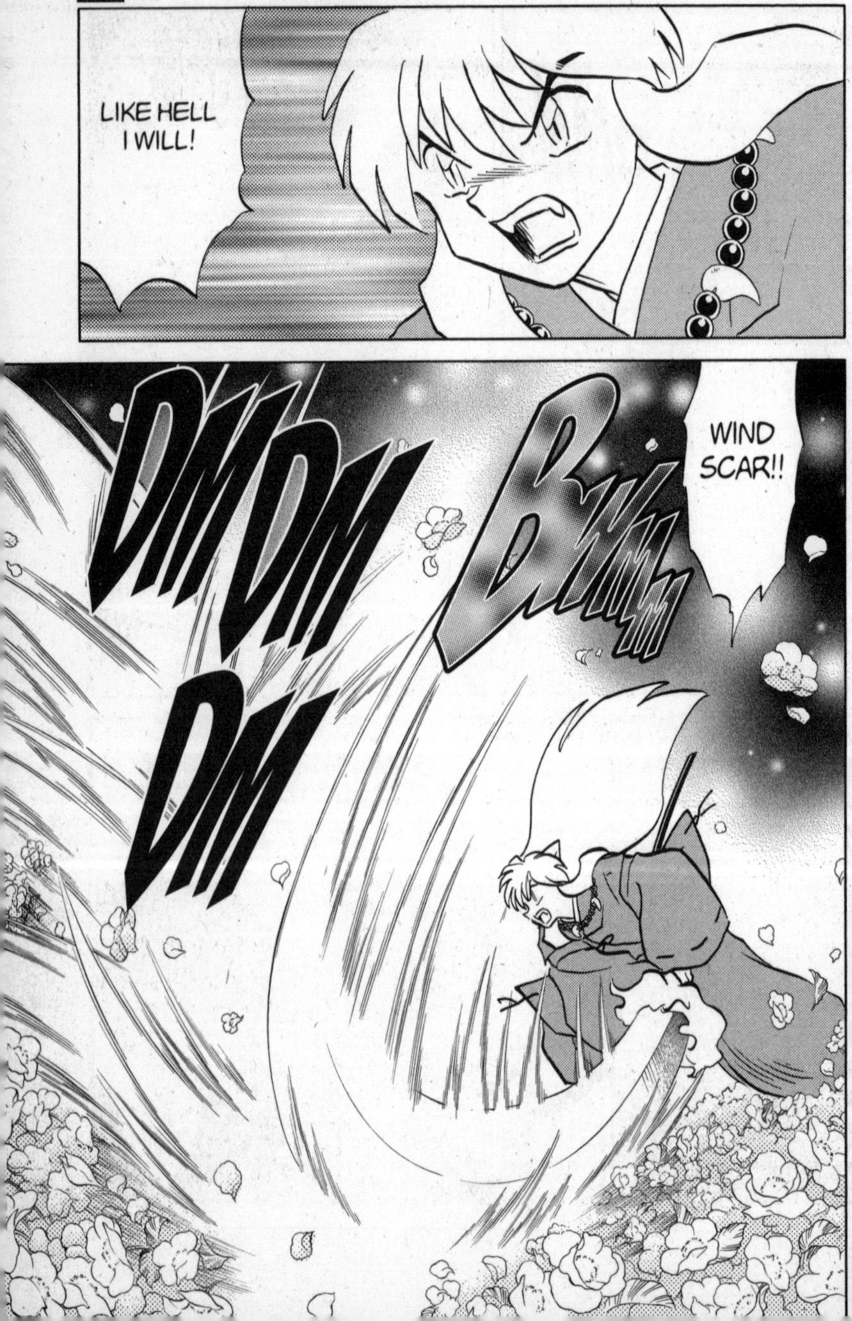
LIKE HELL
I WILL!
WIND
SCAR!!
BWHM
DMDMDM

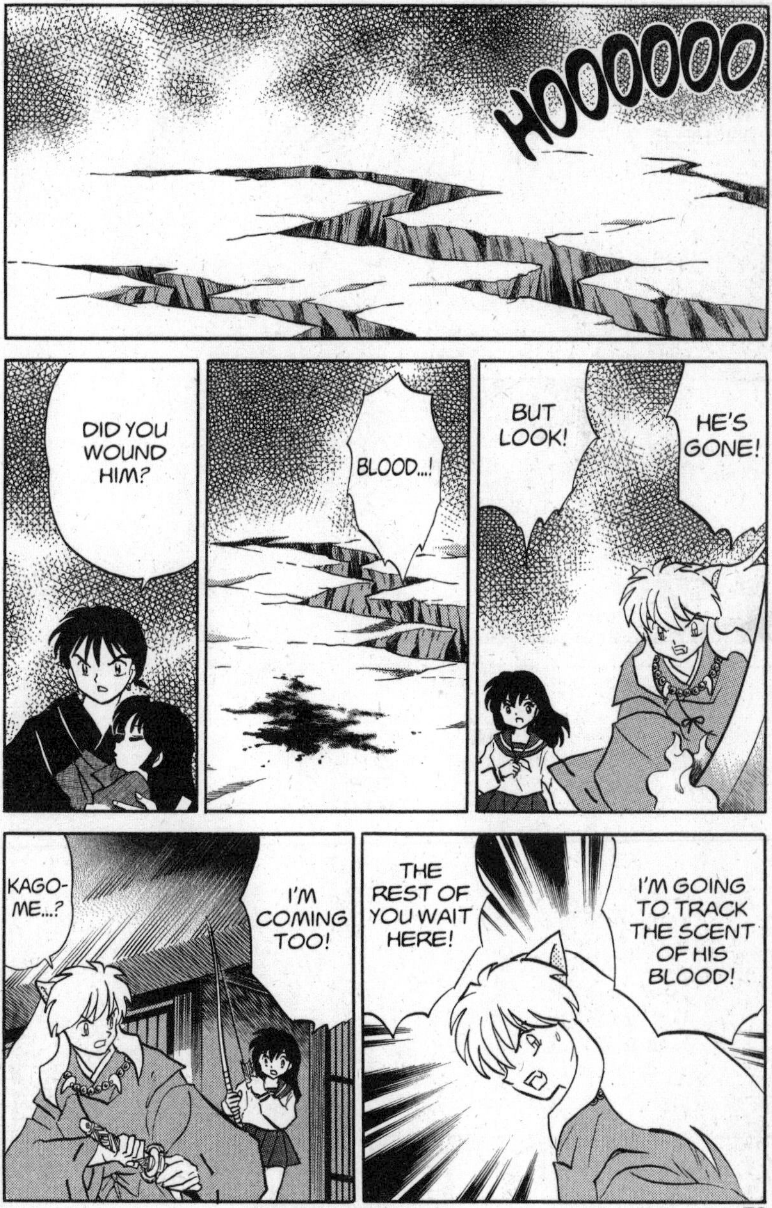
HOOOOOO
HE'S GONE!
BUT LOOK!
BLOOD...!
DID YOU WOUND HIM?
I'M GOING TO TRACK THE SCENT OF HIS BLOOD!
THE REST OF YOU WAIT HERE!
I'M COMING TOO!
KAGO-ME...?

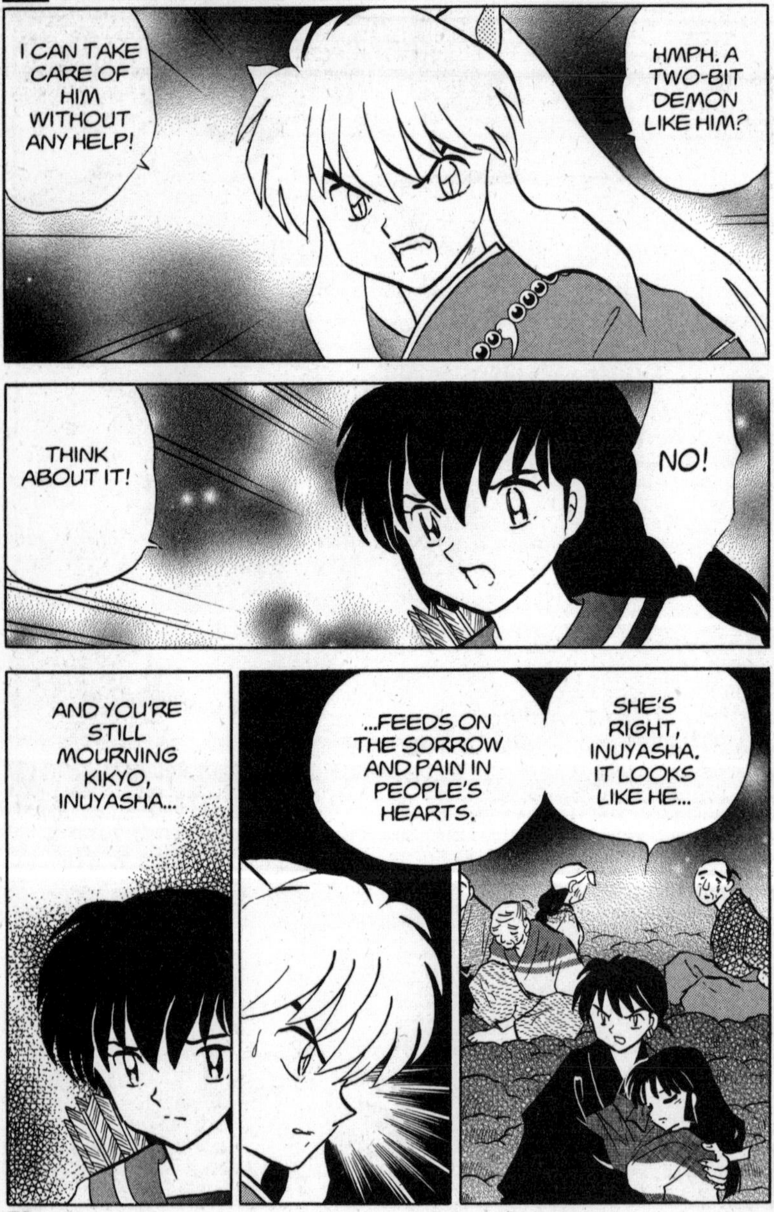
HMPH. A TWO-BIT DEMON LIKE HIM?
I CAN TAKE CARE OF HIM WITHOUT ANY HELP!
NO!
THINK ABOUT IT!
SHE'S RIGHT, INUYASHA. IT LOOKS LIKE HE...
...FEEDS ON THE SORROW AND PAIN IN PEOPLE'S HEARTS.
AND YOU'RE STILL MOURNING KIKYO, INUYASHA...

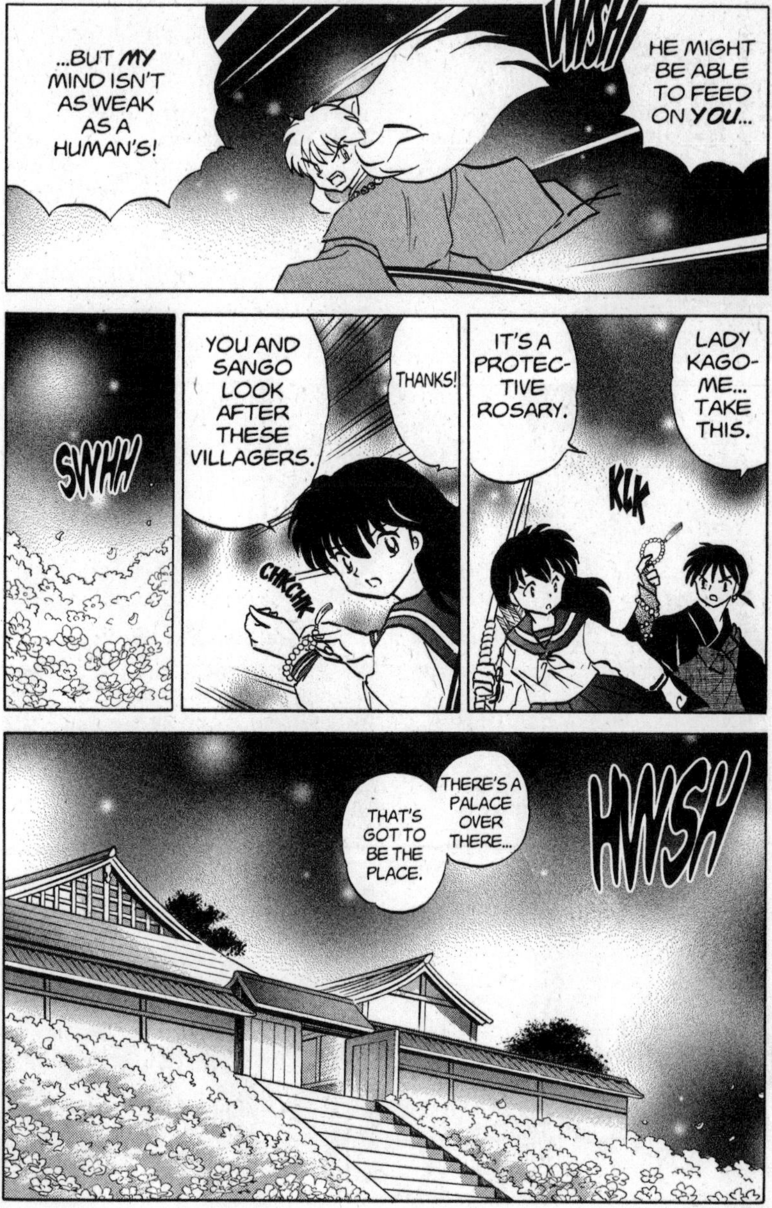

HE MIGHT BE ABLE TO FEED ON *YOU*...
VWSH
...BUT *MY* MIND ISN'T AS WEAK AS A HUMAN'S!
LADY KAGOME... TAKE THIS.
KLK
IT'S A PROTECTIVE ROSARY.
THANKS!
YOU AND SANGO LOOK AFTER THESE VILLAGERS.
CHKCHK
SWHH
HWSH
THERE'S A PALACE OVER THERE...
THAT'S GOT TO BE THE PLACE.

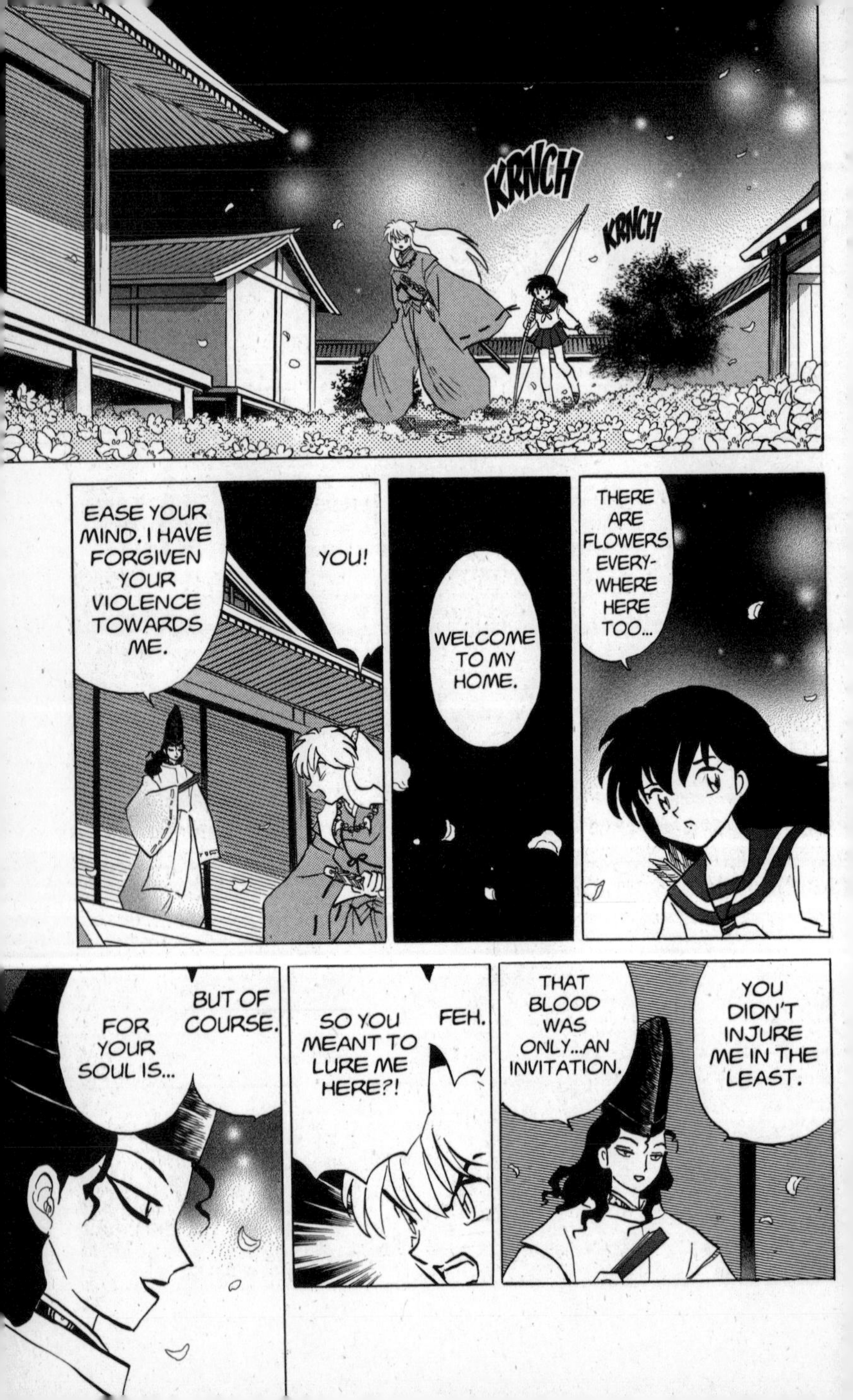
KRNCH
KRNCH
THERE ARE FLOWERS EVERY-WHERE HERE TOO...
WELCOME TO MY HOME.
YOU!
EASE YOUR MIND. I HAVE FORGIVEN YOUR VIOLENCE TOWARDS ME.
YOU DIDN'T INJURE ME IN THE LEAST.
THAT BLOOD WAS ONLY...AN INVITATION.
FEH.
SO YOU MEANT TO LURE ME HERE?!
BUT OF COURSE.
FOR YOUR SOUL IS...

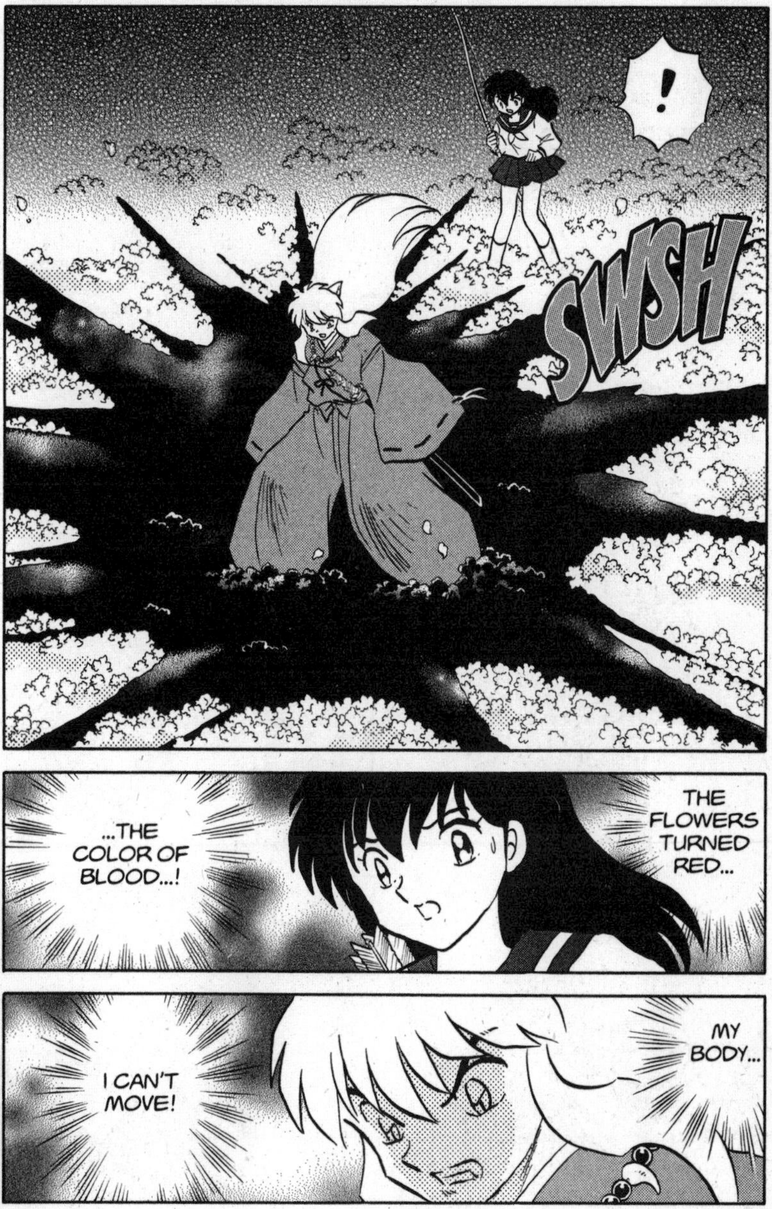
!
SWISH
THE FLOWERS TURNED RED...
...THE COLOR OF BLOOD...!
MY BODY...
I CAN'T MOVE!

SCROLL 5

TEARS OF BLOOD

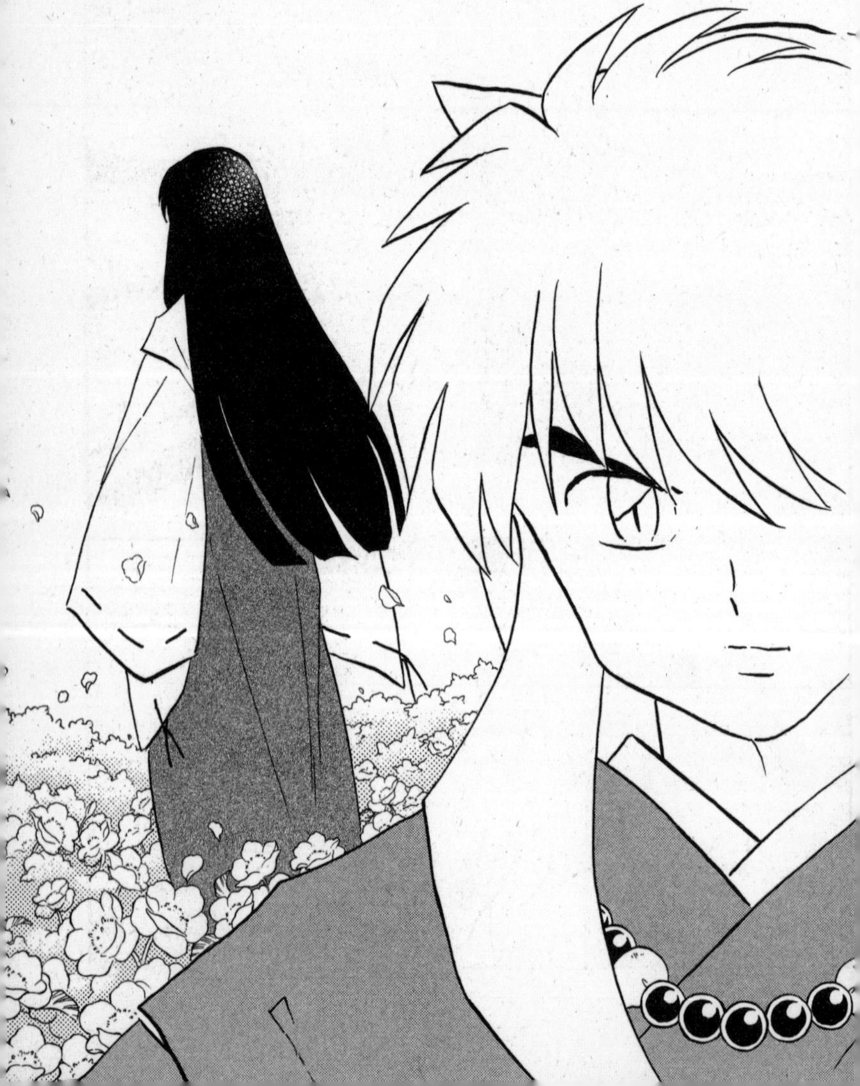

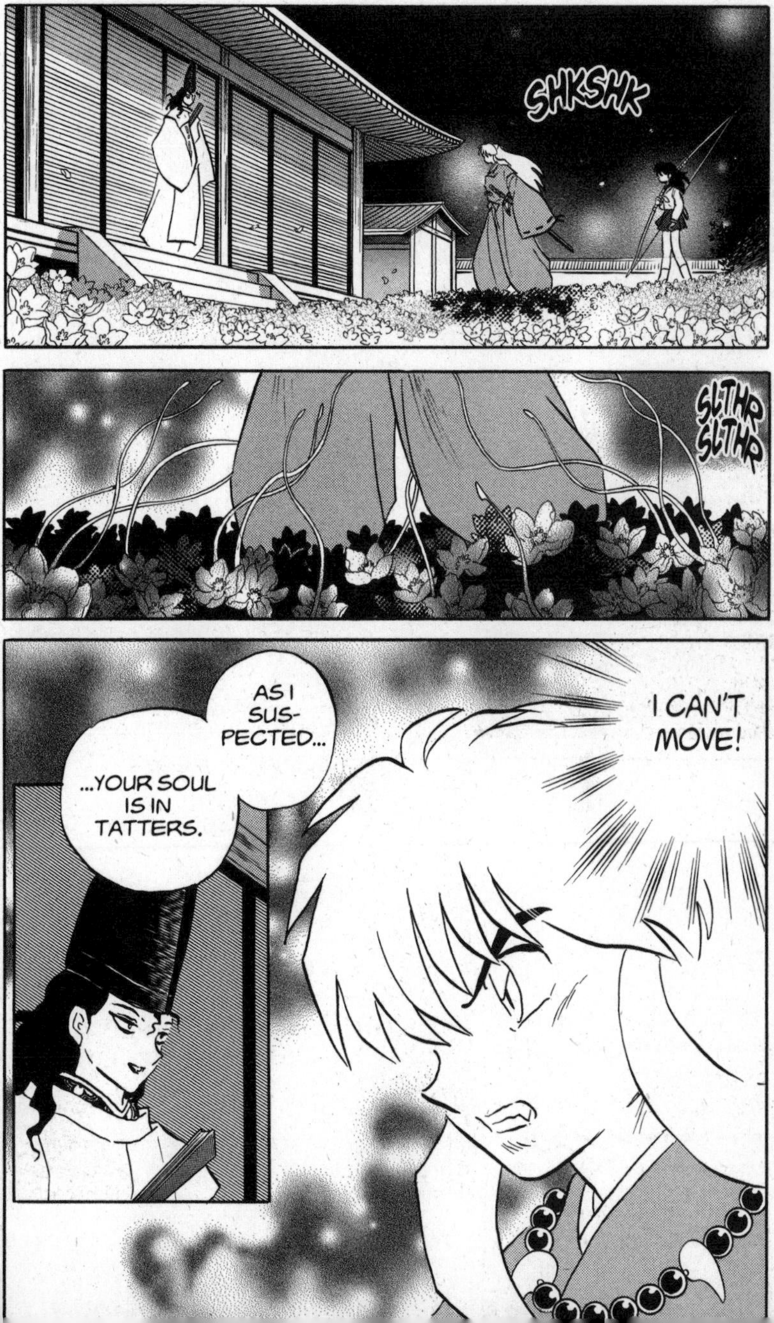
SHKSHK
SLTHR SLTHR
I CAN'T MOVE!
AS I SUS-PECTED...
...YOUR SOUL IS IN TATTERS.

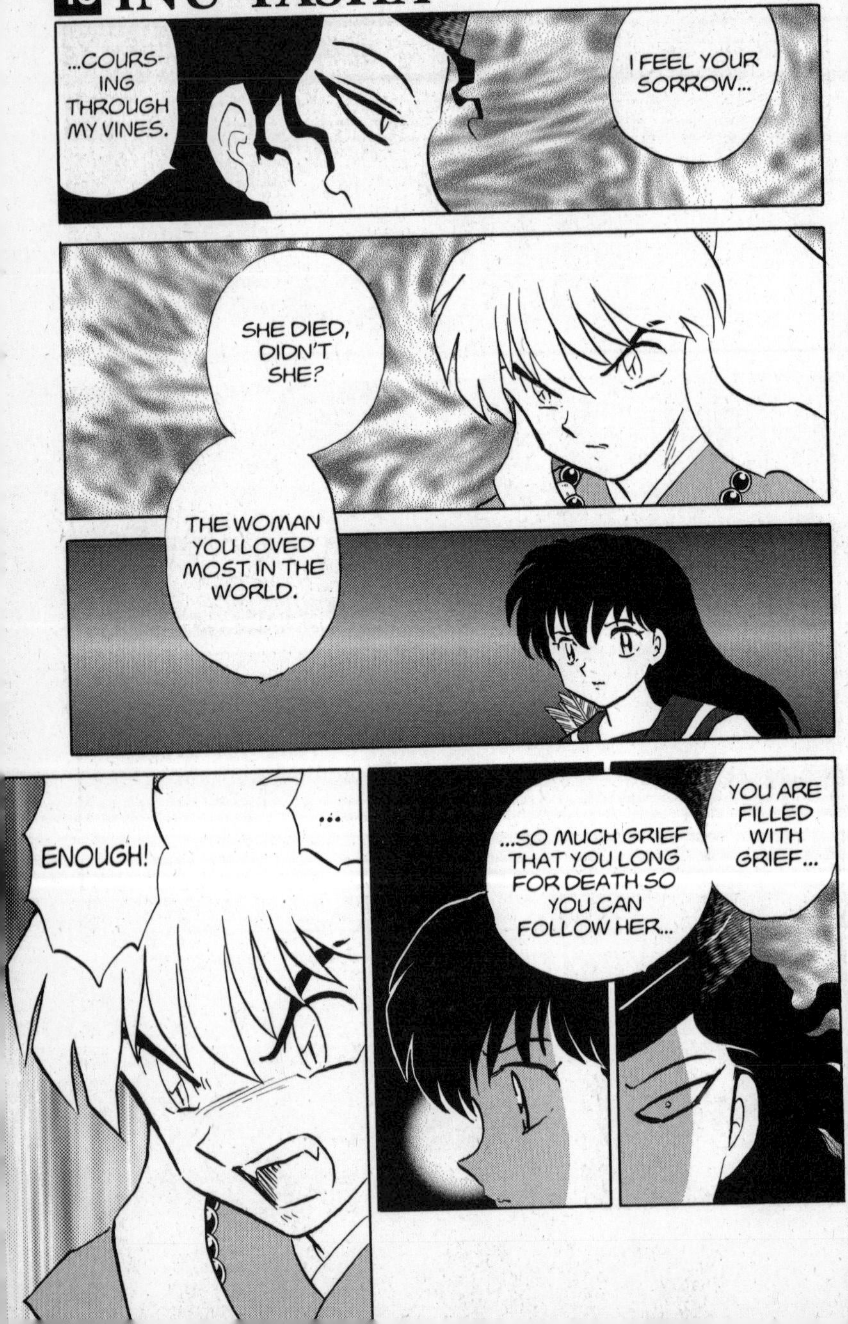
I FEEL YOUR SORROW...
...COURSING THROUGH MY VINES.
SHE DIED, DIDN'T SHE?
THE WOMAN YOU LOVED MOST IN THE WORLD.
YOU ARE FILLED WITH GRIEF...
...SO MUCH GRIEF THAT YOU LONG FOR DEATH SO YOU CAN FOLLOW HER...
...
ENOUGH!

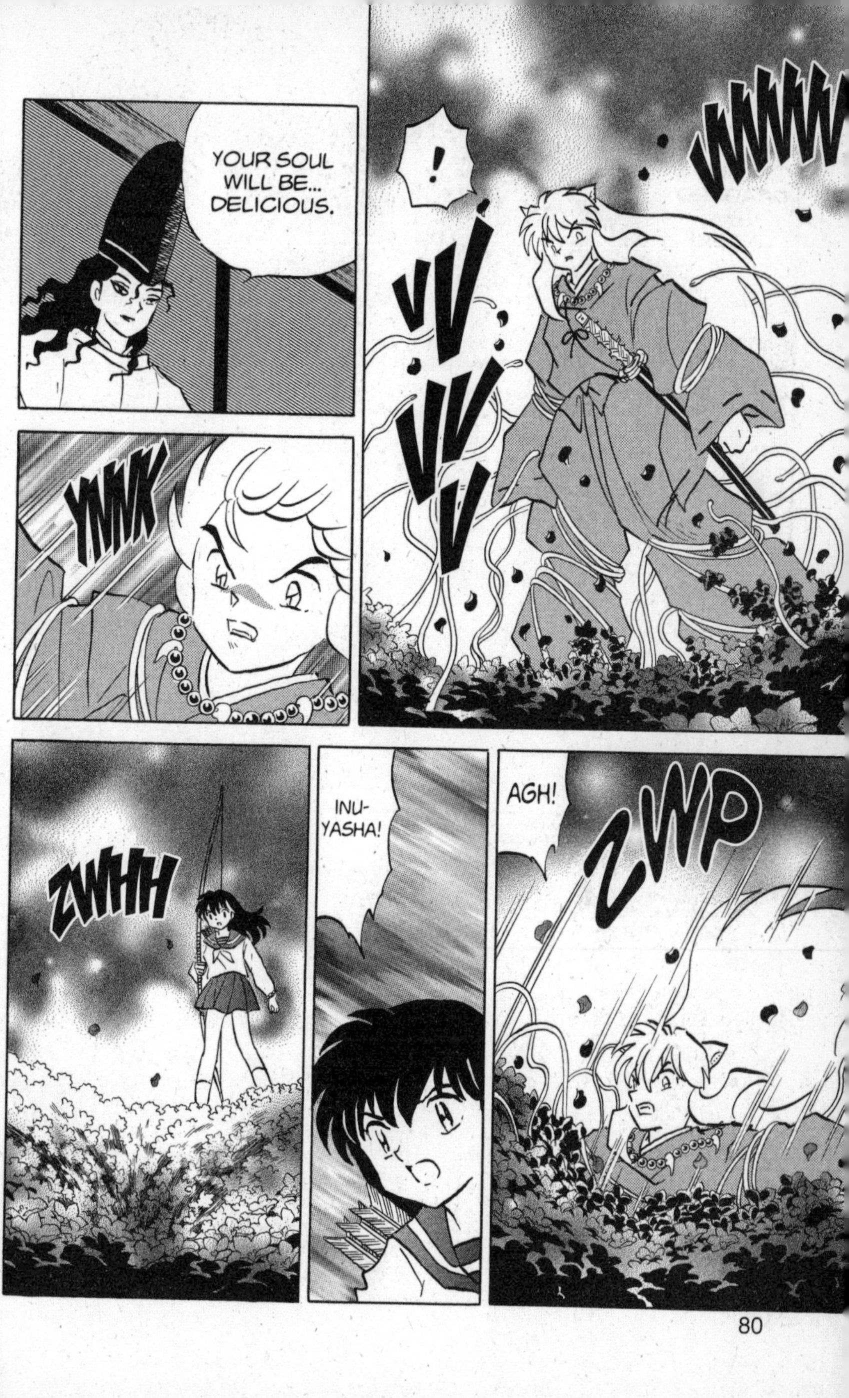
!
YOUR SOUL WILL BE... DELICIOUS.
YNNK
AGH!
ZWP
INU-YASHA!
ZWHH

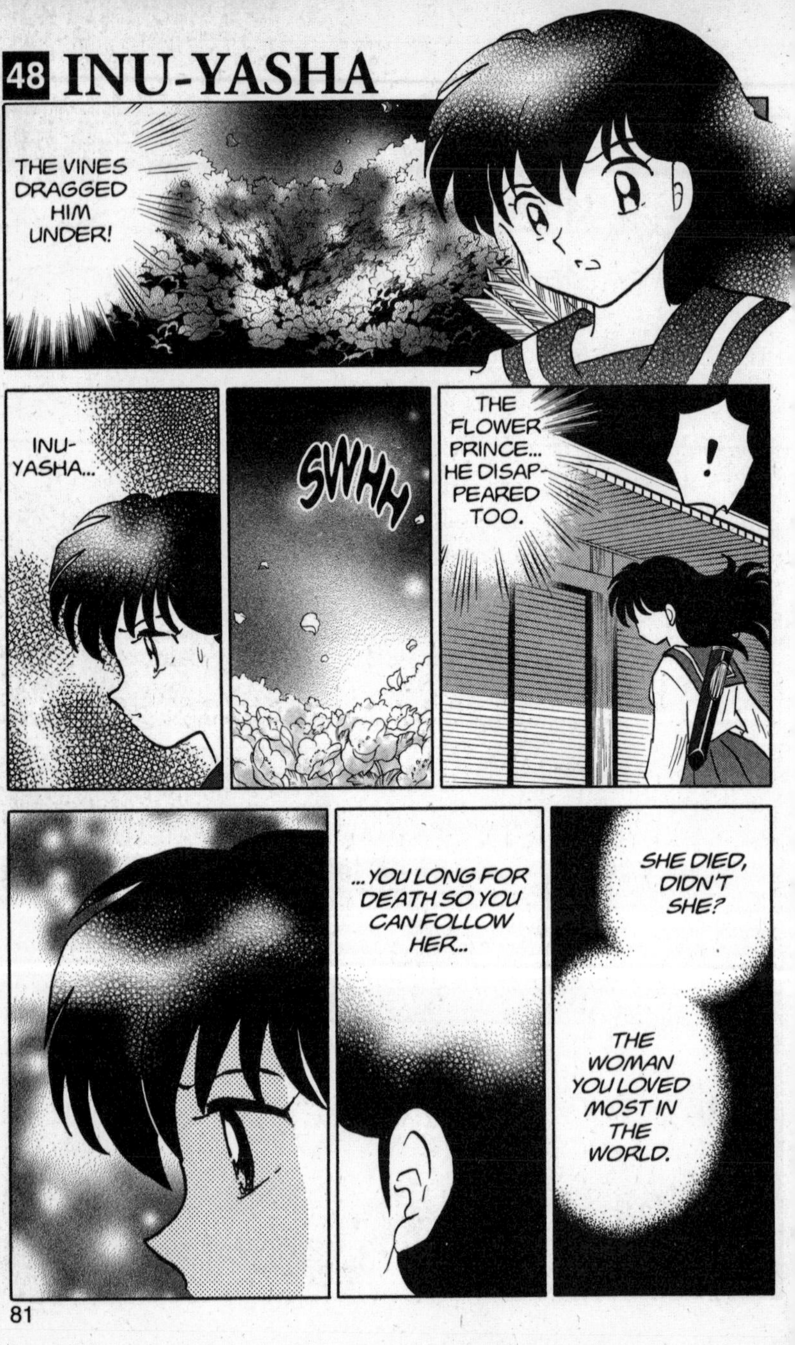
THE VINES DRAGGED HIM UNDER!
THE FLOWER PRINCE... HE DISAPPEARED TOO.
!
SWHH
INU-YASHA...
SHE DIED, DIDN'T SHE?
THE WOMAN YOU LOVED MOST IN THE WORLD.
...YOU LONG FOR DEATH SO YOU CAN FOLLOW HER...

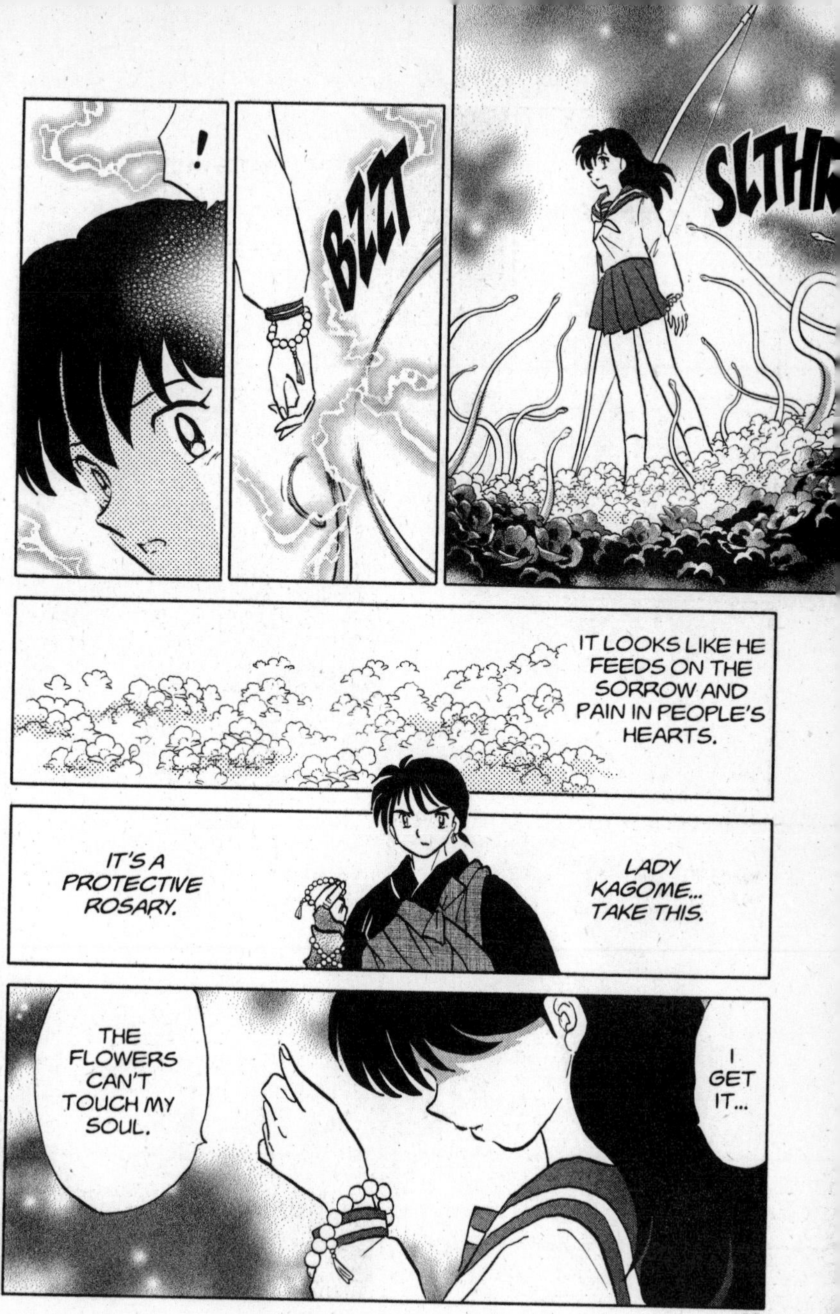
SLTHR
BZZT
!
IT LOOKS LIKE HE FEEDS ON THE SORROW AND PAIN IN PEOPLE'S HEARTS.
LADY KAGOME... TAKE THIS.
IT'S A PROTECTIVE ROSARY.
I GET IT...
THE FLOWERS CAN'T TOUCH MY SOUL.

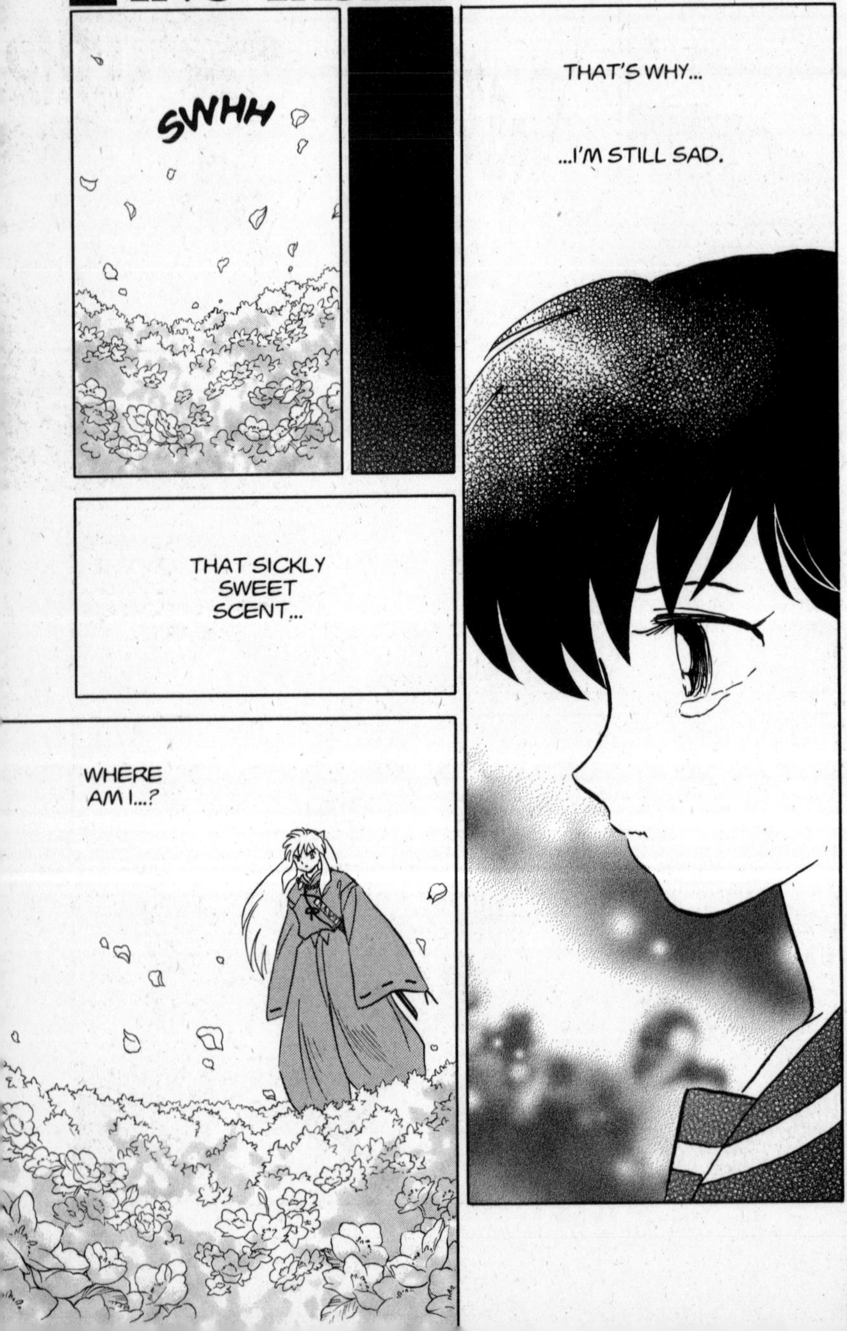
THAT'S WHY...
...I'M STILL SAD.
SWHH
THAT SICKLY SWEET SCENT...
WHERE AM I...?

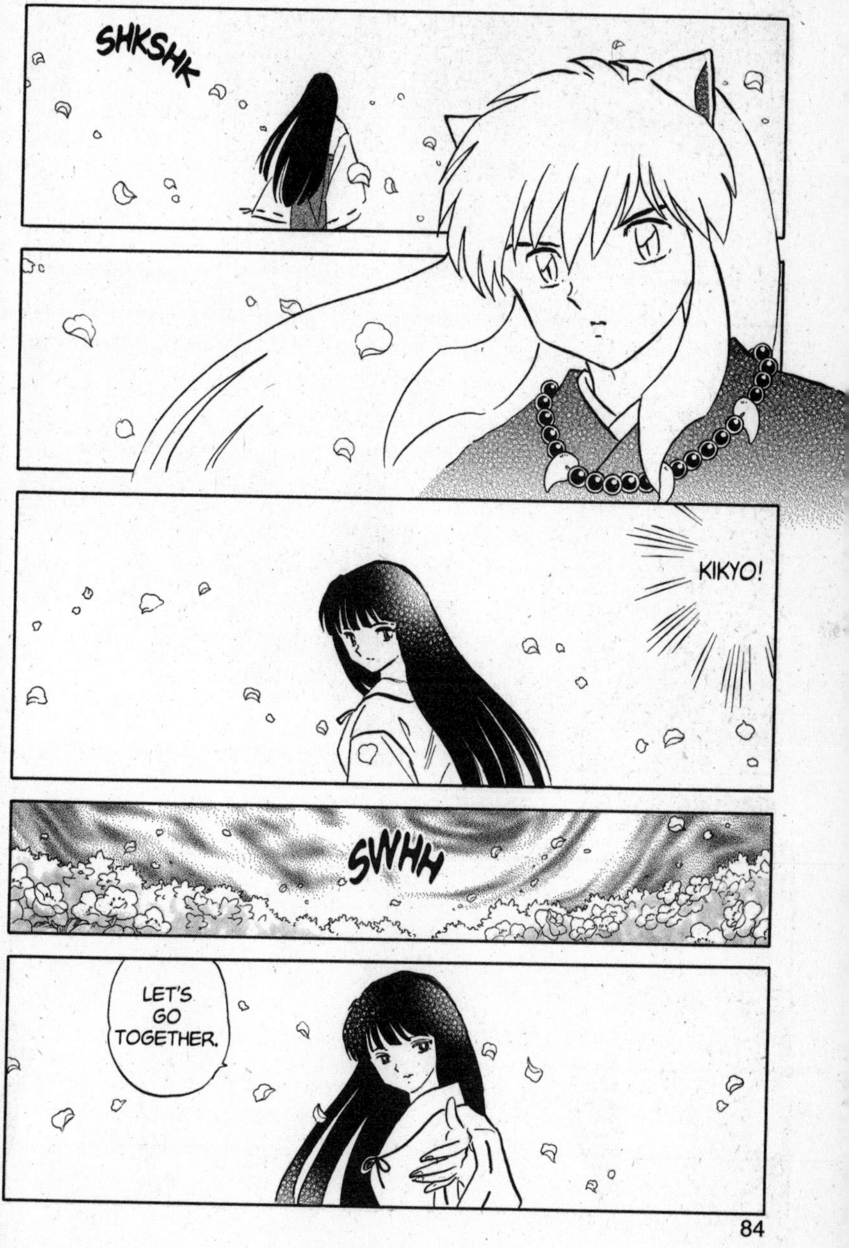
SHKSHK
KIKYO!
SWHH
LET'S GO TOGETHER.

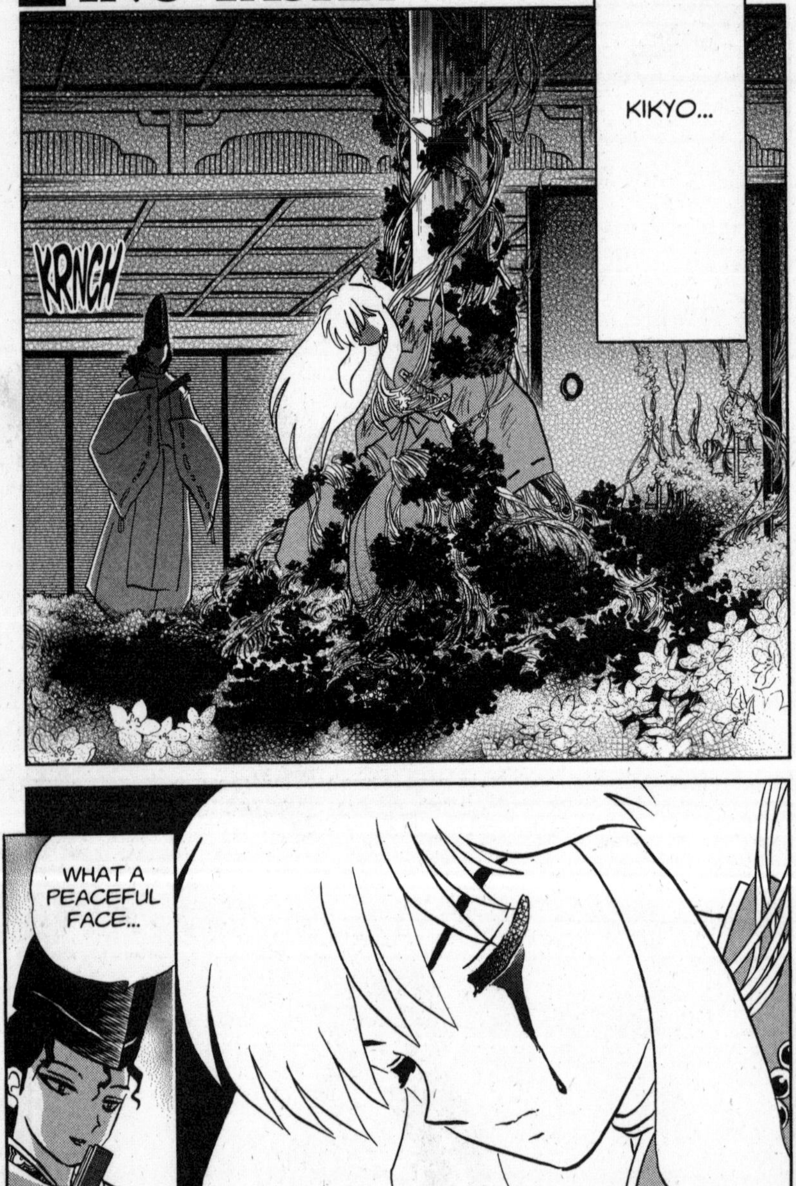
KIKYO...
KRNCH
WHAT A PEACEFUL FACE...

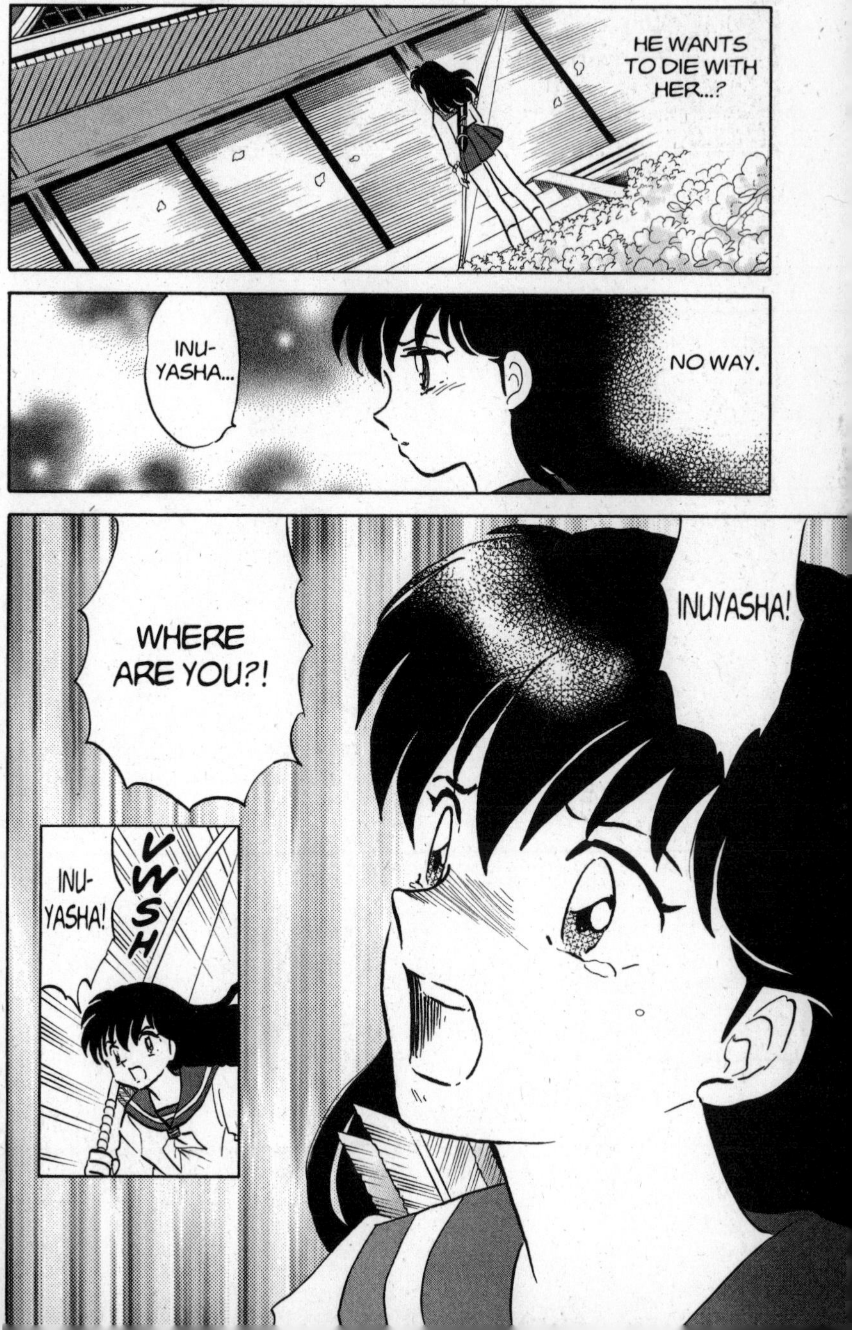
HE WANTS TO DIE WITH HER...?
NO WAY.
INU-YASHA...
INUYASHA!
WHERE ARE YOU?!
VWSH
INU-YASHA!

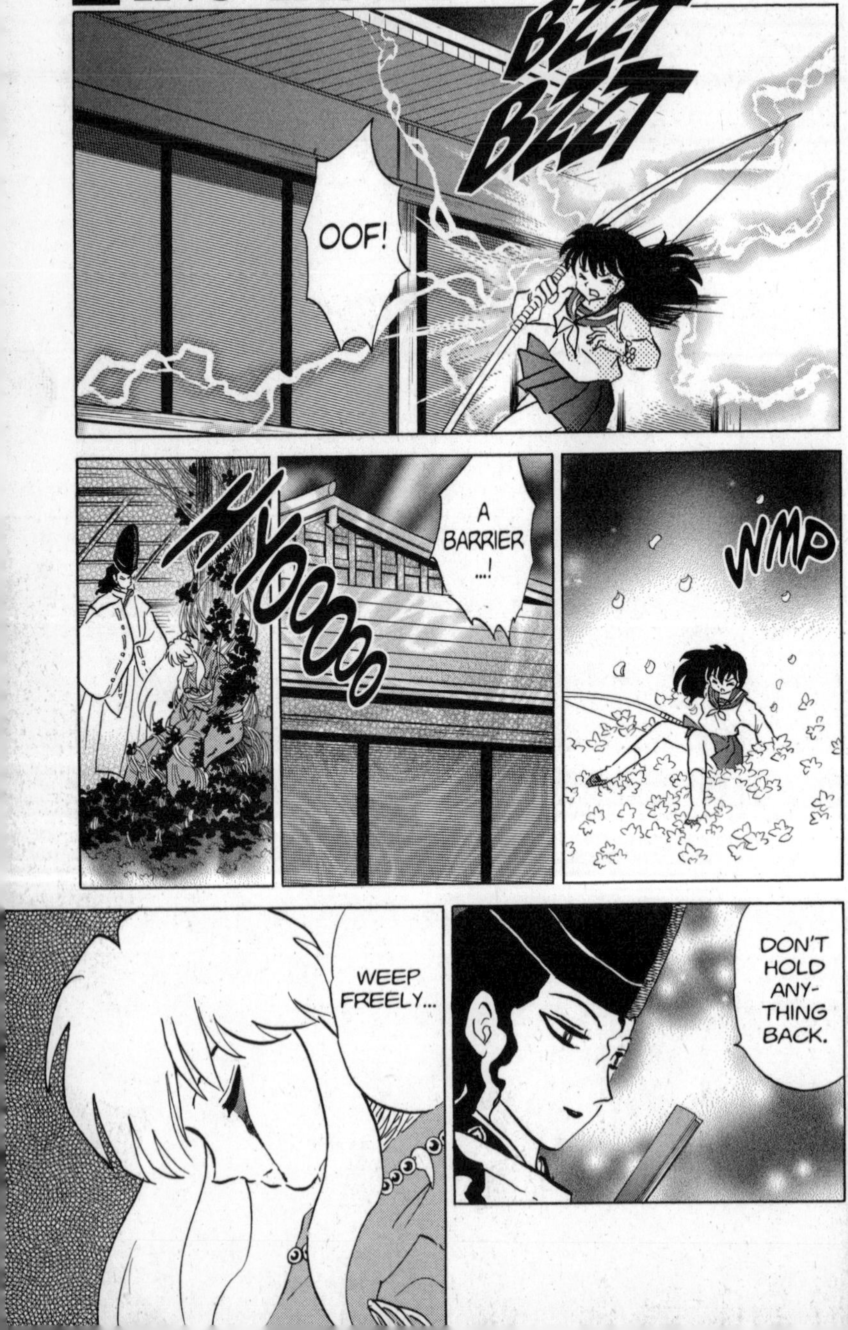
BZZT BZZT
OOF!
WMP
A BARRIER ...!
HYOOOOO
DON'T HOLD ANY-THING BACK.
WEEP FREELY...

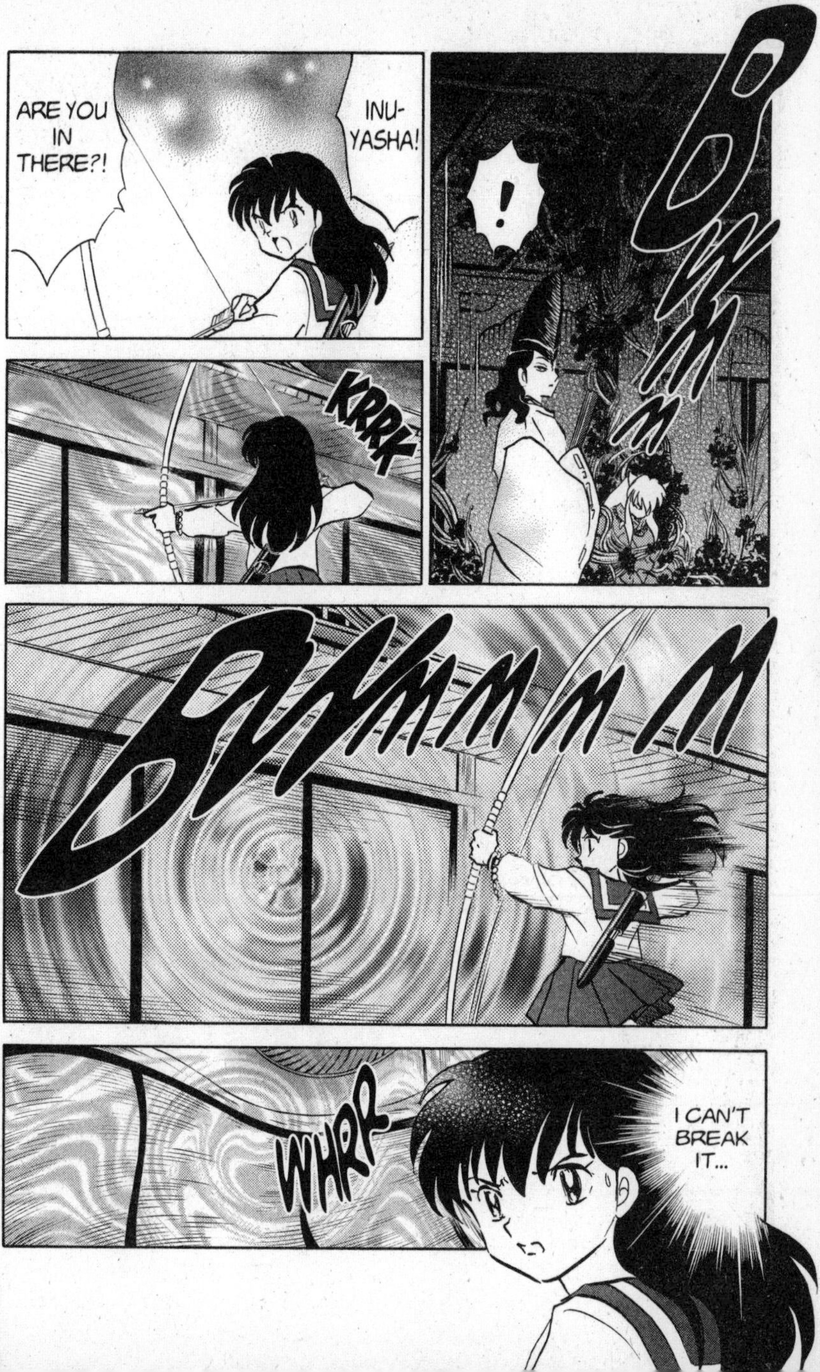

BOWMMMM
!
INU-YASHA!
ARE YOU IN THERE?!
KRRK
BWMMMMM
I CAN'T BREAK IT...
WHRR

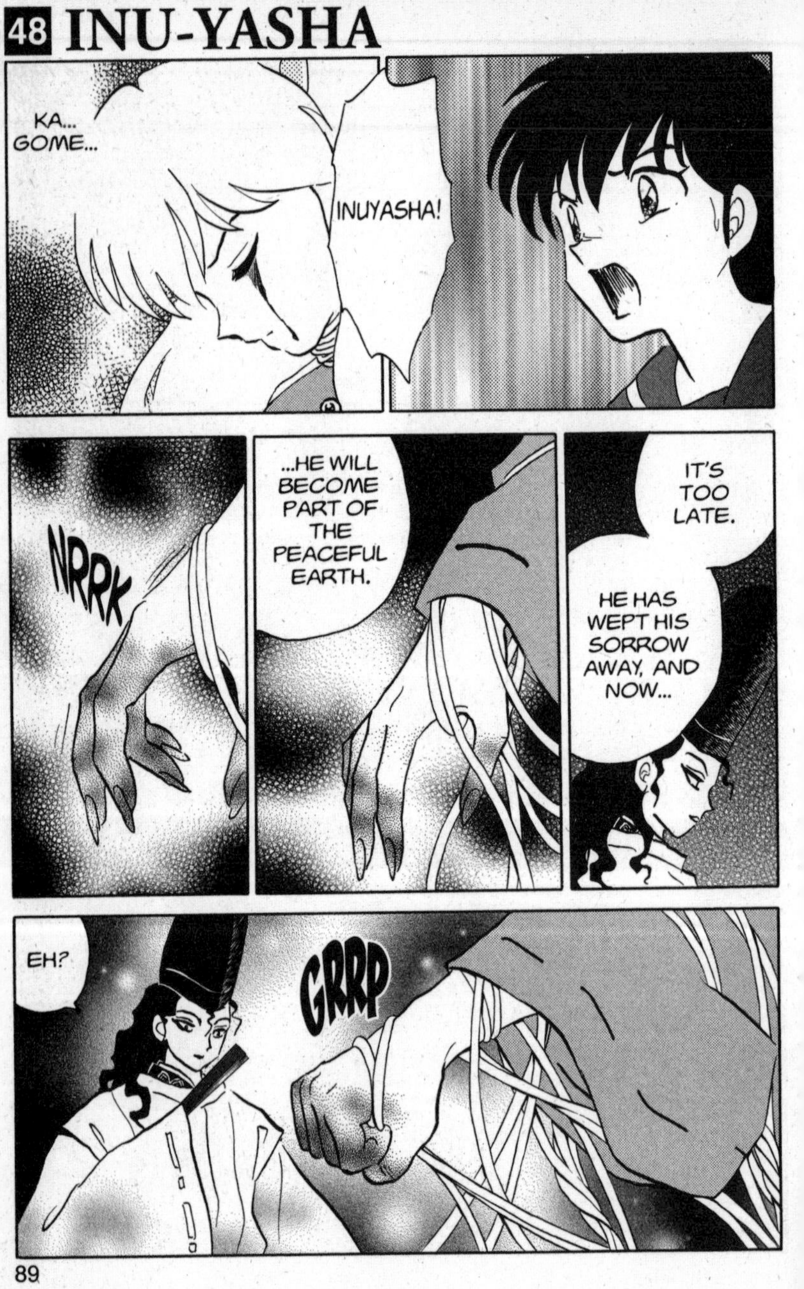
INUYASHA!
KA... GOME...
IT'S TOO LATE.
HE HAS WEPT HIS SORROW AWAY, AND NOW...
...HE WILL BECOME PART OF THE PEACEFUL EARTH.
NRRK
GRRP
EH?

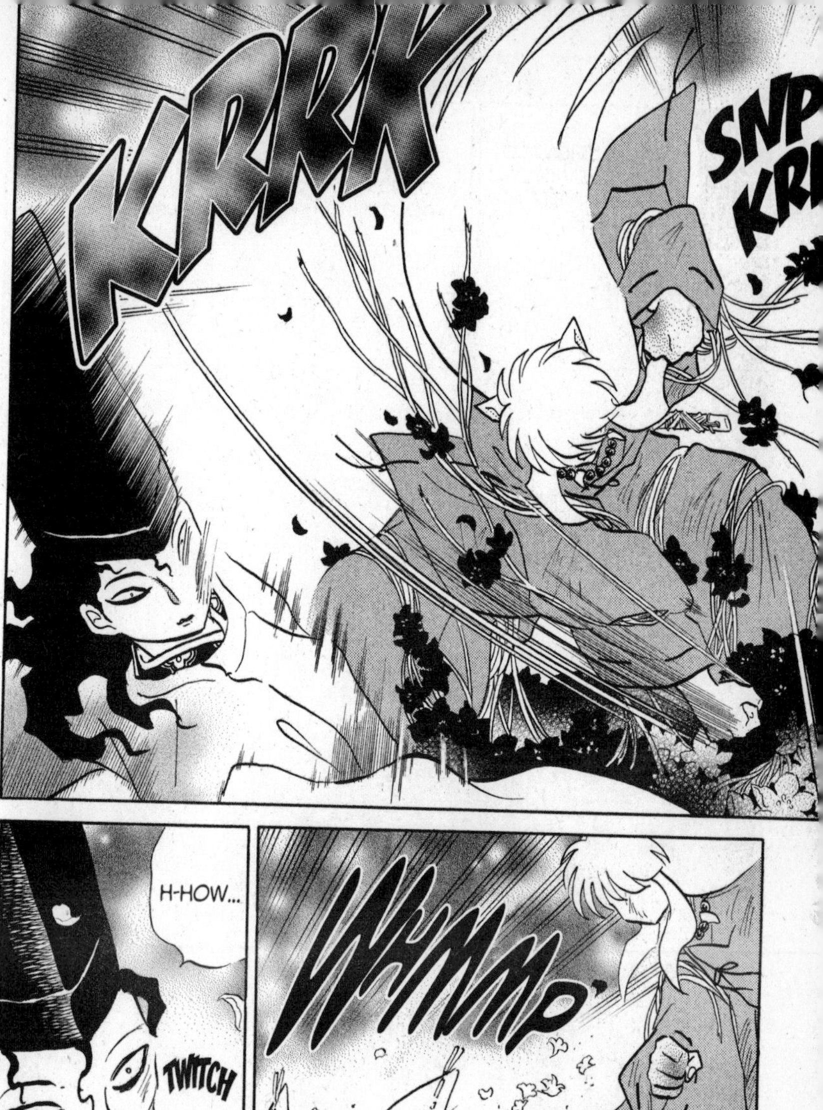
SNP
KR
KRRK
WHMP
H-HOW...
TWITCH

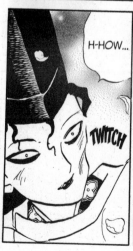

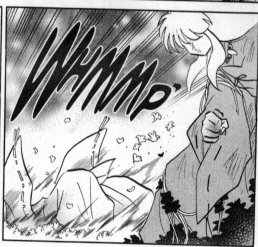

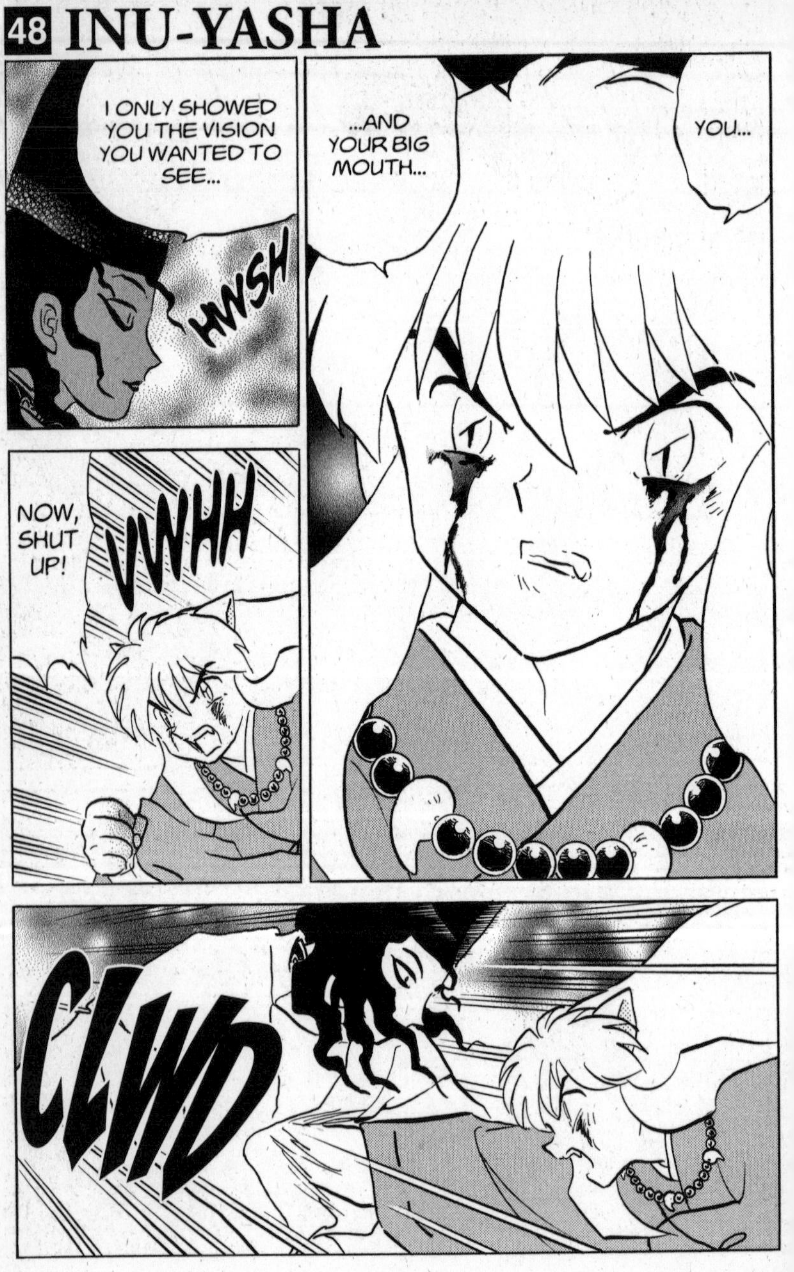
YOU...
...AND YOUR BIG MOUTH...
I ONLY SHOWED YOU THE VISION YOU WANTED TO SEE...
HWSH
NOW, SHUT UP!
VWHH
CLWD

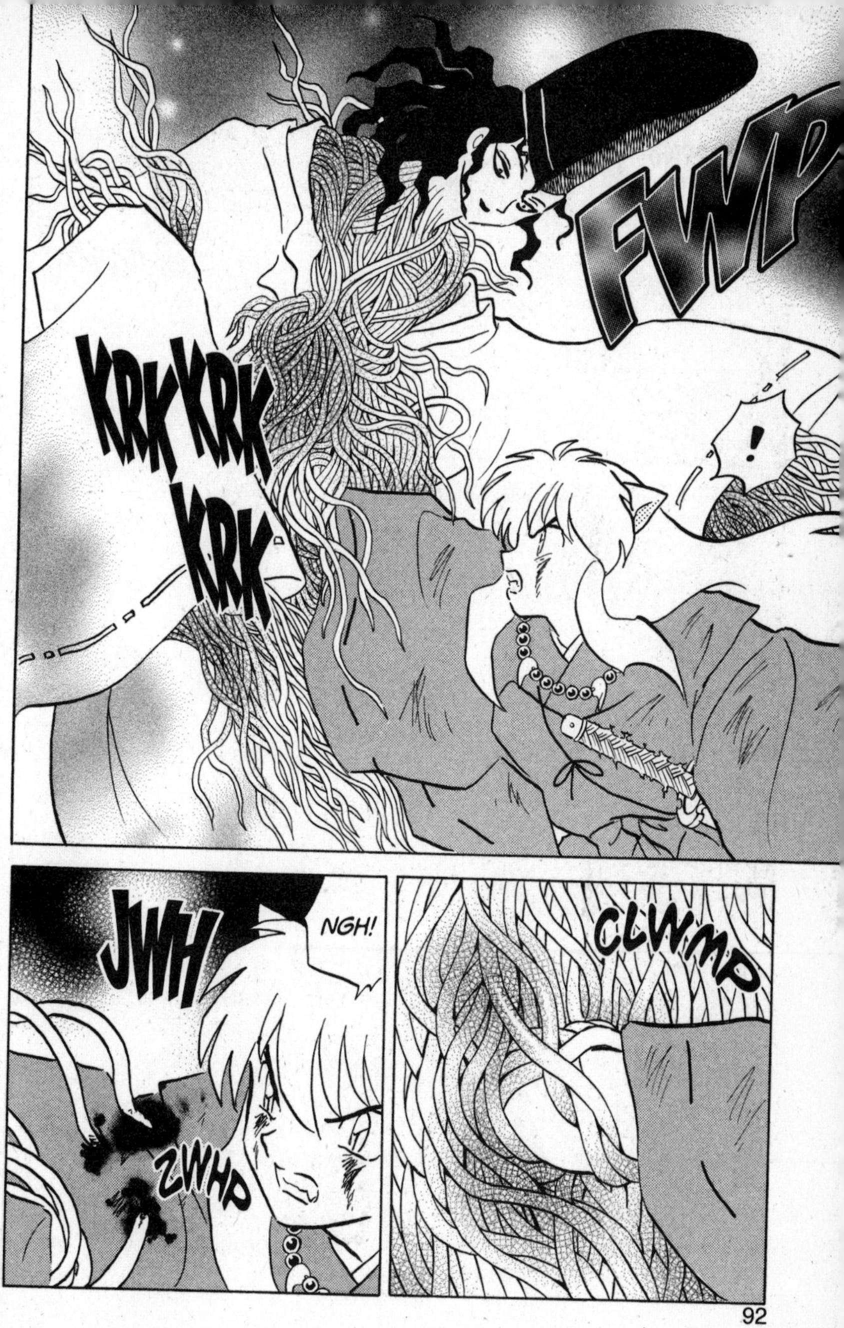
FWP
!
KRK KRK
KRK
CLWMP
NGH!
JWH
ZWHP

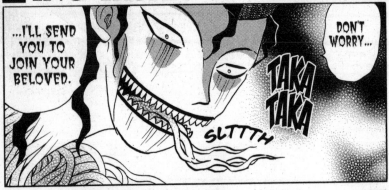

...I'LL SEND YOU TO JOIN YOUR BELOVED.

DON'T WORRY...

TAKA TAKA

SLTTTH

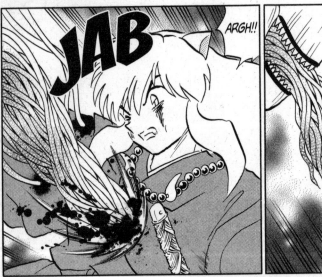

JAB

ARGH!!

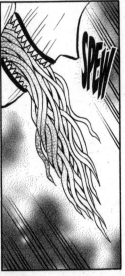

SPEW

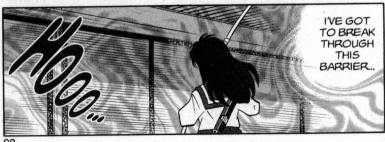

HOOO...

I'VE GOT TO BREAK THROUGH THIS BARRIER...

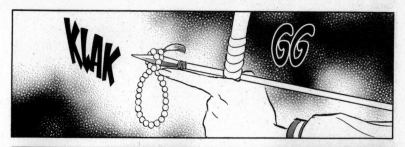

KLAK

GG

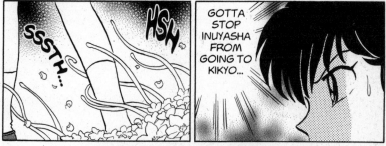

SSSTH...

HSH

GOTTA STOP INUYASHA FROM GOING TO KIKYO...

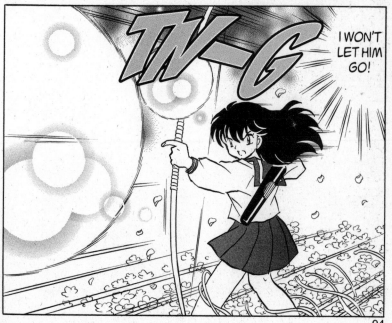

TV-G

I WON'T LET HIM GO!

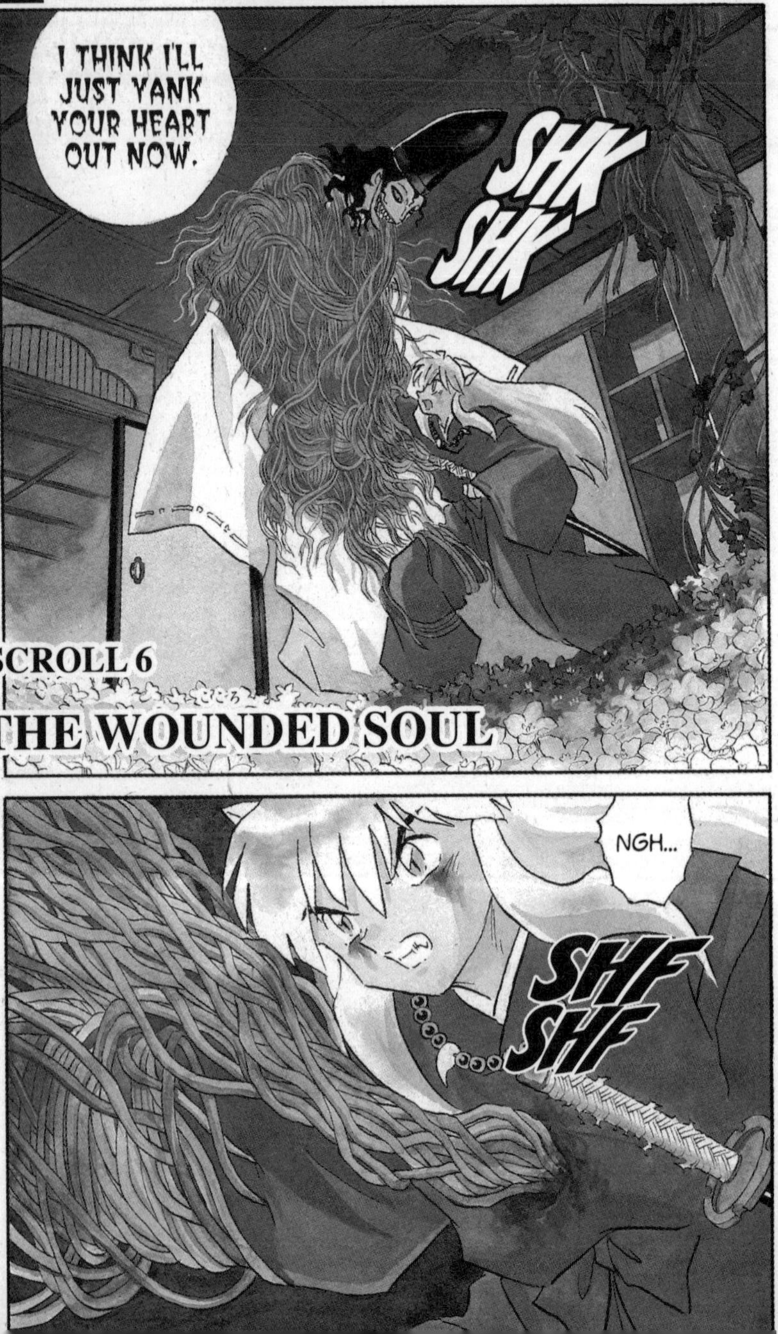
I THINK I'LL JUST YANK YOUR HEART OUT NOW.
SHK SHK
SCROLL 6
THE WOUNDED SOUL
NGH...
SHF SHF

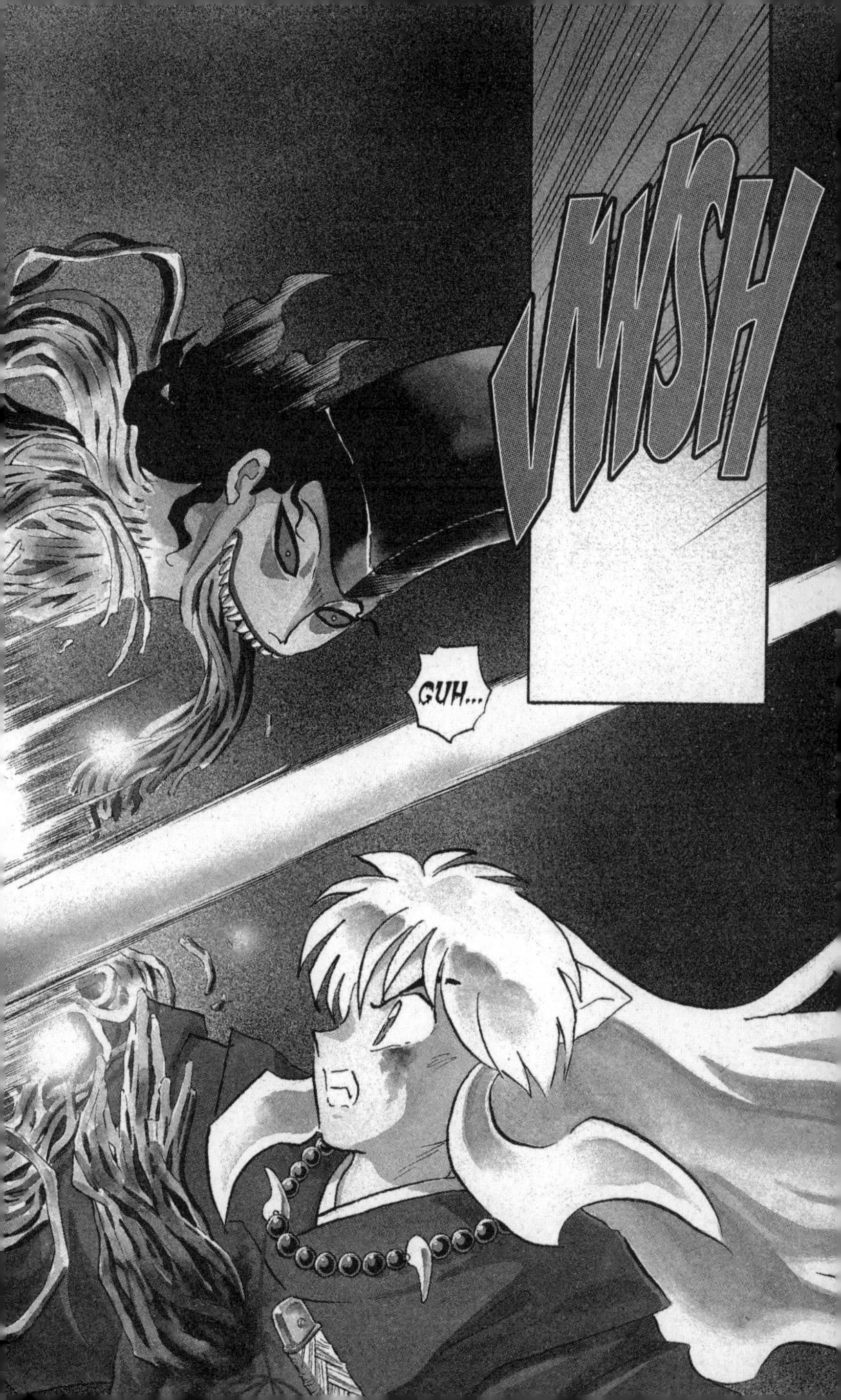
VWOOSH
GUH...

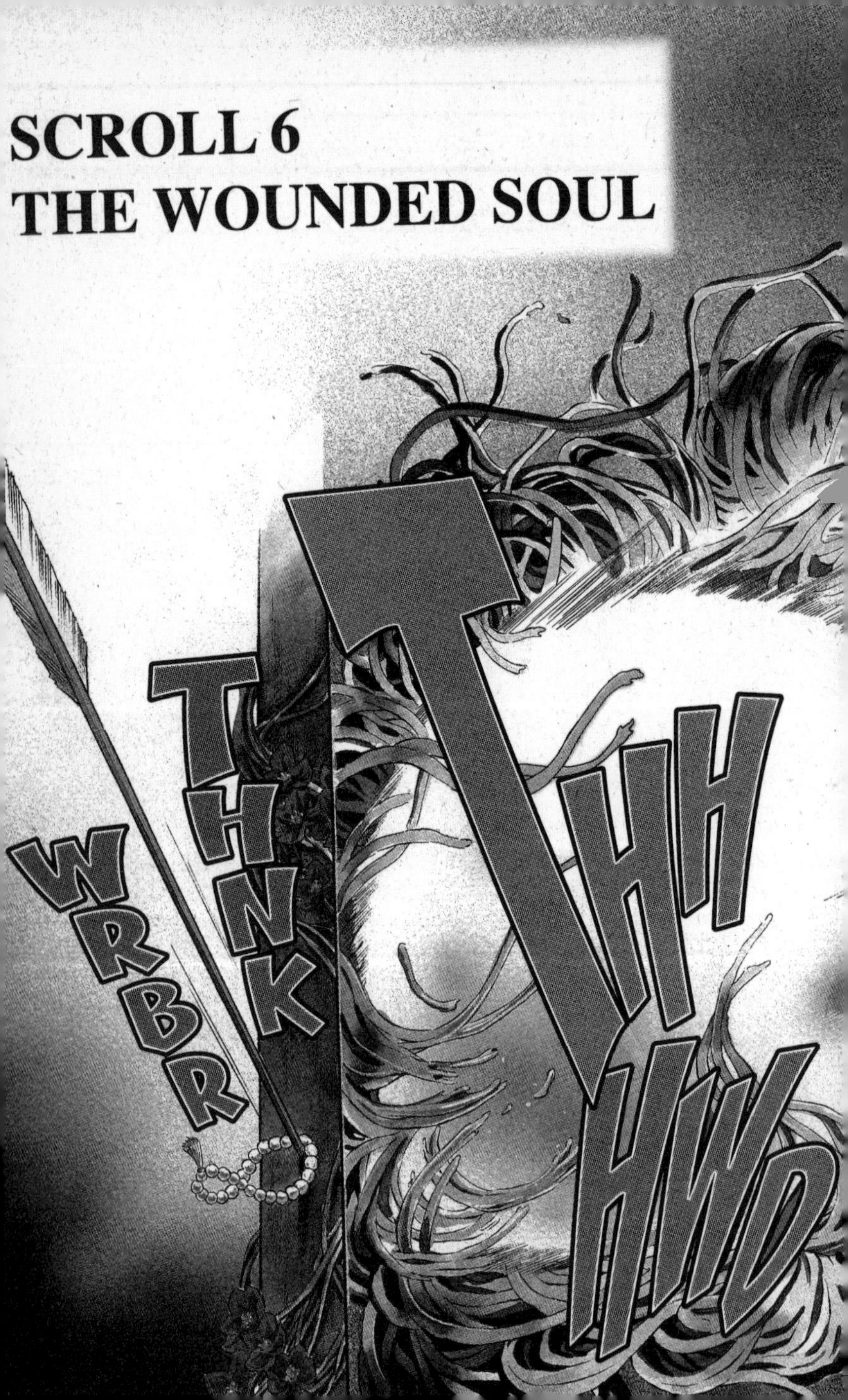
SCROLL 6
THE WOUNDED SOUL
THNK
WRBR

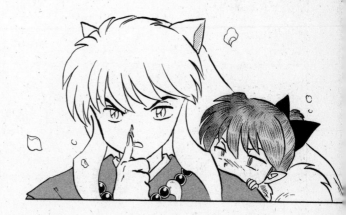

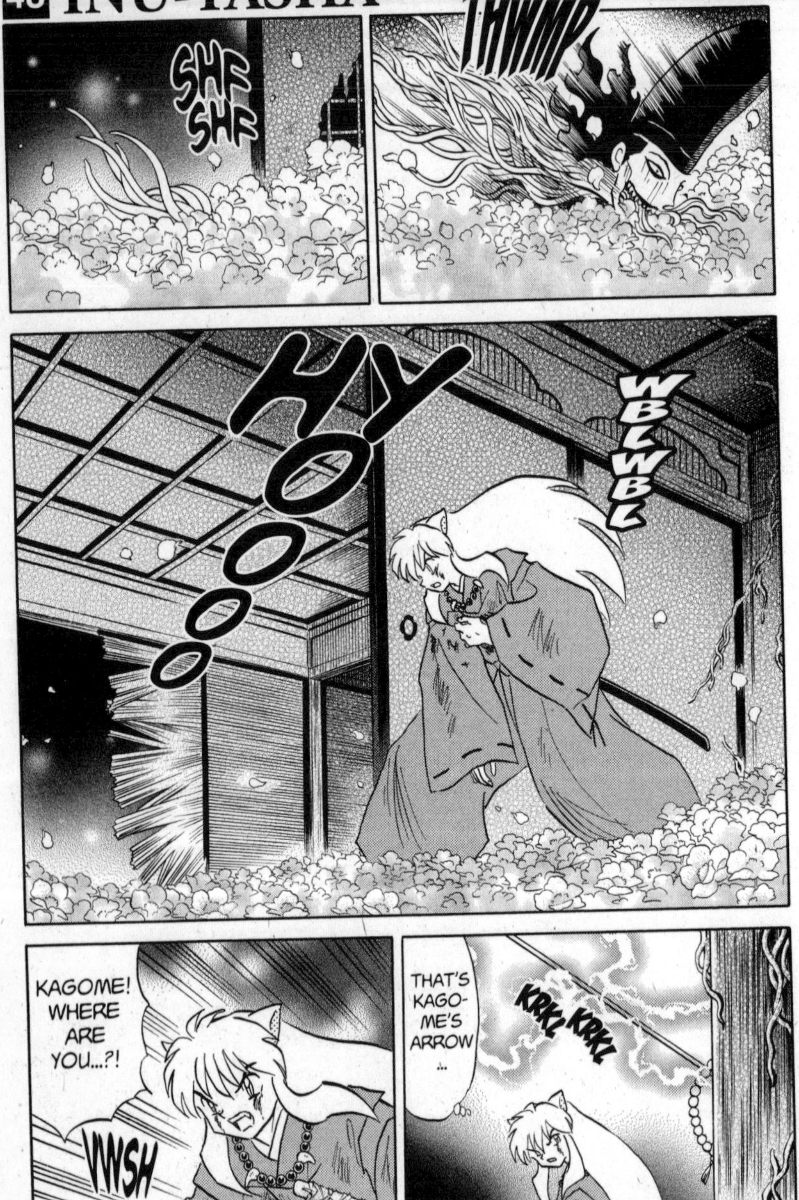
THWMP
SHF SHF
WBLWBL
HYOOOOOO
THAT'S KAGO-ME'S ARROW...
KRKL KRKL
KAGOME! WHERE ARE YOU...?!
VWSH

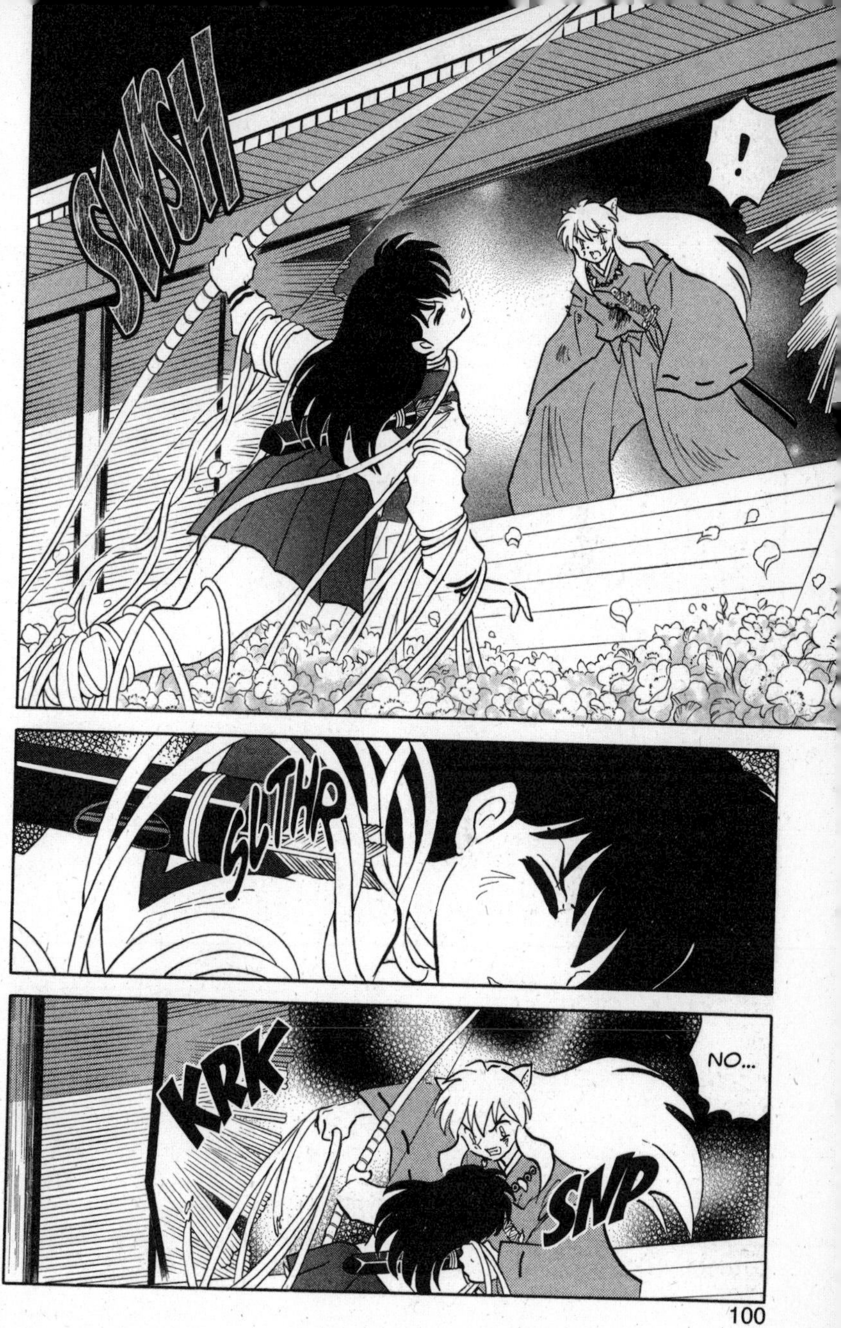
SWISH
!
SLITHR
NO...
SNP
KRK

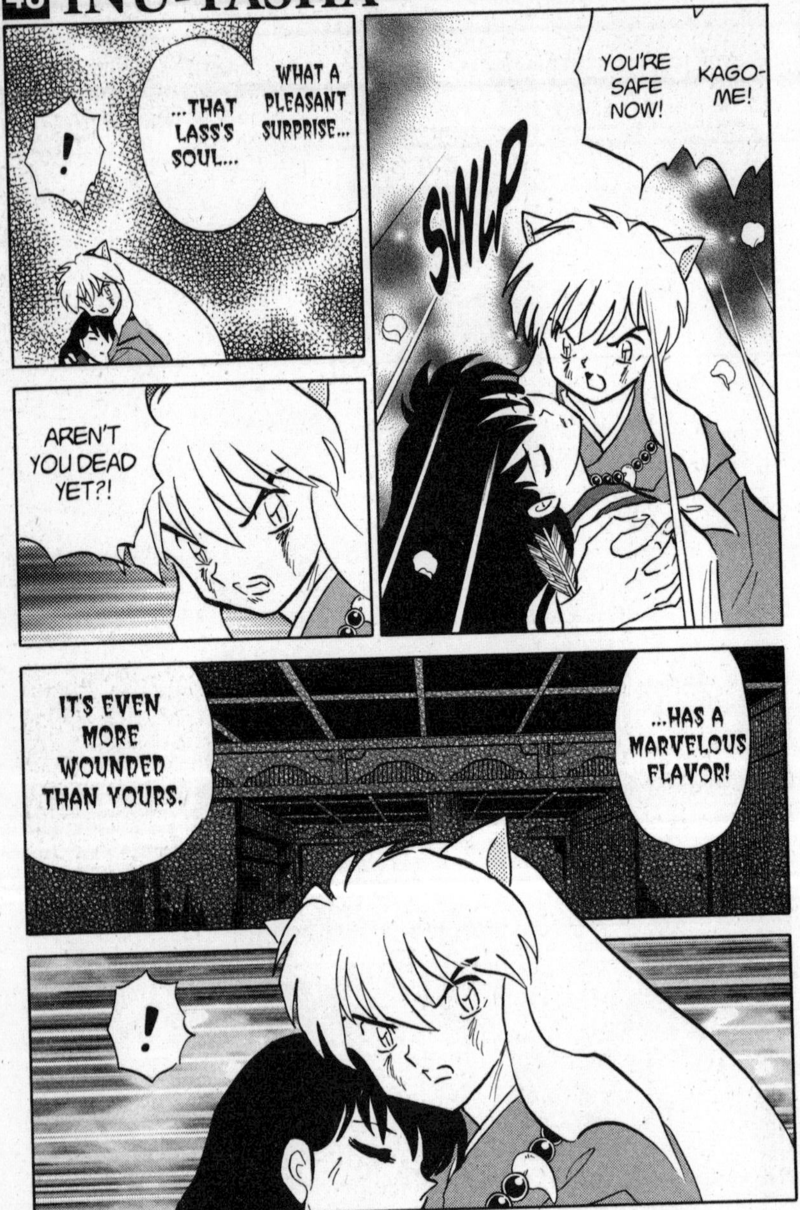
KAGO-ME!
YOU'RE SAFE NOW!
SWLP
WHAT A PLEASANT SURPRISE...
...THAT LASS'S SOUL...
!
AREN'T YOU DEAD YET?!
...HAS A MARVELOUS FLAVOR!
IT'S EVEN MORE WOUNDED THAN YOURS.
!

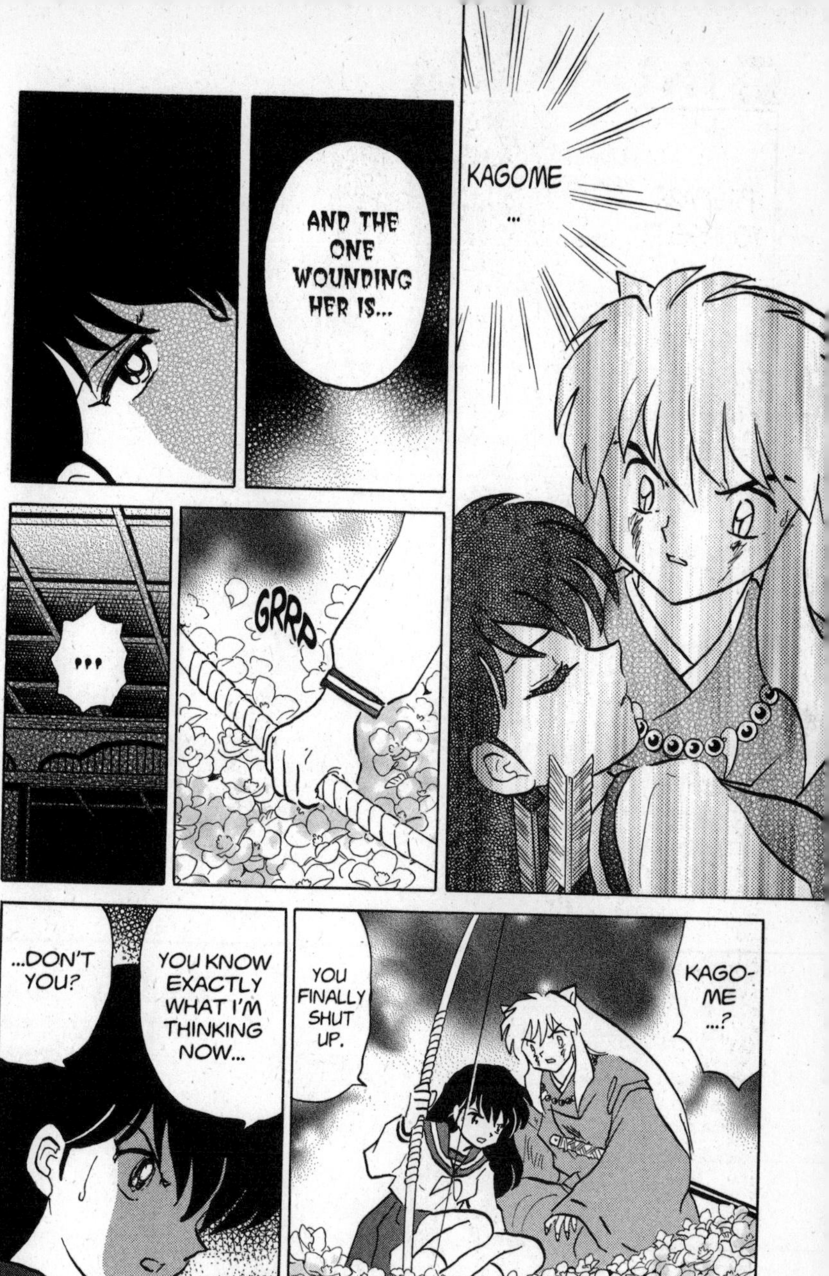
KAGOME ...
AND THE ONE WOUNDING HER IS...
GRRP
...
KAGO-ME ...?
YOU FINALLY SHUT UP.
YOU KNOW EXACTLY WHAT I'M THINKING NOW...
...DON'T YOU?

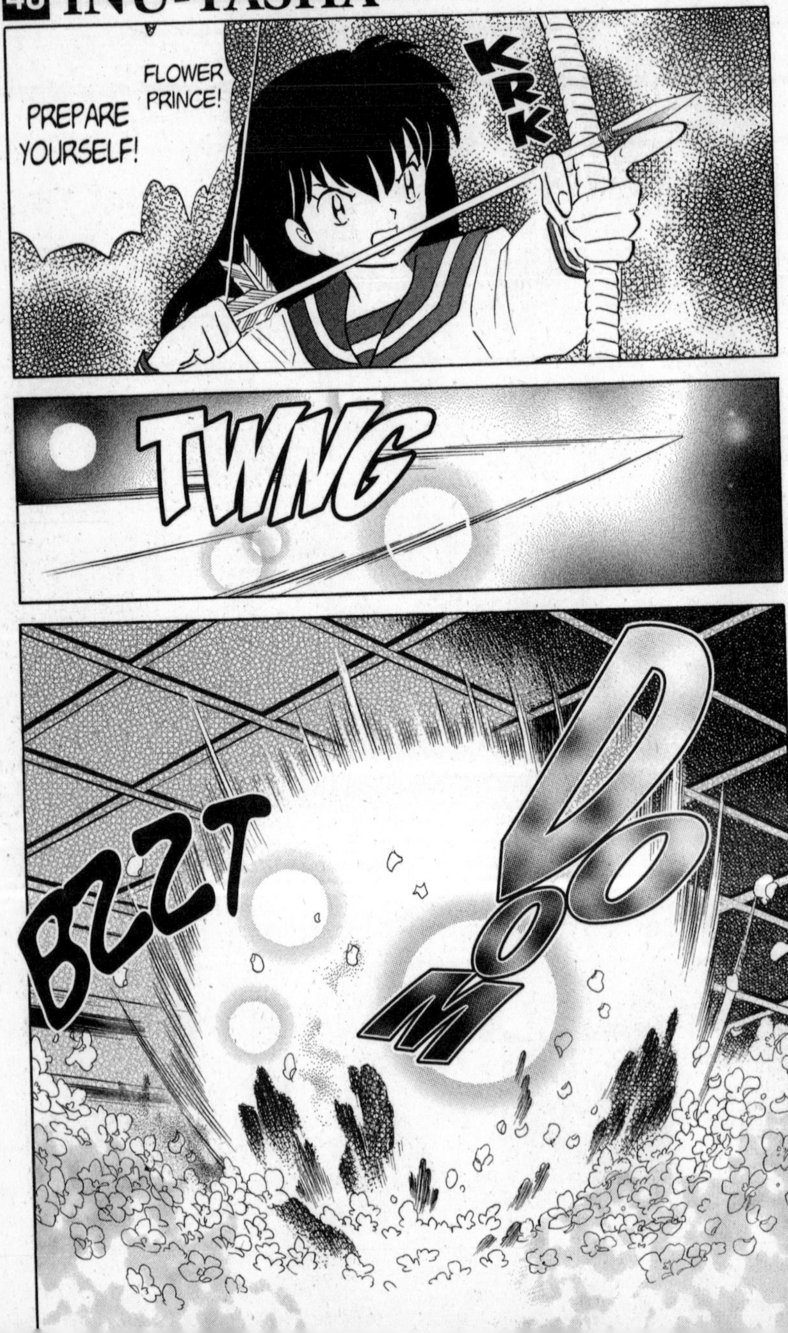
KRK
FLOWER PRINCE!
PREPARE YOURSELF!
TWNG
DOOM
BZZT

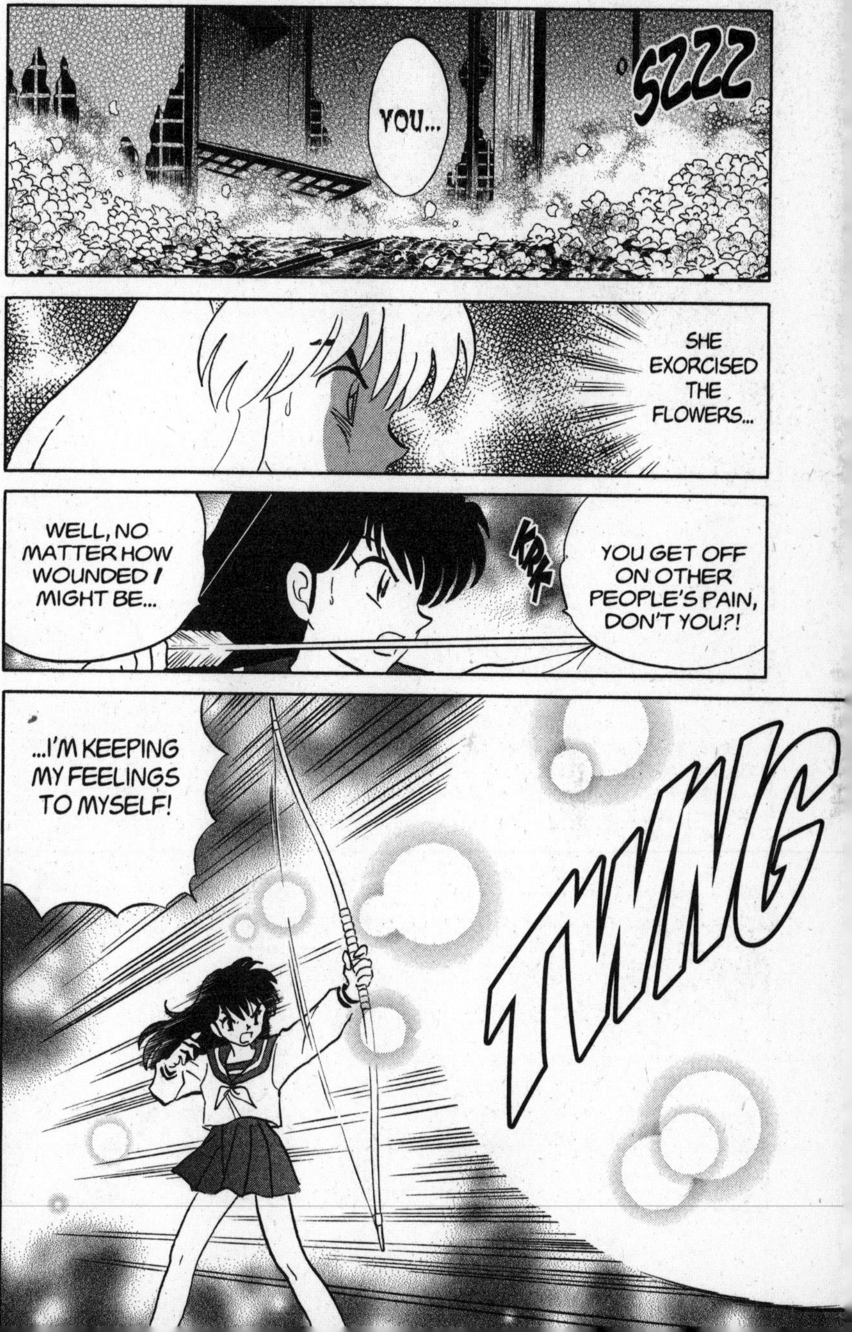
SZZZ
YOU...
SHE EXORCISED THE FLOWERS...
YOU GET OFF ON OTHER PEOPLE'S PAIN, DON'T YOU?!
KRK
WELL, NO MATTER HOW WOUNDED I MIGHT BE...
TWNG
...I'M KEEPING MY FEELINGS TO MYSELF!

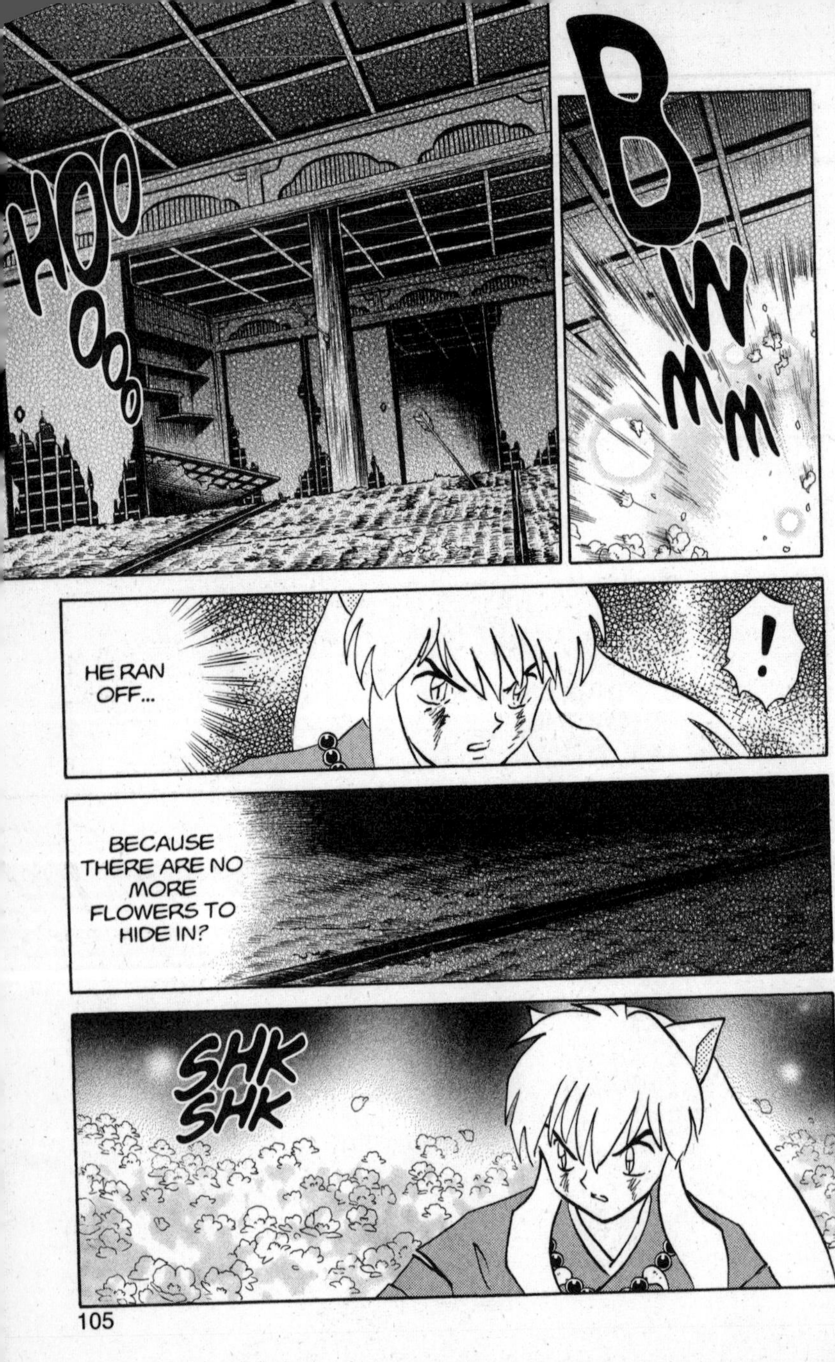
BWMMM
HOOOOO
!
HE RAN OFF...
BECAUSE THERE ARE NO MORE FLOWERS TO HIDE IN?
SHK SHK

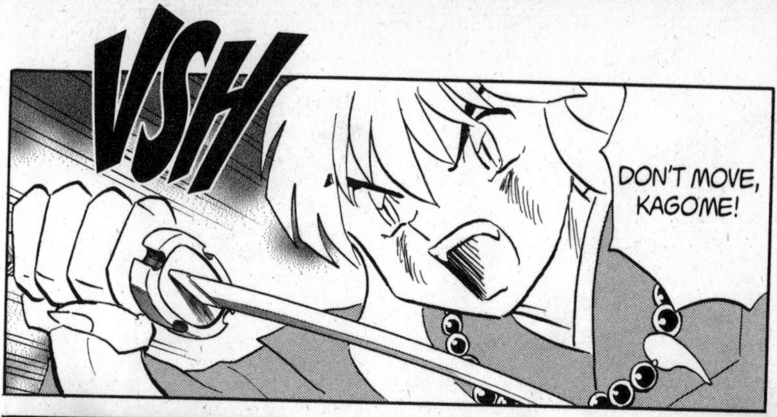
VSH
DON'T MOVE, KAGOME!

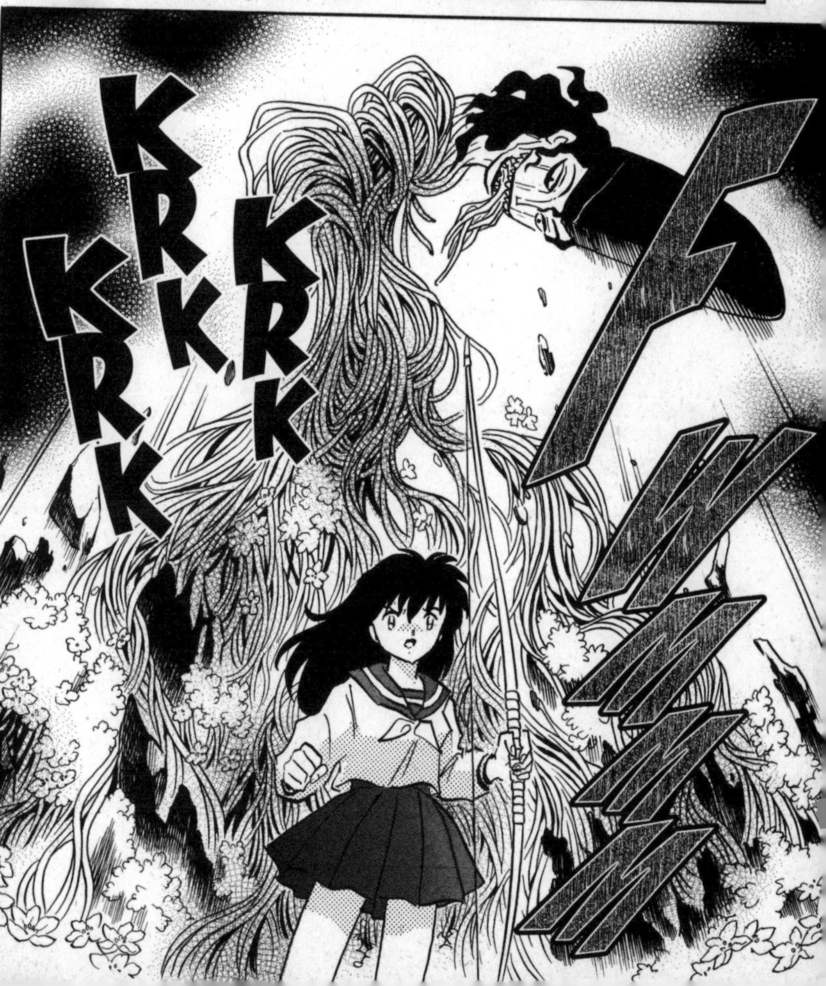
KRK
KRK
KRK

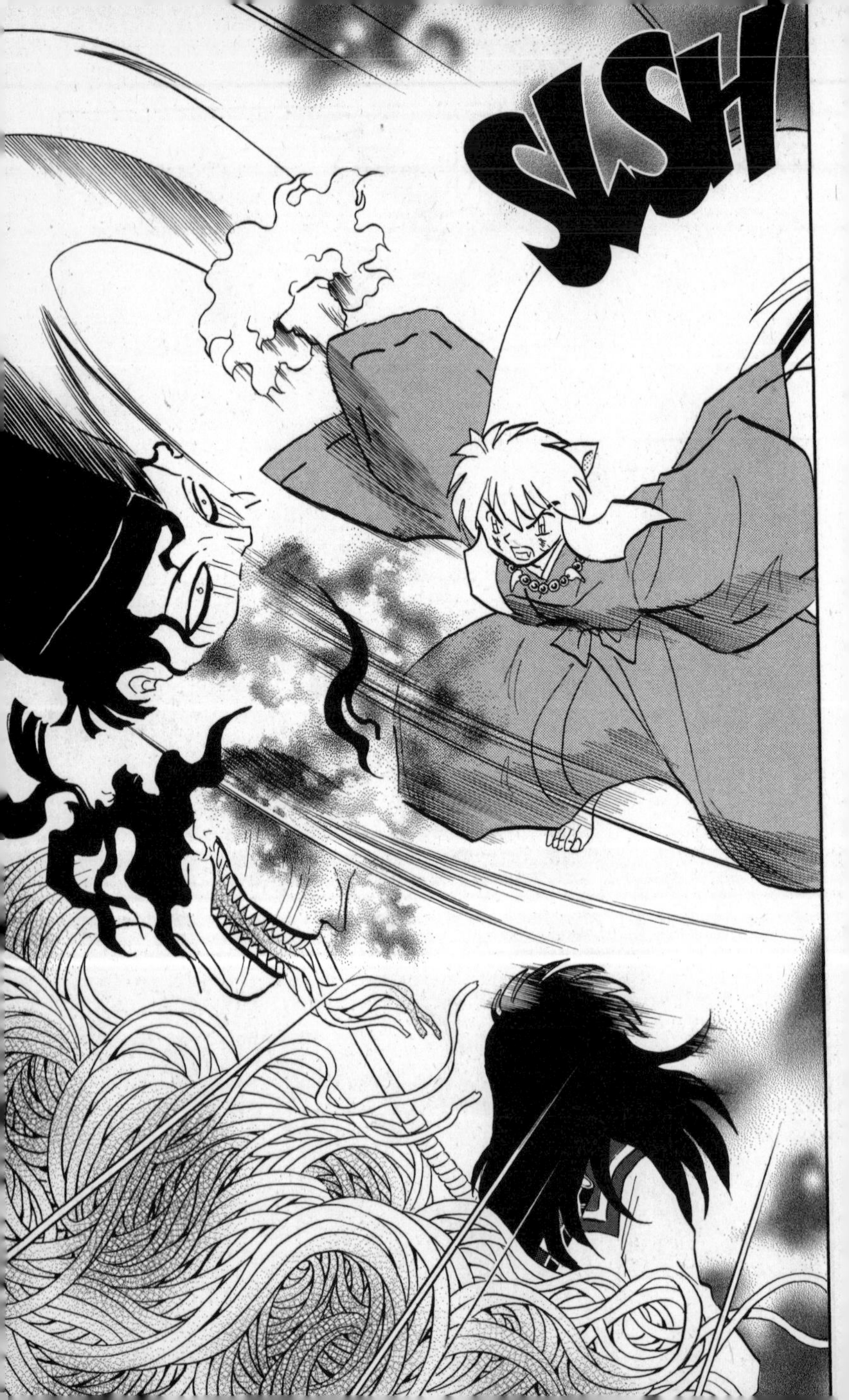
SLSH!

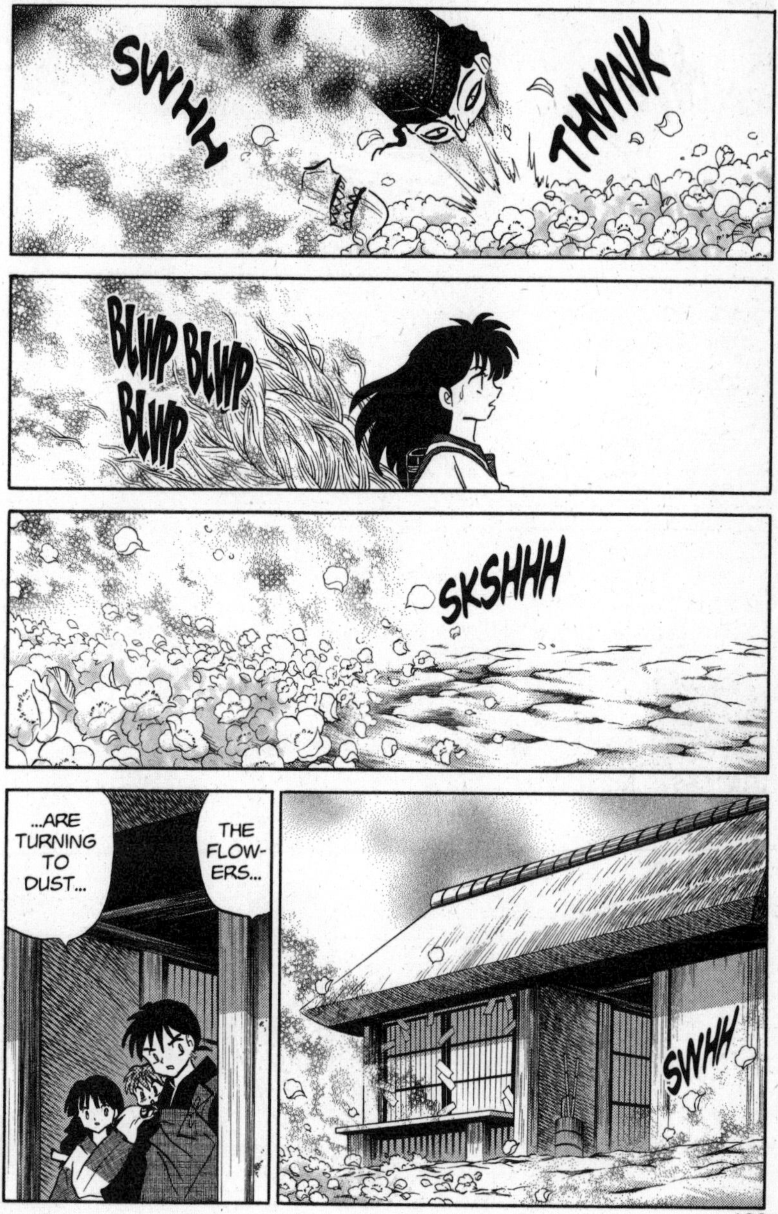
THWNK
SWHH
BLWP BLWP
BLWP
SKSHHH
SWHH
THE FLOW-ERS...
...ARE TURNING TO DUST...

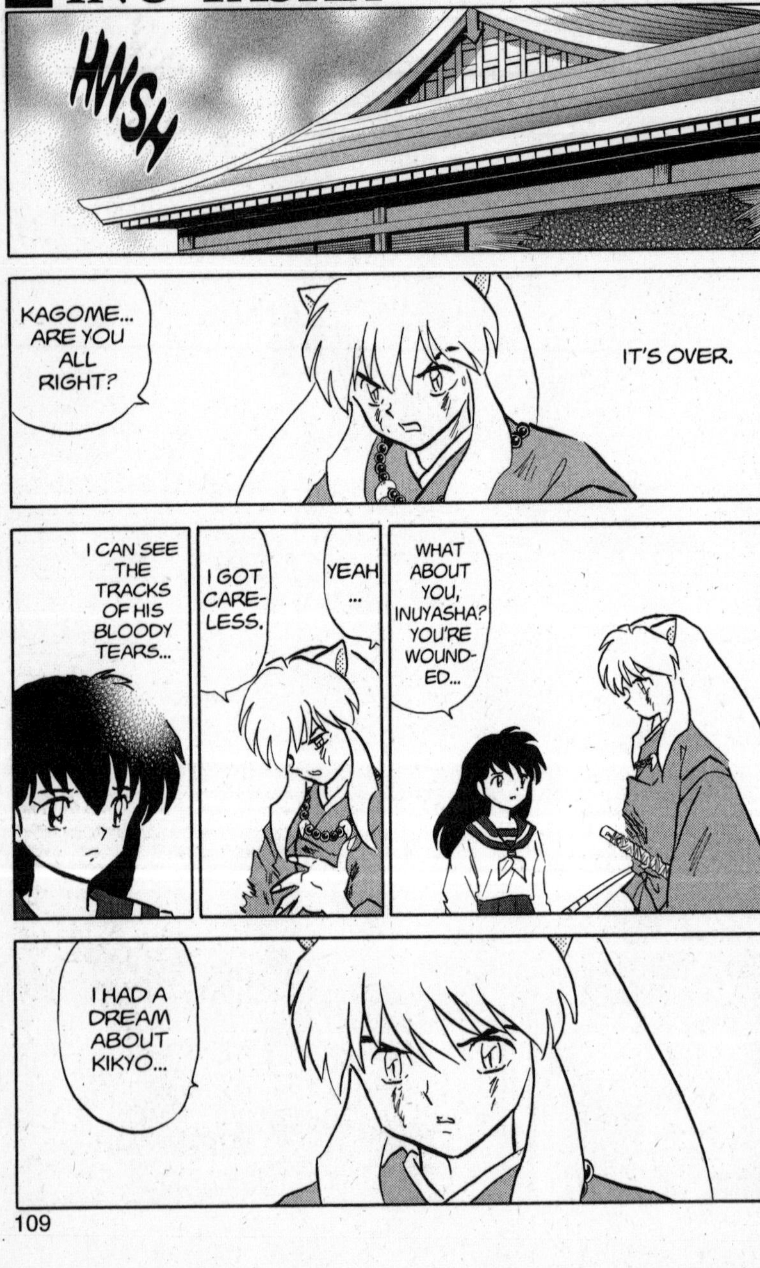
HWSH
IT'S OVER.
KAGOME... ARE YOU ALL RIGHT?
WHAT ABOUT YOU, INUYASHA? YOU'RE WOUND-ED...
YEAH...
I GOT CARE-LESS.
I CAN SEE THE TRACKS OF HIS BLOODY TEARS...
I HAD A DREAM ABOUT KIKYO...

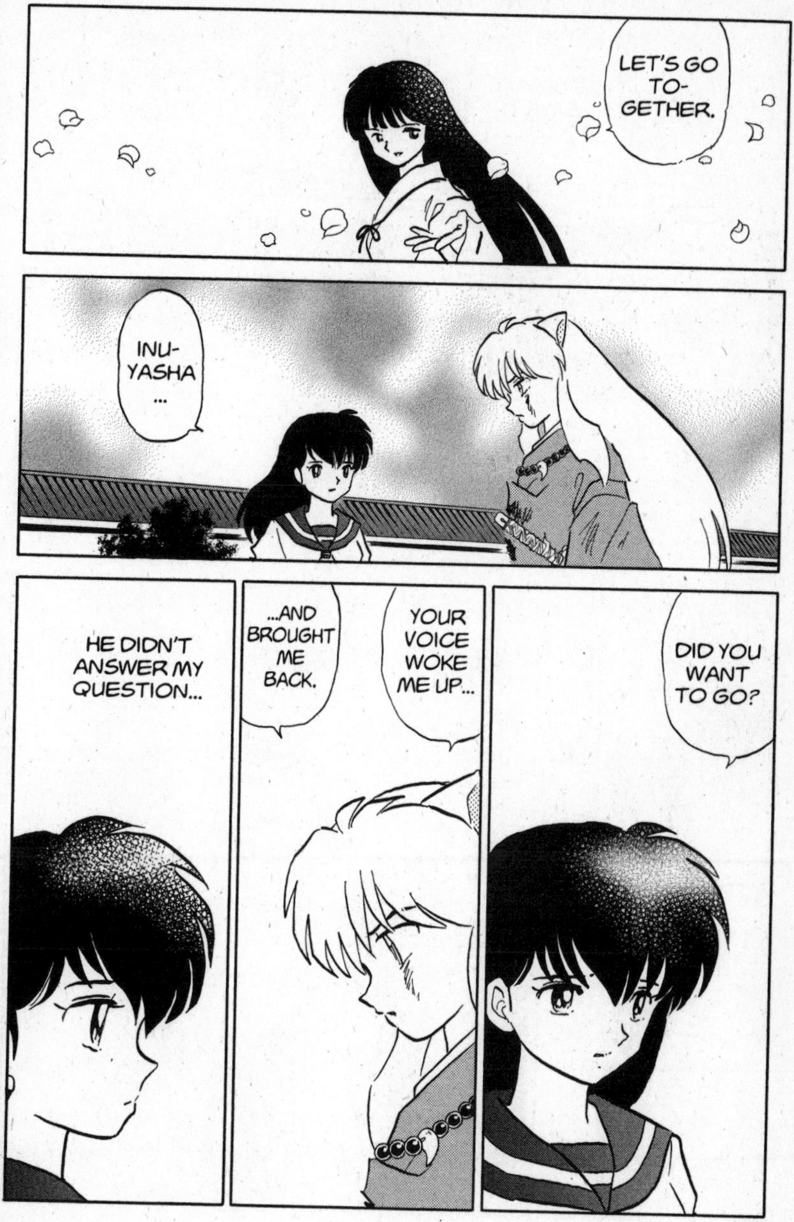
LET'S GO TO-GETHER.
INU-YASHA ...
DID YOU WANT TO GO?
YOUR VOICE WOKE ME UP...
...AND BROUGHT ME BACK.
HE DIDN'T ANSWER MY QUESTION...

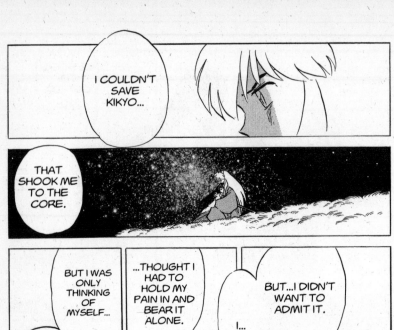

I COULDN'T SAVE KIKYO...
THAT SHOOK ME TO THE CORE.
BUT...I DIDN'T WANT TO ADMIT IT.
I...
...THOUGHT I HAD TO HOLD MY PAIN IN AND BEAR IT ALONE.
BUT I WAS ONLY THINKING OF MYSELF...
I DIDN'T PAY ANY ATTENTION TO WHAT YOU WERE GOING THROUGH, KAGOME ...

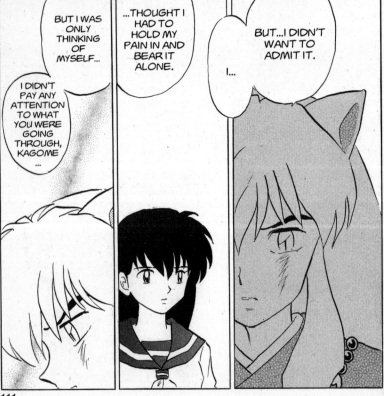

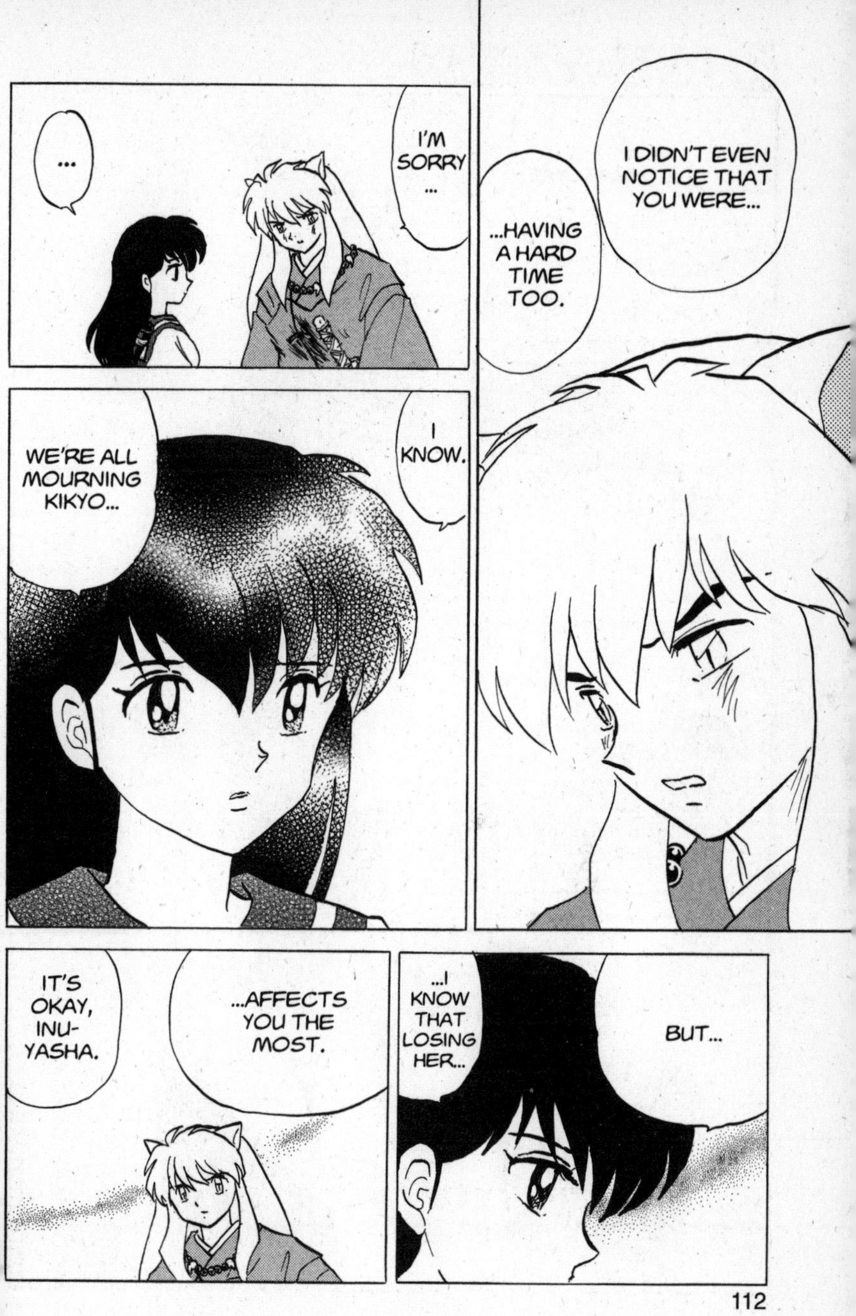
I DIDN'T EVEN NOTICE THAT YOU WERE...
...HAVING A HARD TIME TOO.
I'M SORRY...
...
I KNOW.
WE'RE ALL MOURNING KIKYO...
BUT...
...I KNOW THAT LOSING HER...
...AFFECTS YOU THE MOST.
IT'S OKAY, INU-YASHA.

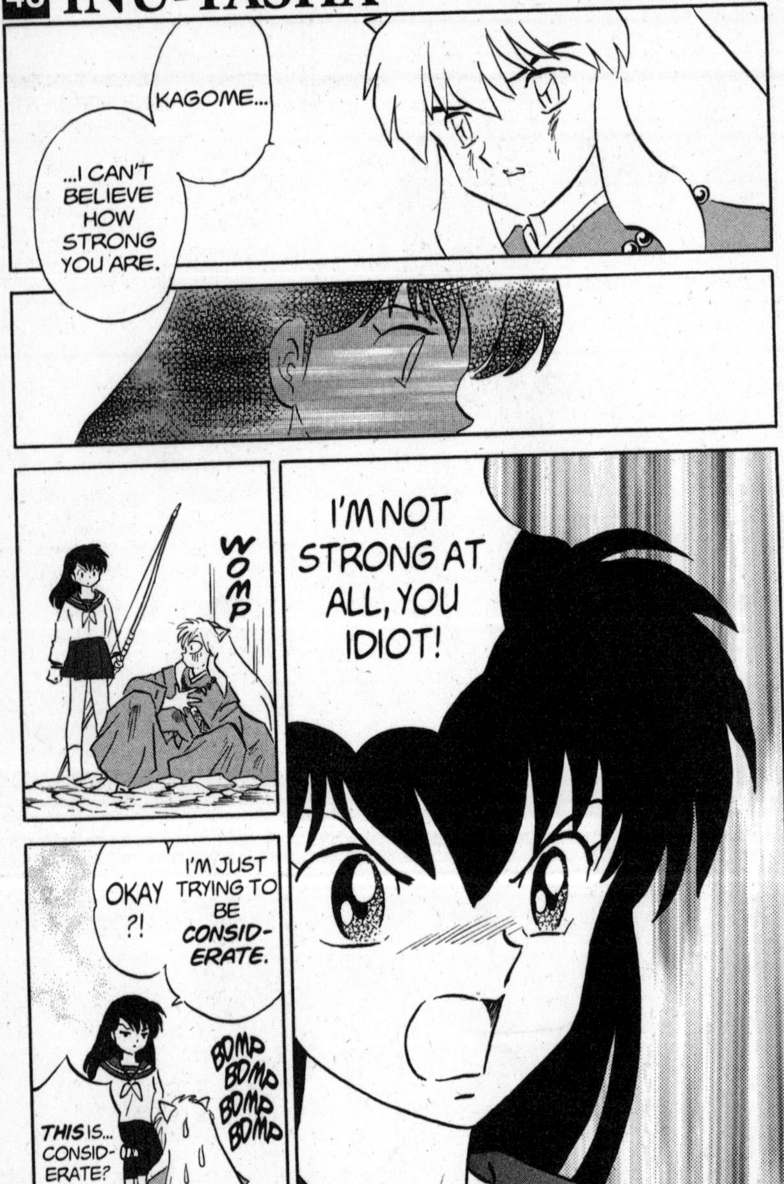
KAGOME...
...I CAN'T BELIEVE HOW STRONG YOU ARE.
I'M NOT STRONG AT ALL, YOU IDIOT!
WOMP
I'M JUST TRYING TO BE CONSIDERATE.
OKAY?!
BDMP BDMP BDMP BDMP
THIS IS... CONSIDERATE?

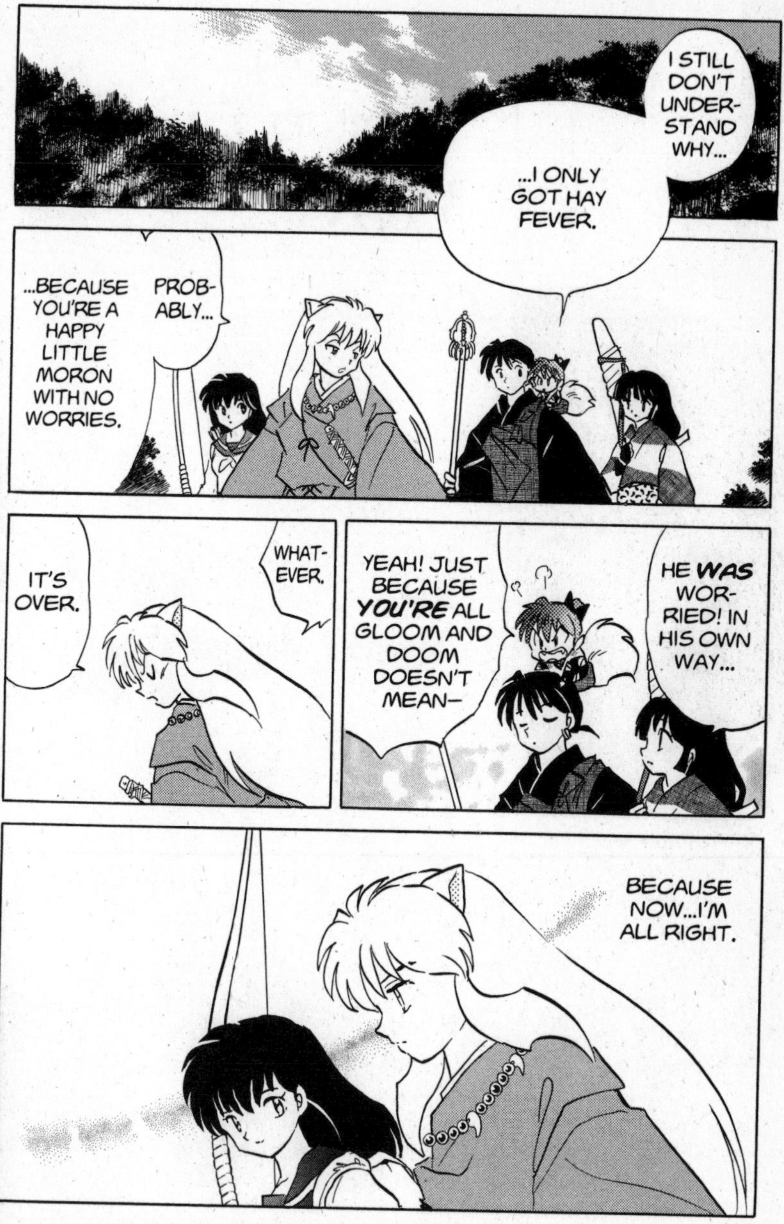
I STILL DON'T UNDER-STAND WHY...
...I ONLY GOT HAY FEVER.
PROB-ABLY...
...BECAUSE YOU'RE A HAPPY LITTLE MORON WITH NO WORRIES.
HE **WAS** WOR-RIED! IN HIS OWN WAY...
YEAH! JUST BECAUSE ***YOU'RE*** ALL GLOOM AND DOOM DOESN'T MEAN—
WHAT-EVER.
IT'S OVER.
BECAUSE NOW...I'M ALL RIGHT.

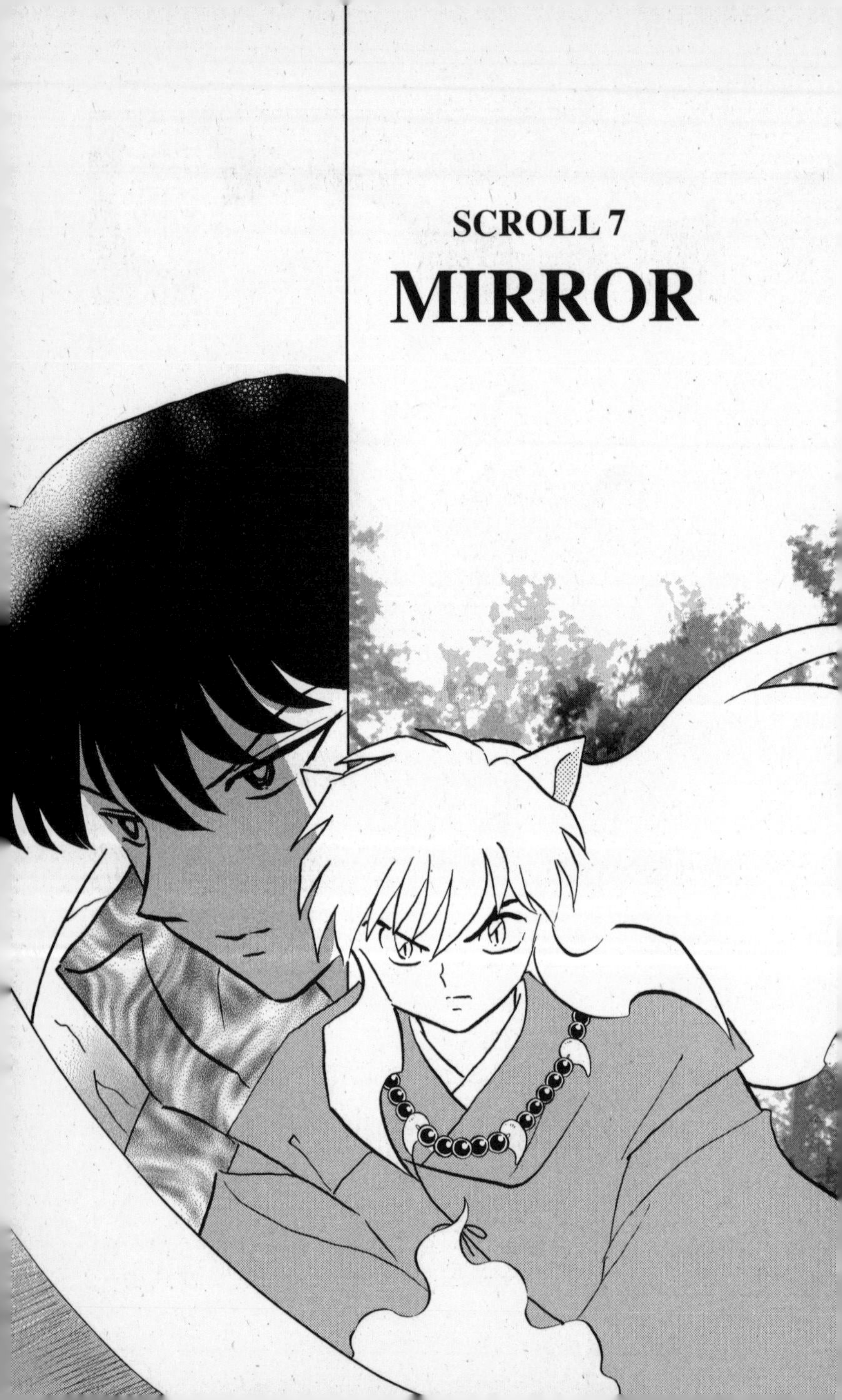
SCROLL 7
MIRROR

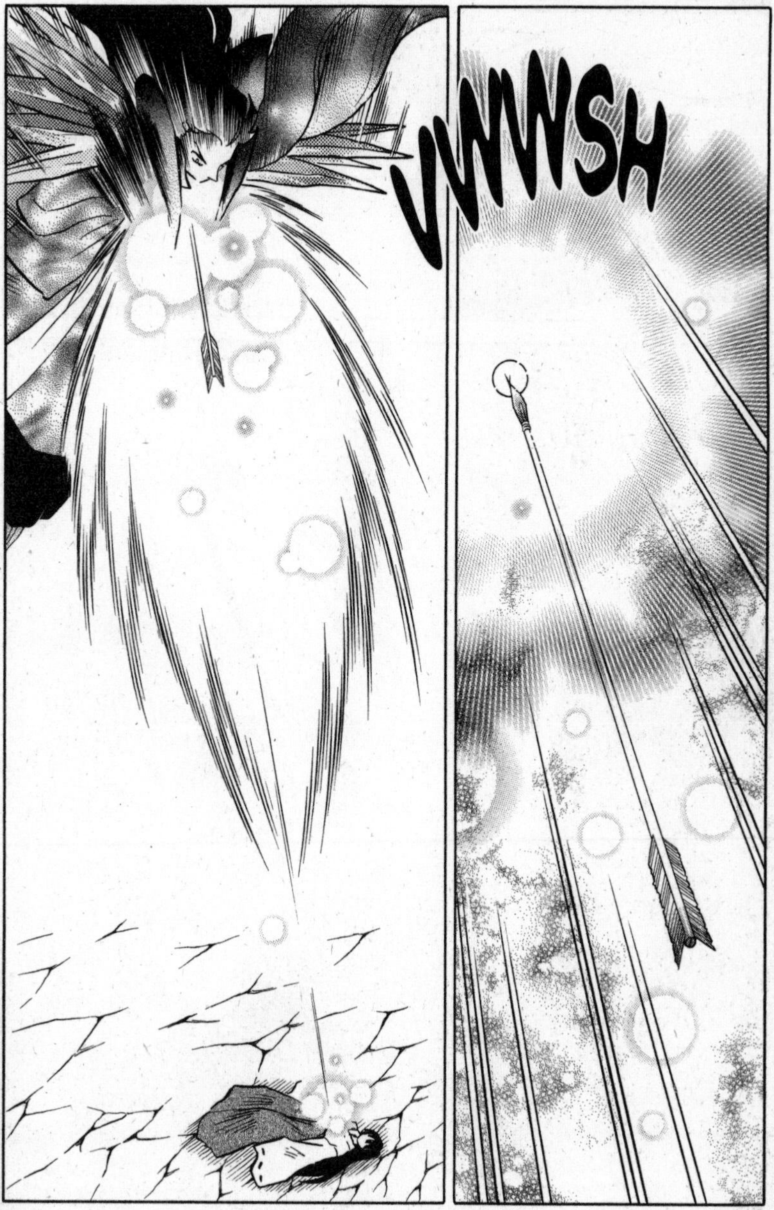
VWWSH

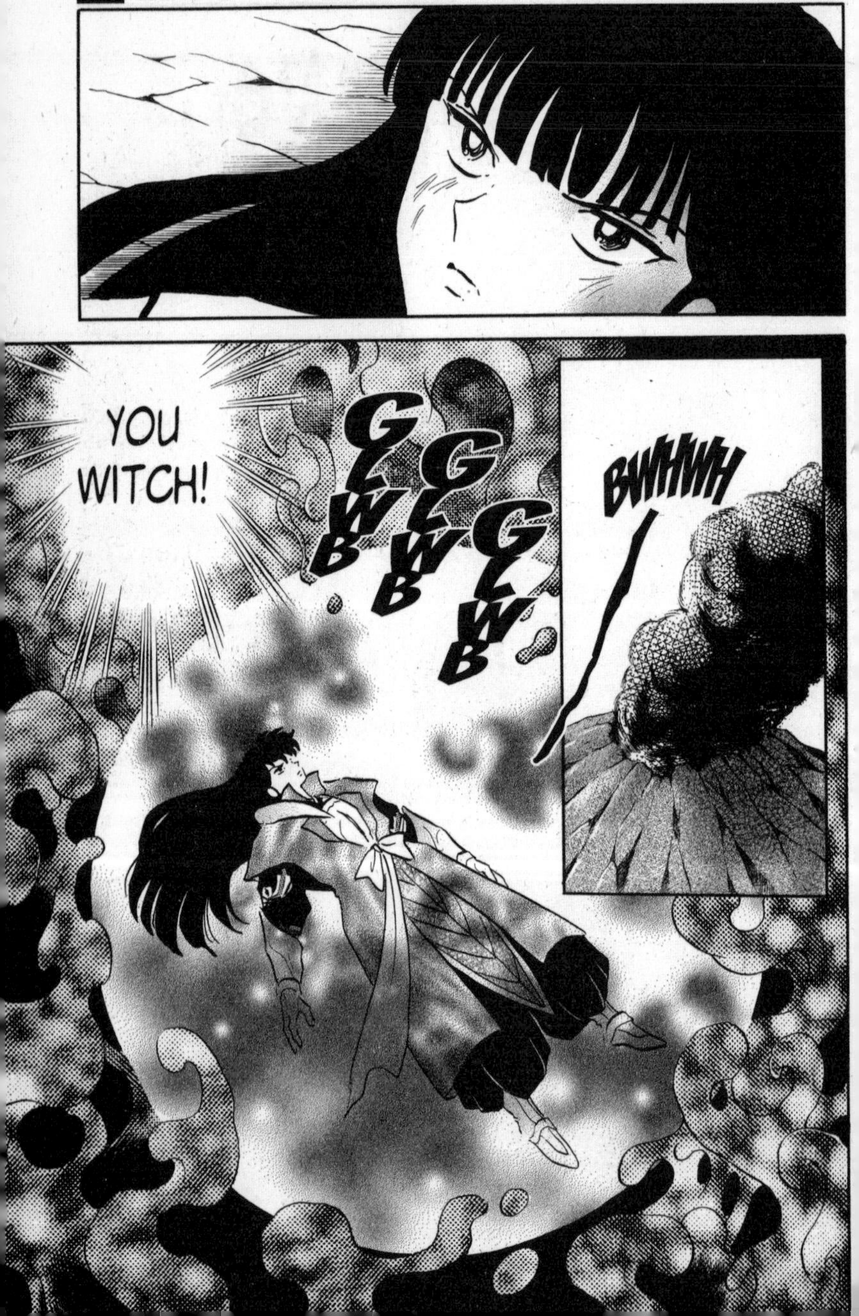
BWHWH
GLWB GLWB GLWB
YOU WITCH!

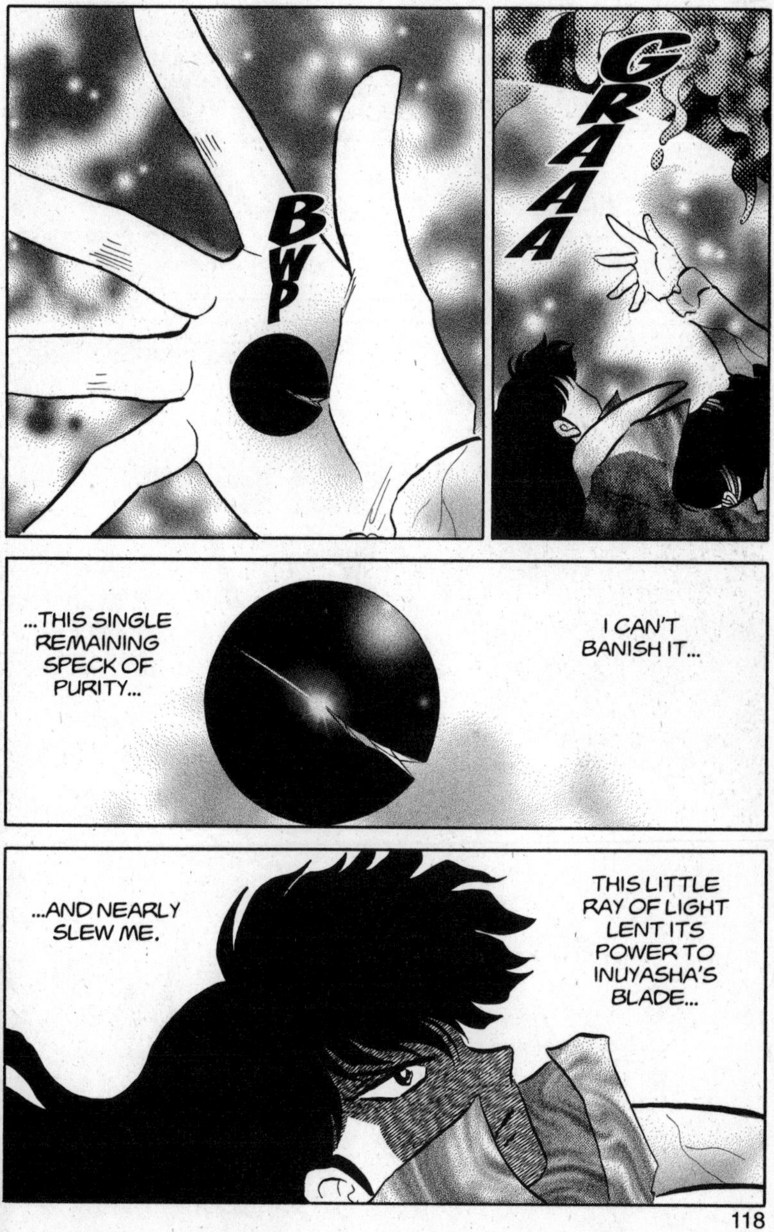
GRAAA
BWP
I CAN'T BANISH IT...
...THIS SINGLE REMAINING SPECK OF PURITY...
THIS LITTLE RAY OF LIGHT LENT ITS POWER TO INUYASHA'S BLADE...
...AND NEARLY SLEW ME.

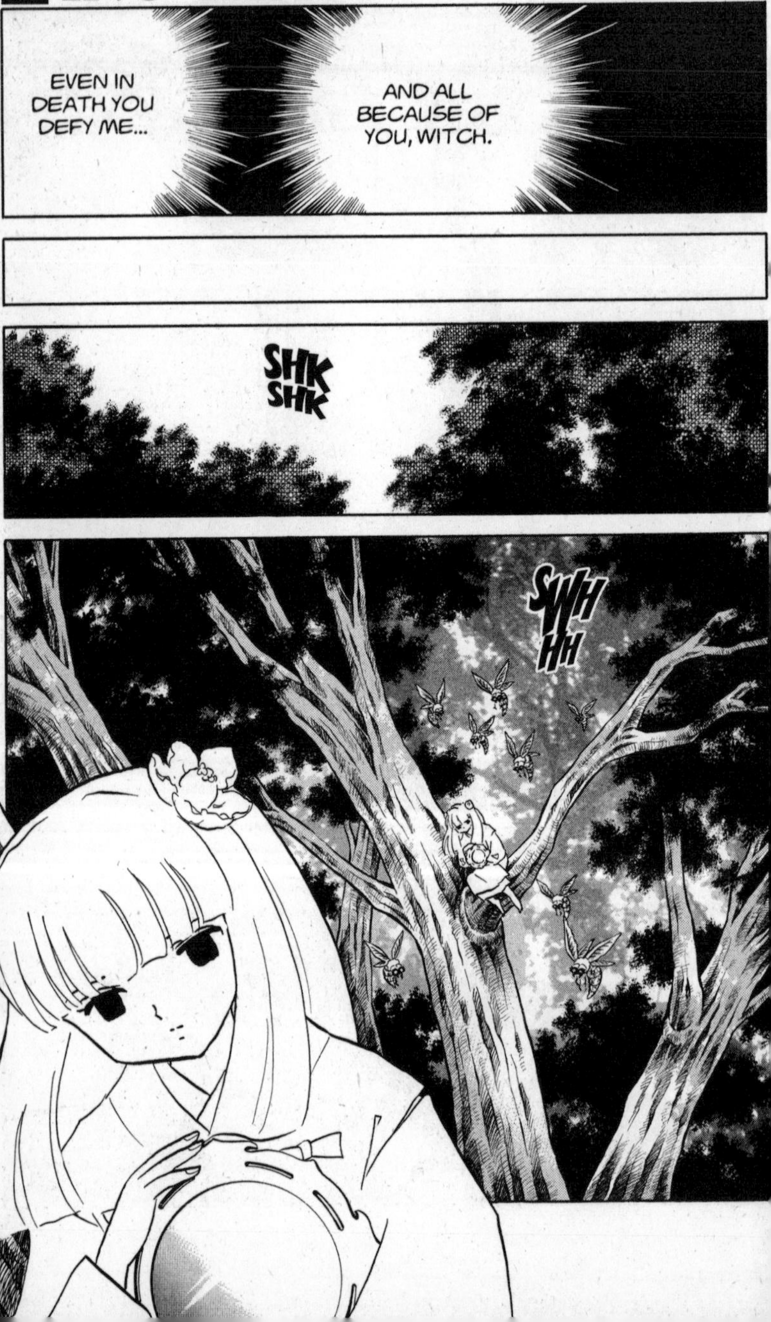
EVEN IN DEATH YOU DEFY ME...
AND ALL BECAUSE OF YOU, WITCH.
SHK SHK
SWHHH

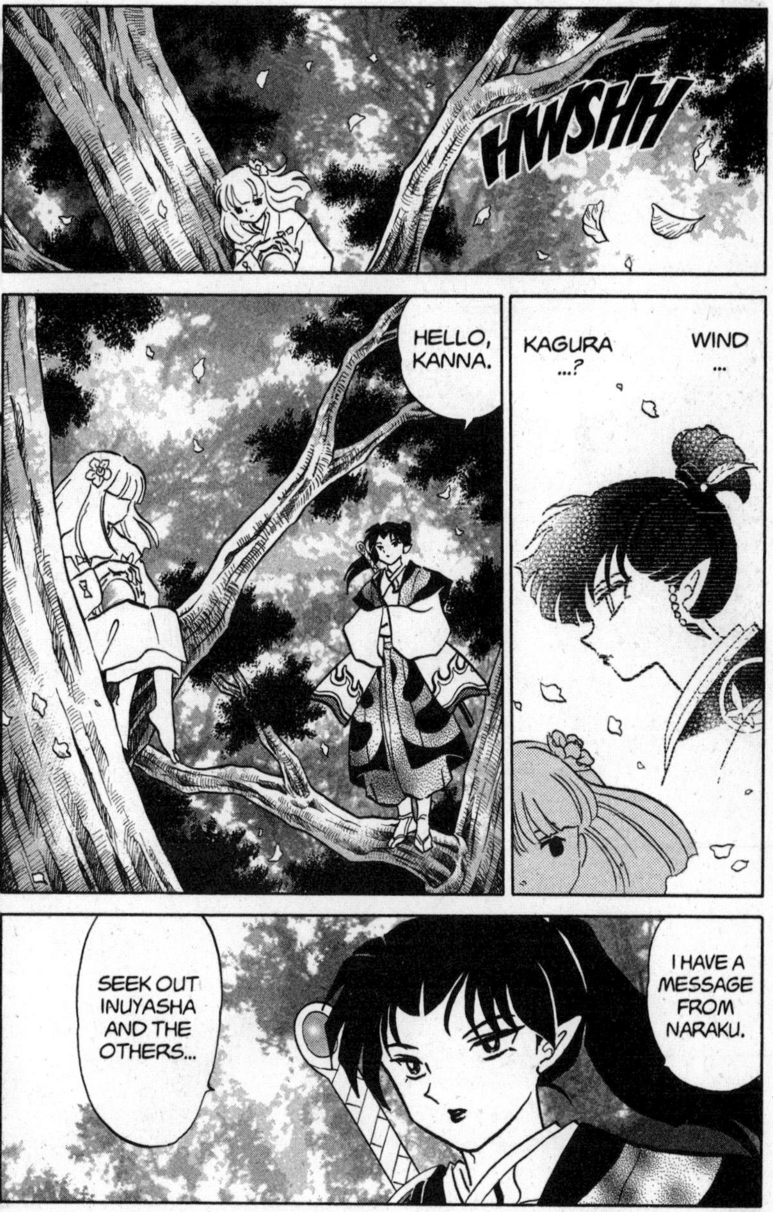
HWSHH
WIND ...
KAGURA ...?
HELLO, KANNA.
I HAVE A MESSAGE FROM NARAKU.
SEEK OUT INUYASHA AND THE OTHERS...

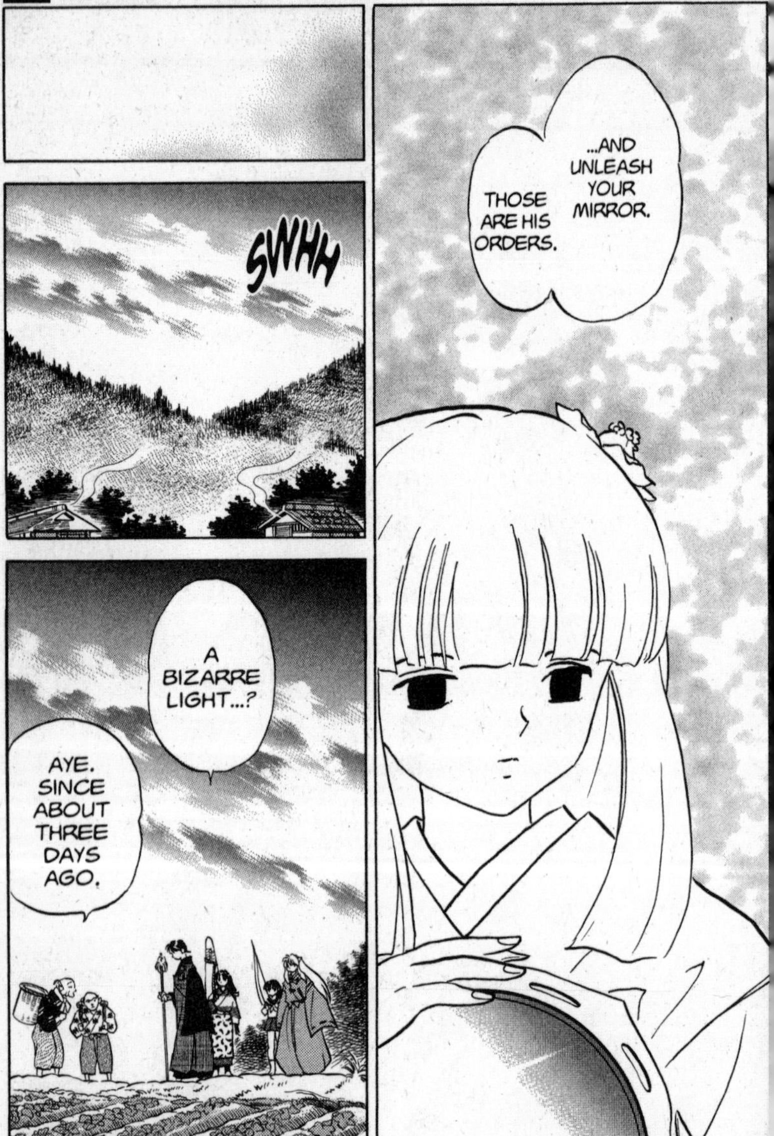
...AND UNLEASH YOUR MIRROR.
THOSE ARE HIS ORDERS.
SWHH
A BIZARRE LIGHT...?
AYE. SINCE ABOUT THREE DAYS AGO.

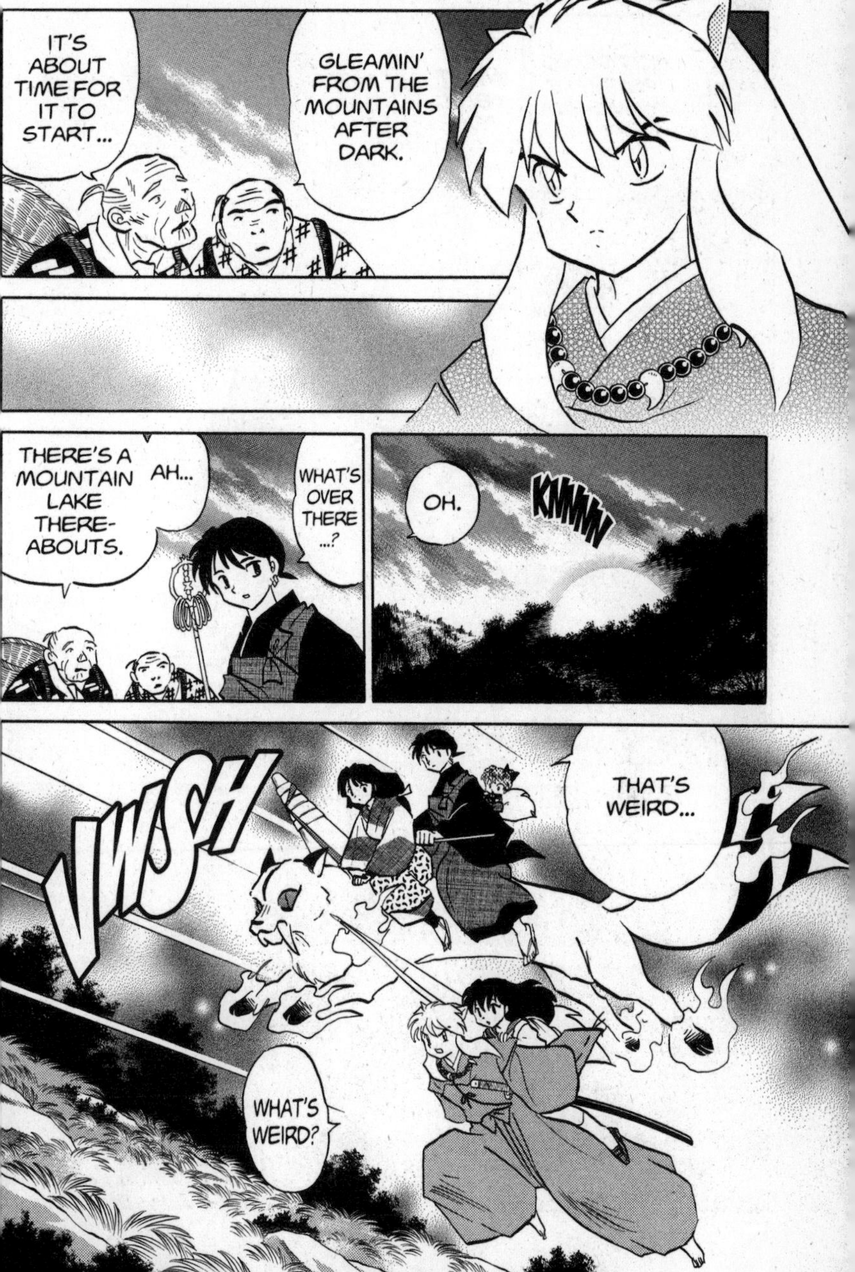
GLEAMIN' FROM THE MOUNTAINS AFTER DARK.
IT'S ABOUT TIME FOR IT TO START...
OH.
KNMMN
WHAT'S OVER THERE ...?
AH...
THERE'S A MOUNTAIN LAKE THERE-ABOUTS.
THAT'S WEIRD...
VWSH
WHAT'S WEIRD?

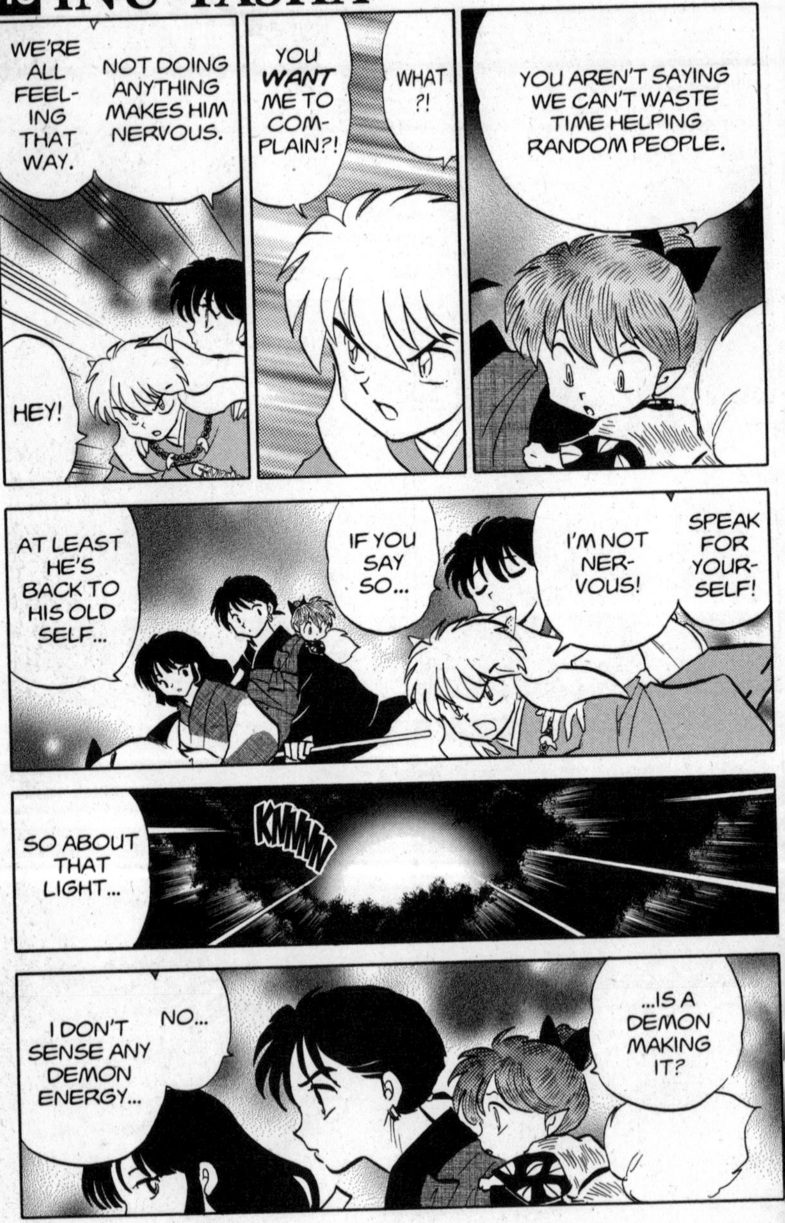
YOU AREN'T SAYING WE CAN'T WASTE TIME HELPING RANDOM PEOPLE.
WHAT?!
YOU *WANT* ME TO COMPLAIN?!
NOT DOING ANYTHING MAKES HIM NERVOUS.
WE'RE ALL FEELING THAT WAY.
HEY!
SPEAK FOR YOURSELF!
I'M NOT NERVOUS!
IF YOU SAY SO...
AT LEAST HE'S BACK TO HIS OLD SELF...
KMMMM
SO ABOUT THAT LIGHT...
...IS A DEMON MAKING IT?
NO...
I DON'T SENSE ANY DEMON ENERGY...

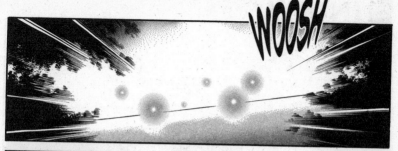

WOOSH

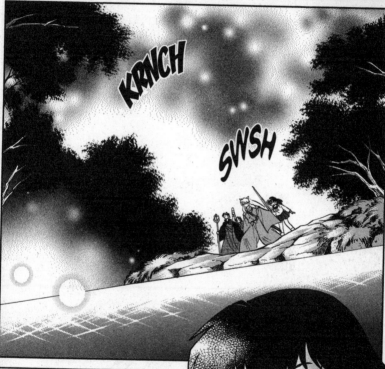

KRNCH

SWSH

THE LAKE...
WHY'S IT ALL LIT UP?!

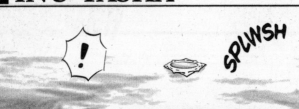

!

SPLWSH

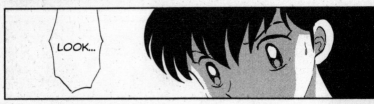

LOOK...

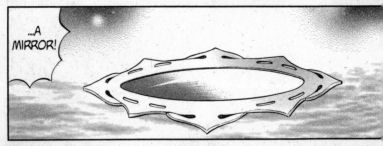

...A MIRROR!

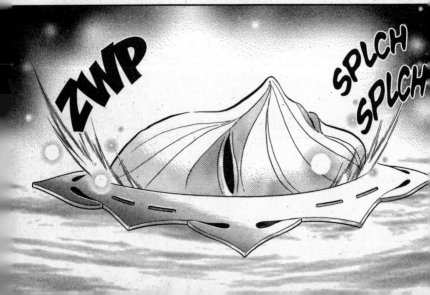

ZWP

SPLCH SPLCH

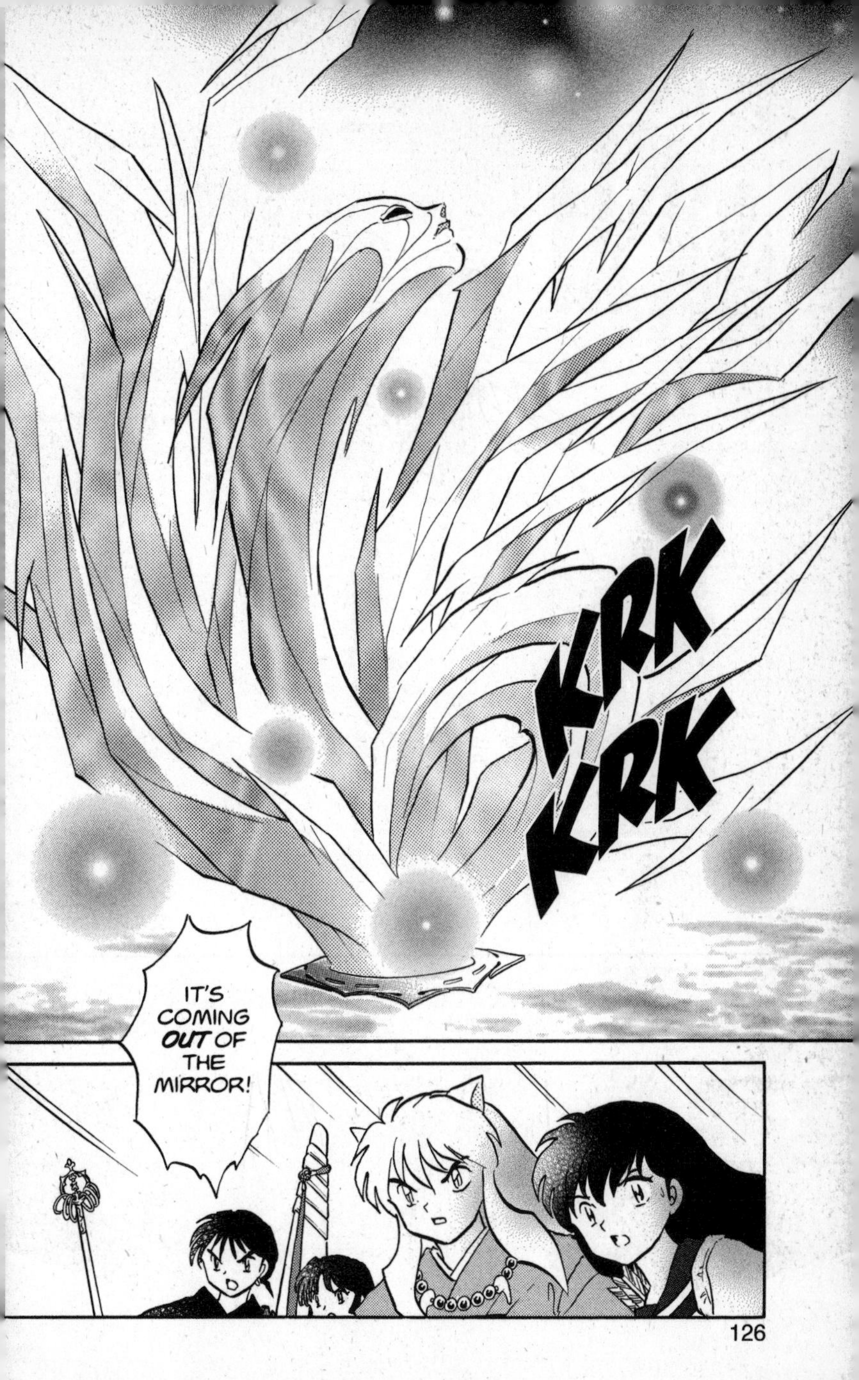

KRK KRK
IT'S COMING *OUT* OF THE MIRROR!

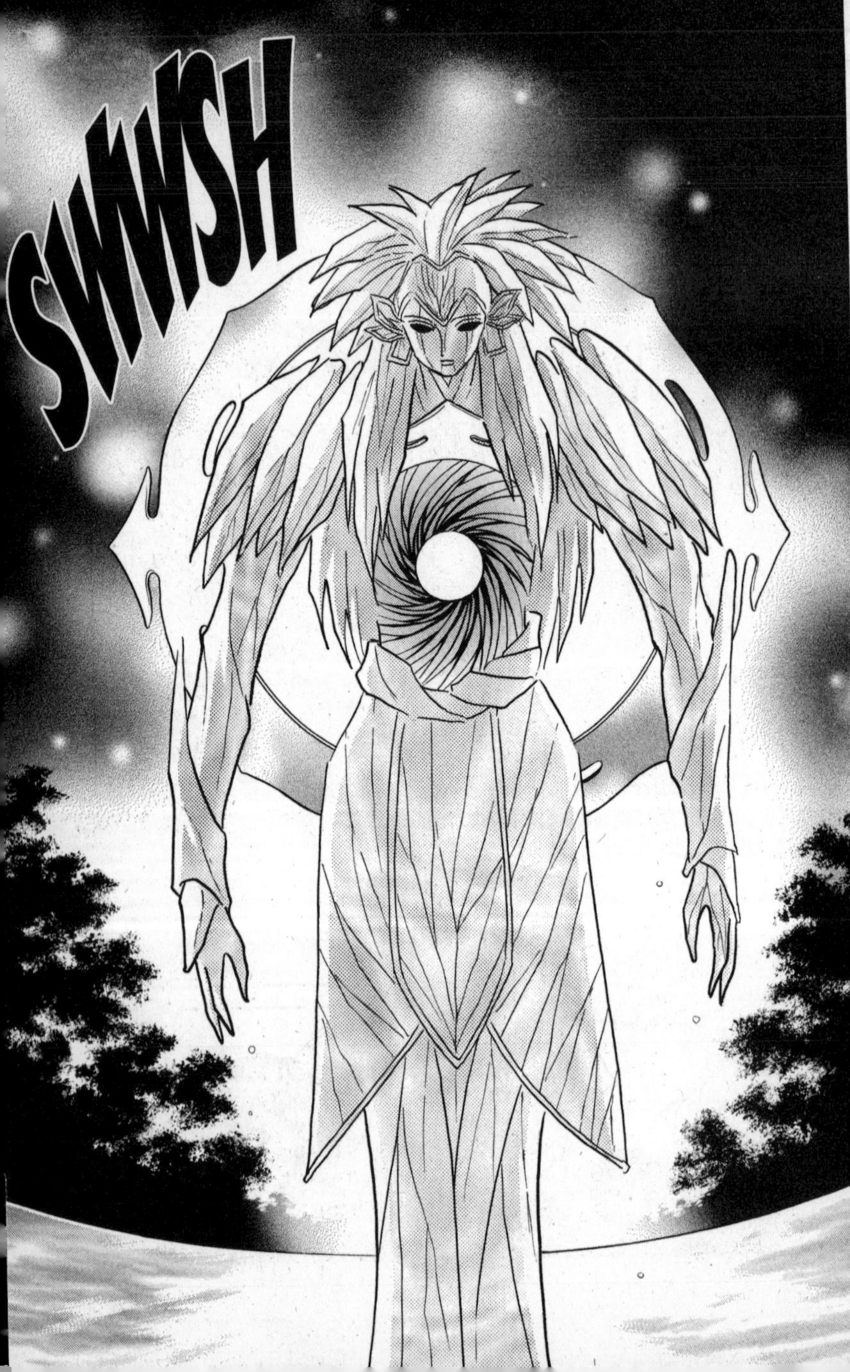
SWWISH

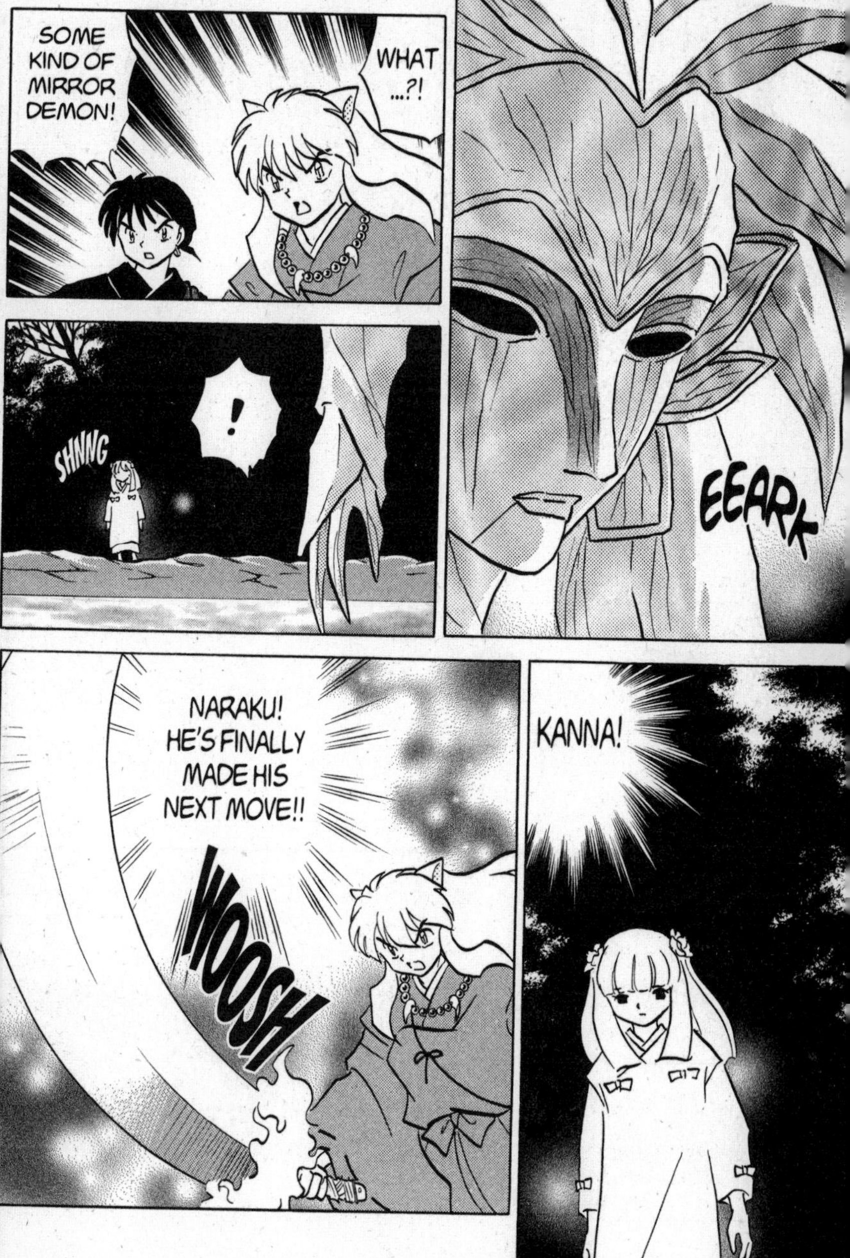
EEARK
WHAT ...?!
SOME KIND OF MIRROR DEMON!
!
SHNNG
KANNA!
NARAKU! HE'S FINALLY MADE HIS NEXT MOVE!!
WOOSH

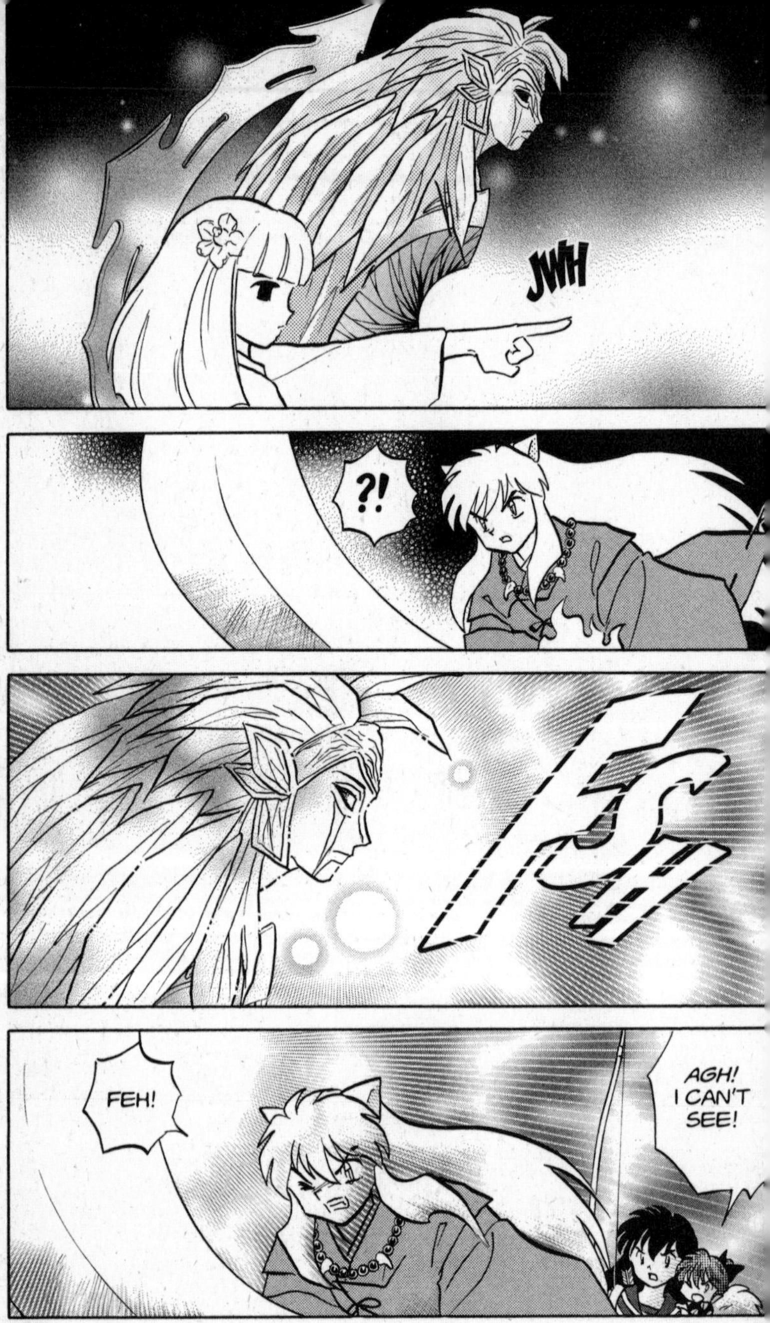
JWH
?!
FSH
AGH! I CAN'T SEE!
FEH!

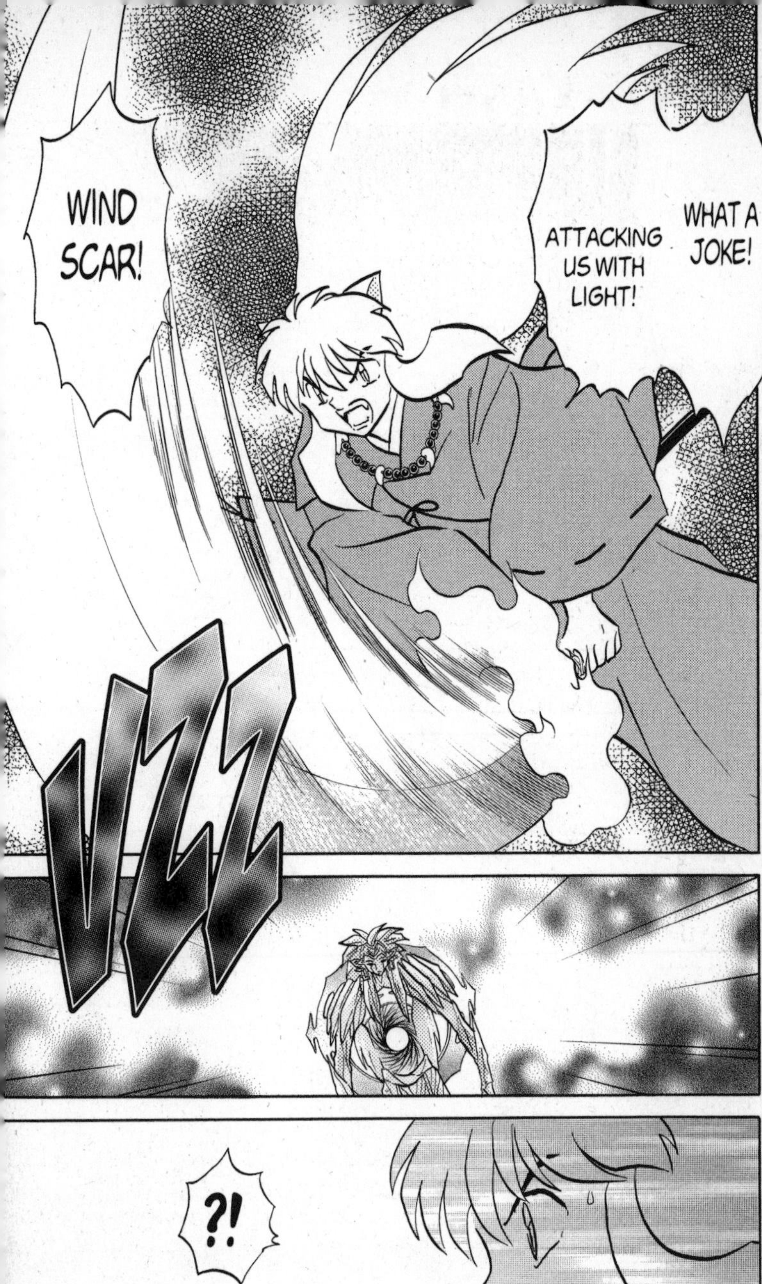
WHAT A JOKE!
ATTACKING US WITH LIGHT!
WIND SCAR!
VZZ
?!

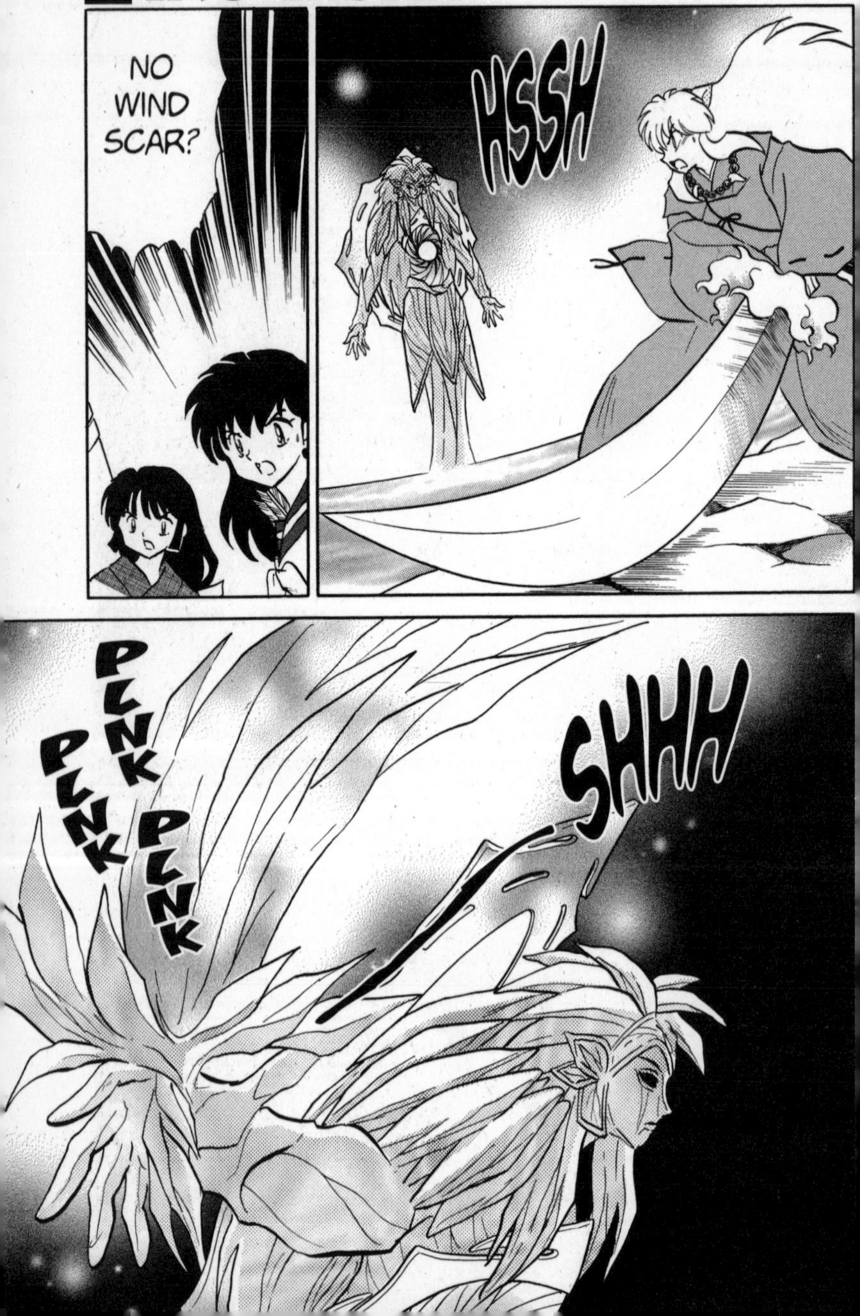

HSSH
NO WIND SCAR?
SHHH
PLNK PLNK
PLNK PLNK

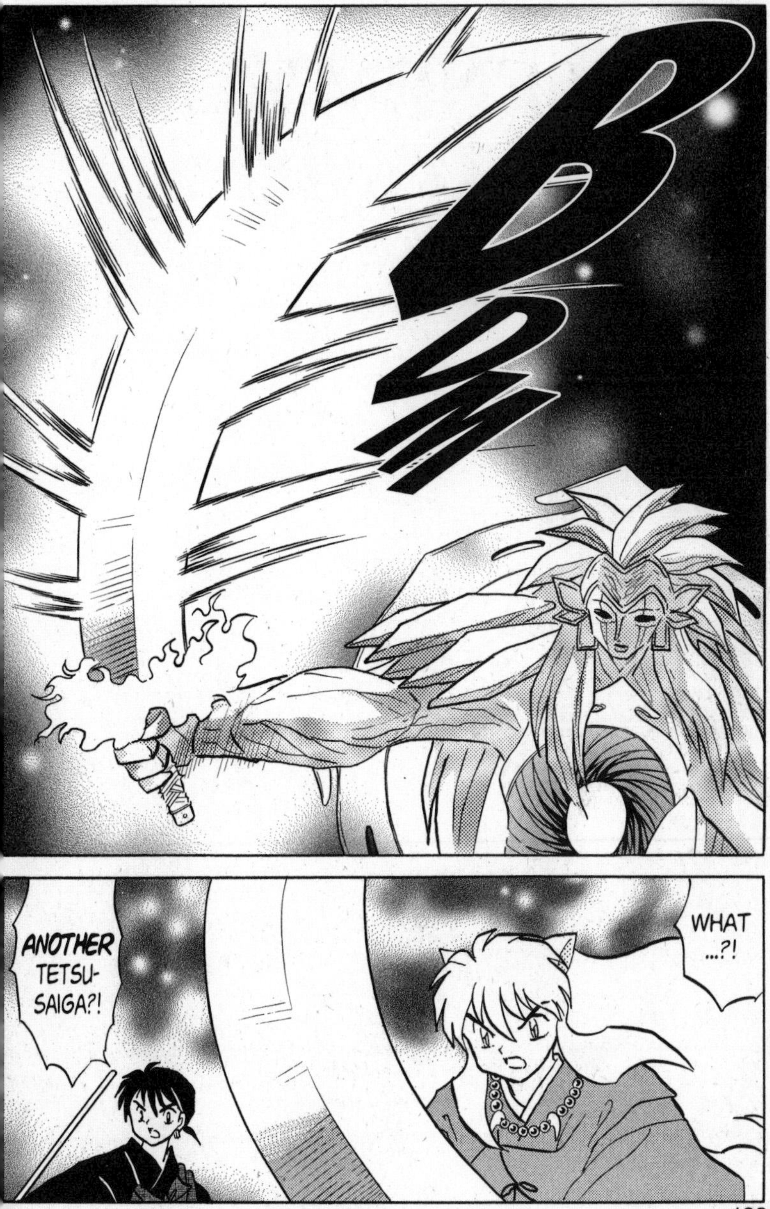
BOOM
WHAT ...?!
ANOTHER TETSU-SAIGA?!

SCROLL 8

MY ENEMY... TETSUSAIGA

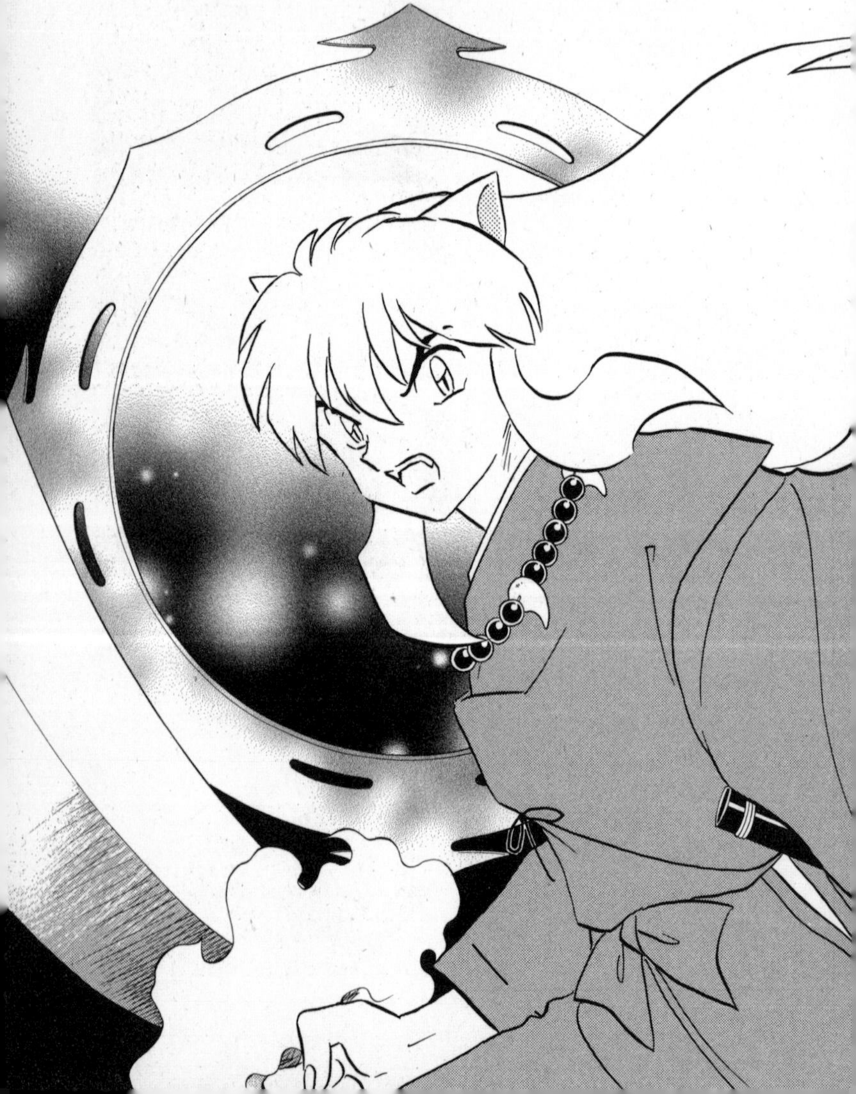

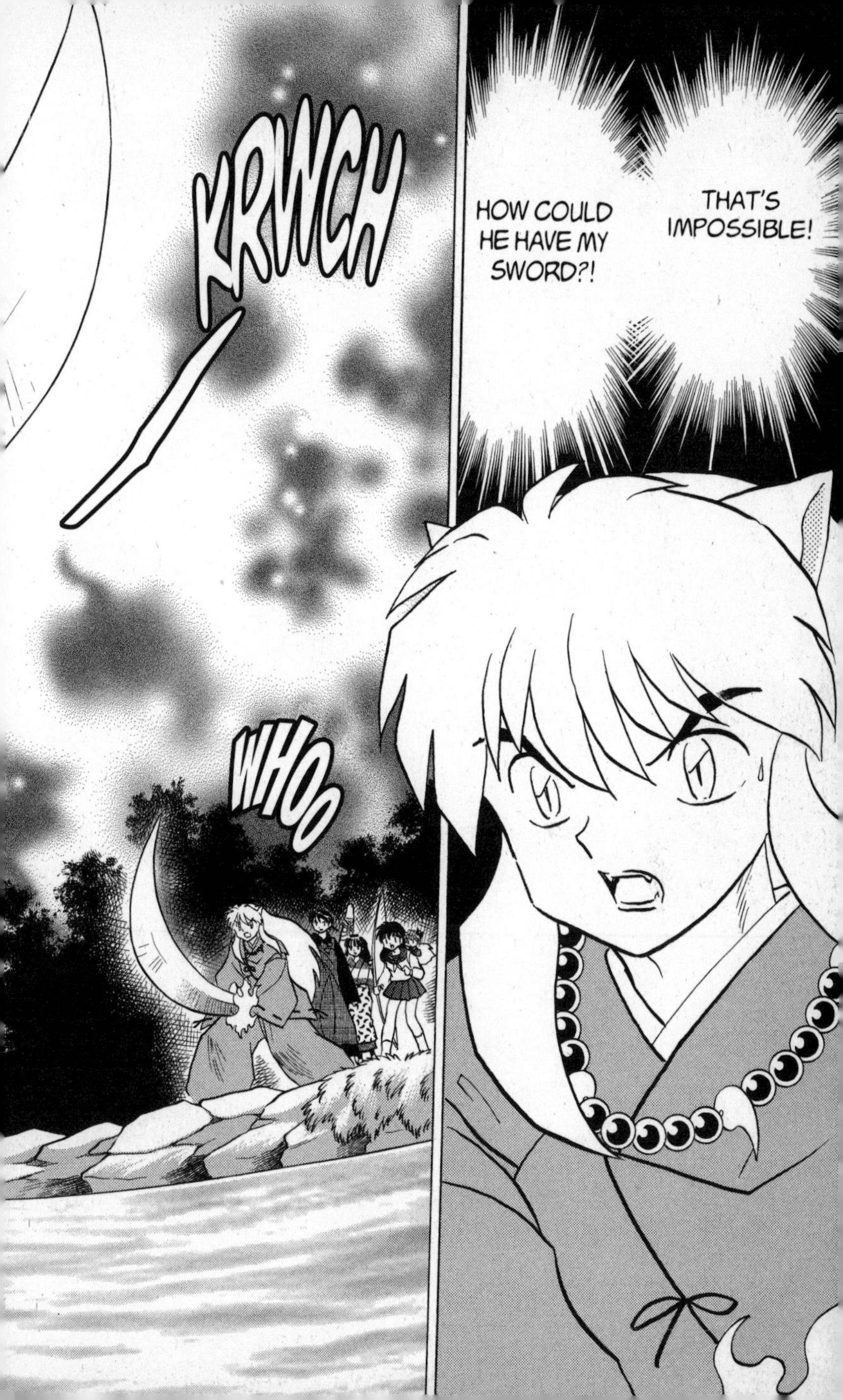
THAT'S IMPOSSIBLE!
HOW COULD HE HAVE MY SWORD?!
KRNCH
WHOO

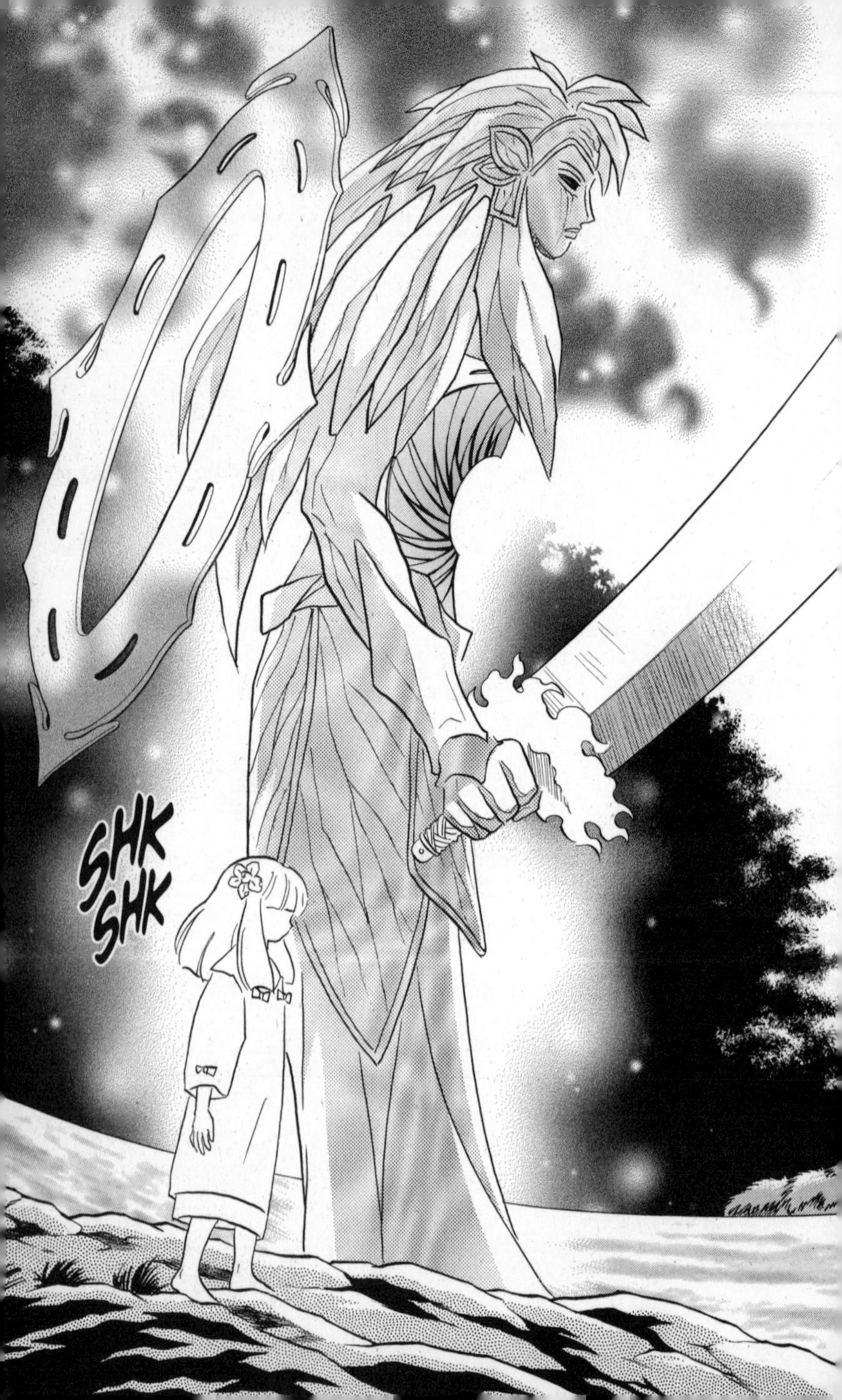
SHK SHK

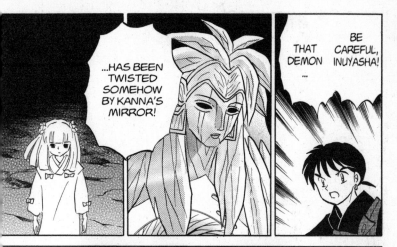

BE CAREFUL, INUYASHA!
THAT DEMON ...
...HAS BEEN TWISTED SOMEHOW BY KANNA'S MIRROR!
THERE'S BOUND TO BE SOMETHING WEIRD ABOUT HIS BLADE TOO!
DON'T WORRY!
HE'S JUST A MIRROR MONSTER!
WHICH MEANS THAT *OTHER* TETSUSAIGA IS JUST AN ILLUSION!
HE CAN'T FOOL ME!
VVNSH

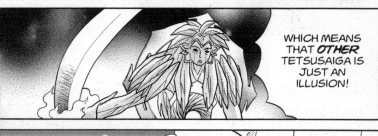

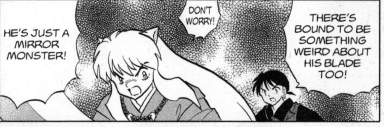

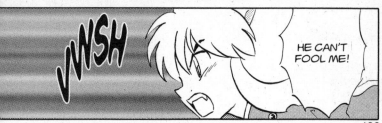

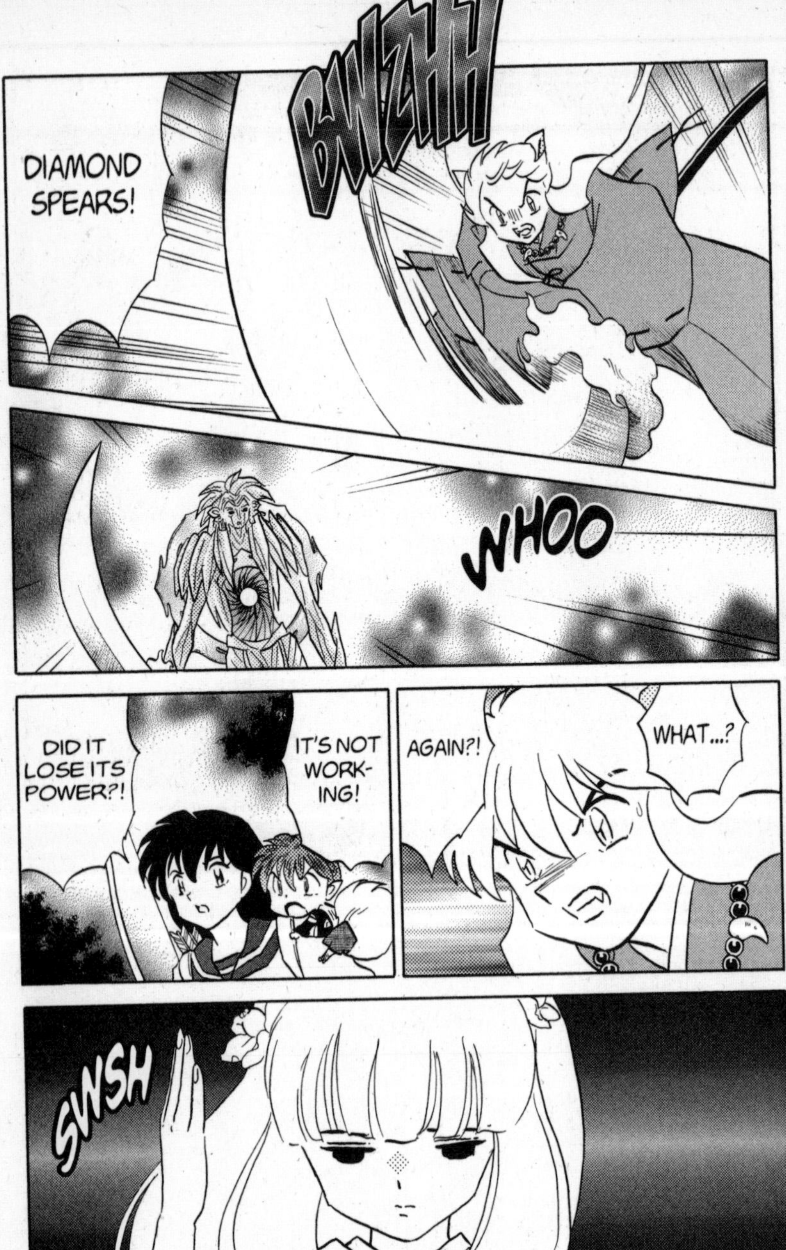
BWZHH
DIAMOND SPEARS!
WHOO
WHAT...?
AGAIN?!
IT'S NOT WORKING!
DID IT LOSE ITS POWER?!
SWSH

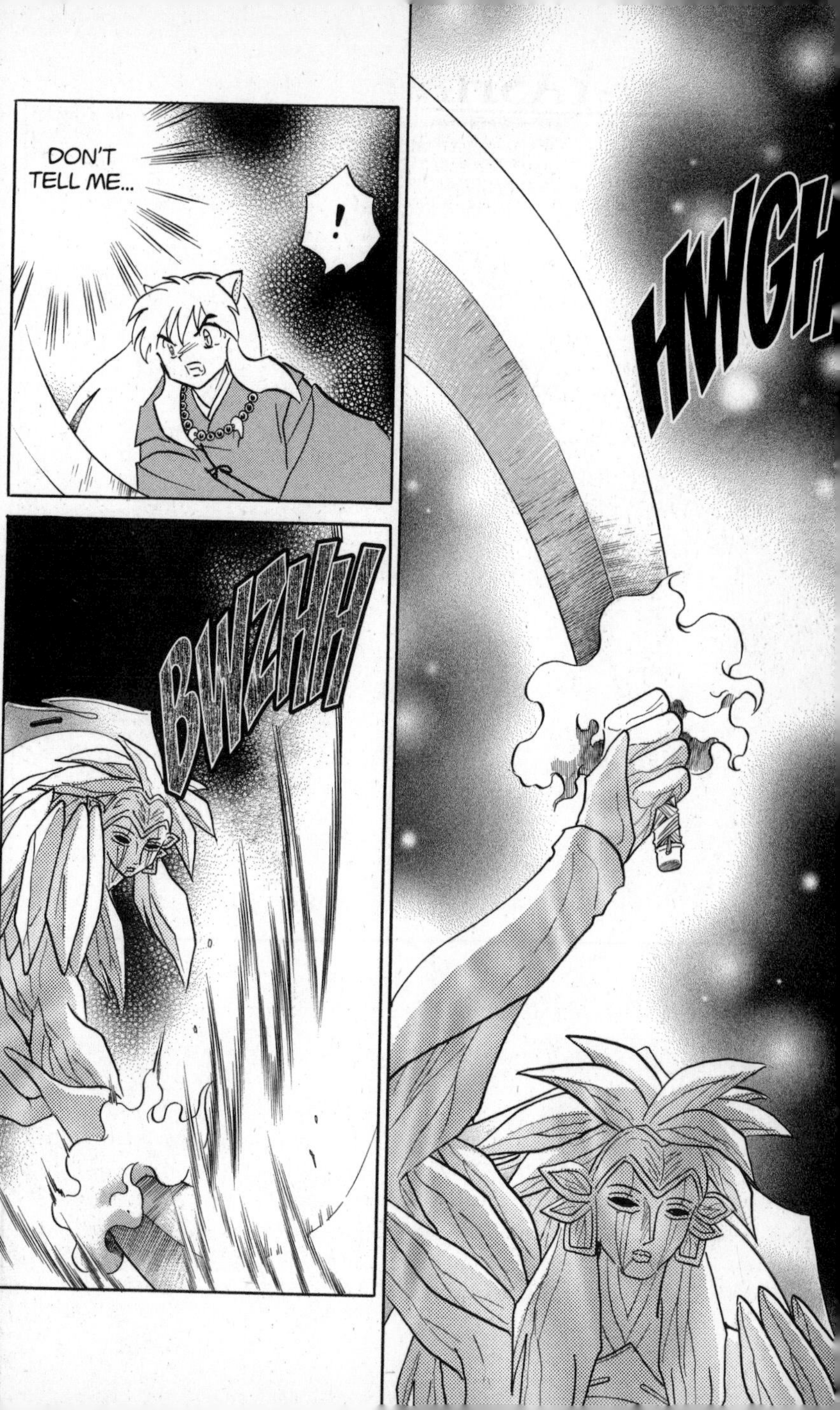
HWGH
DON'T TELL ME...
!
BWZHH

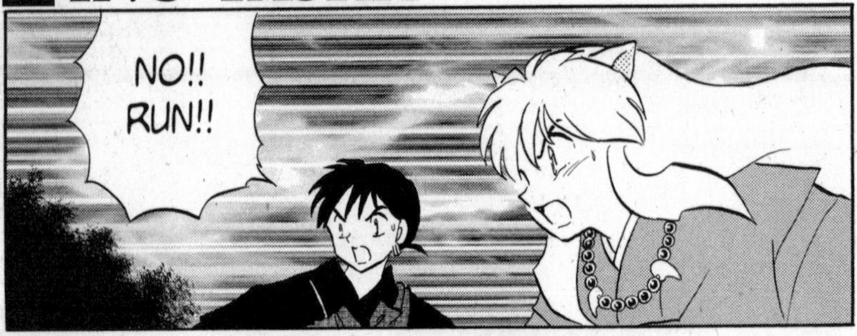
NO!! RUN!!

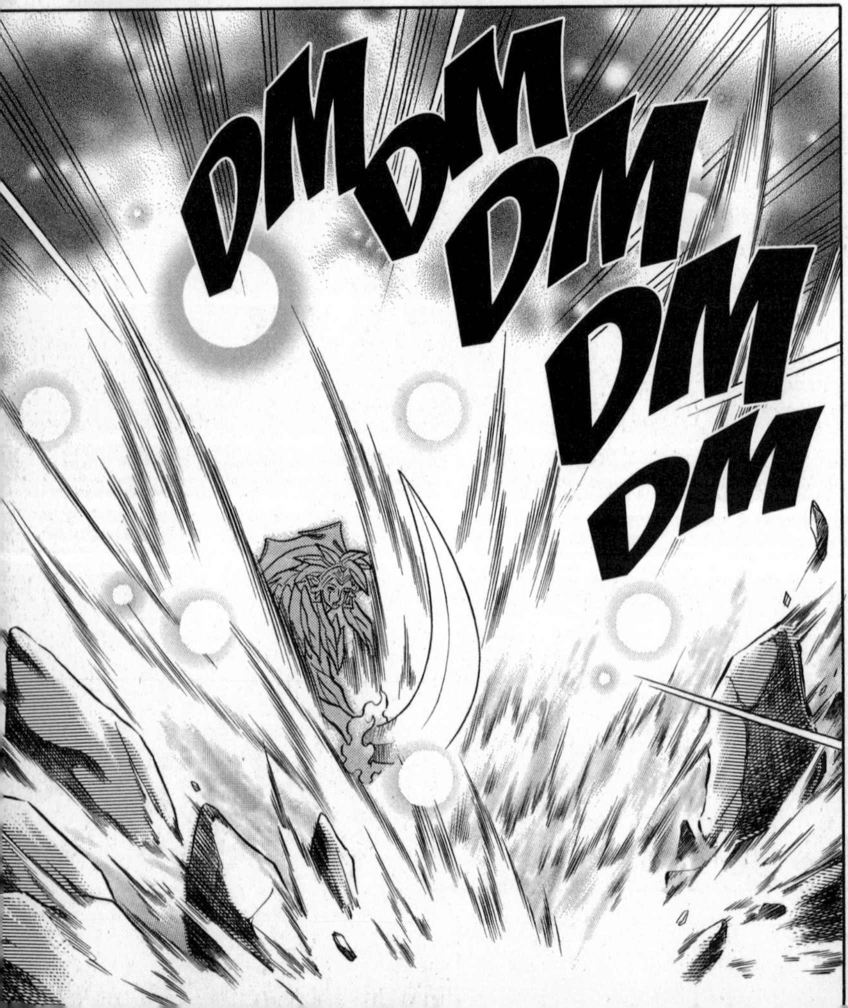
DM DM DM DM DM

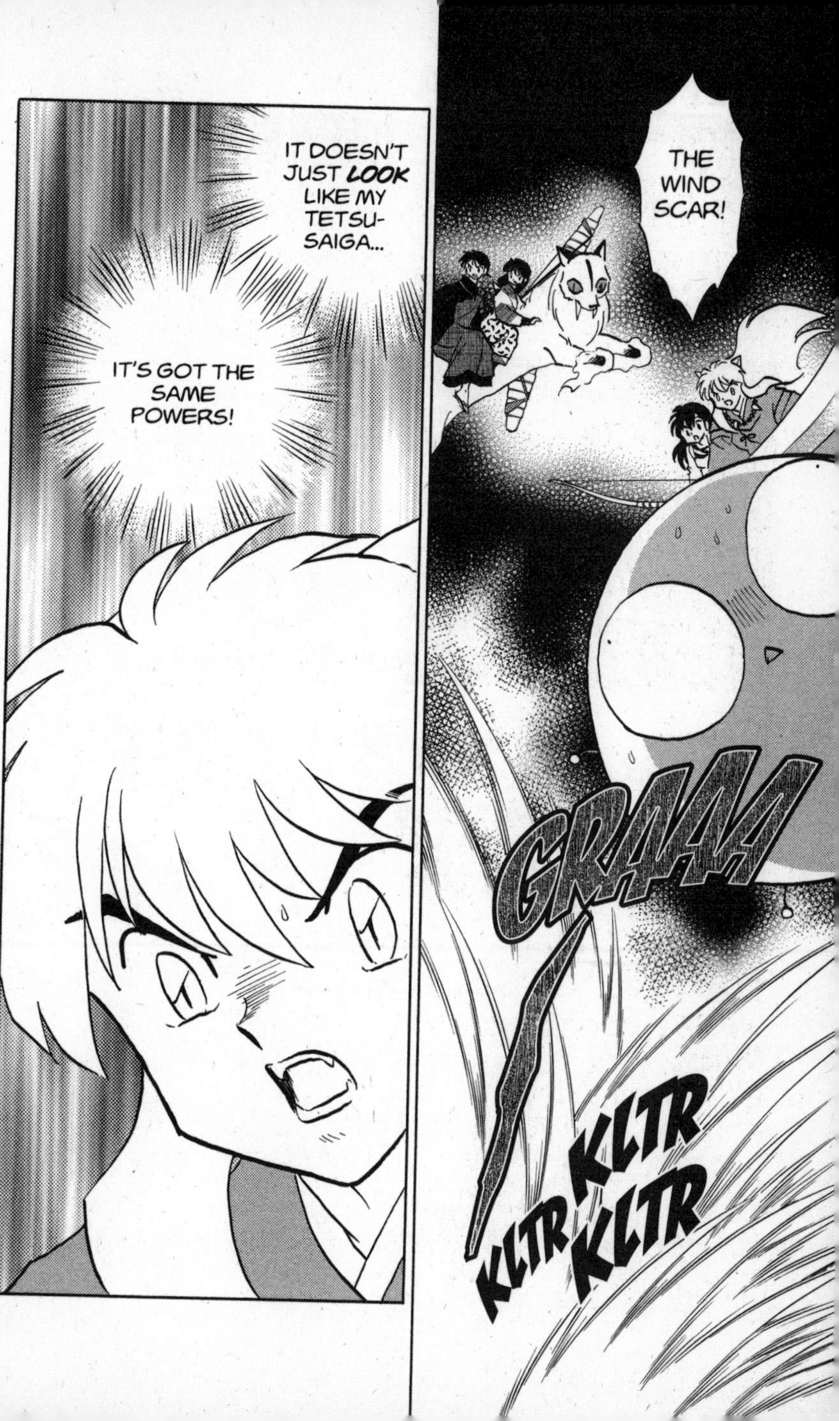
THE WIND SCAR!
GRAAA
KLTR KLTR
KLTR KLTR
IT DOESN'T JUST LOOK LIKE MY TETSU-SAIGA...
IT'S GOT THE SAME POWERS!

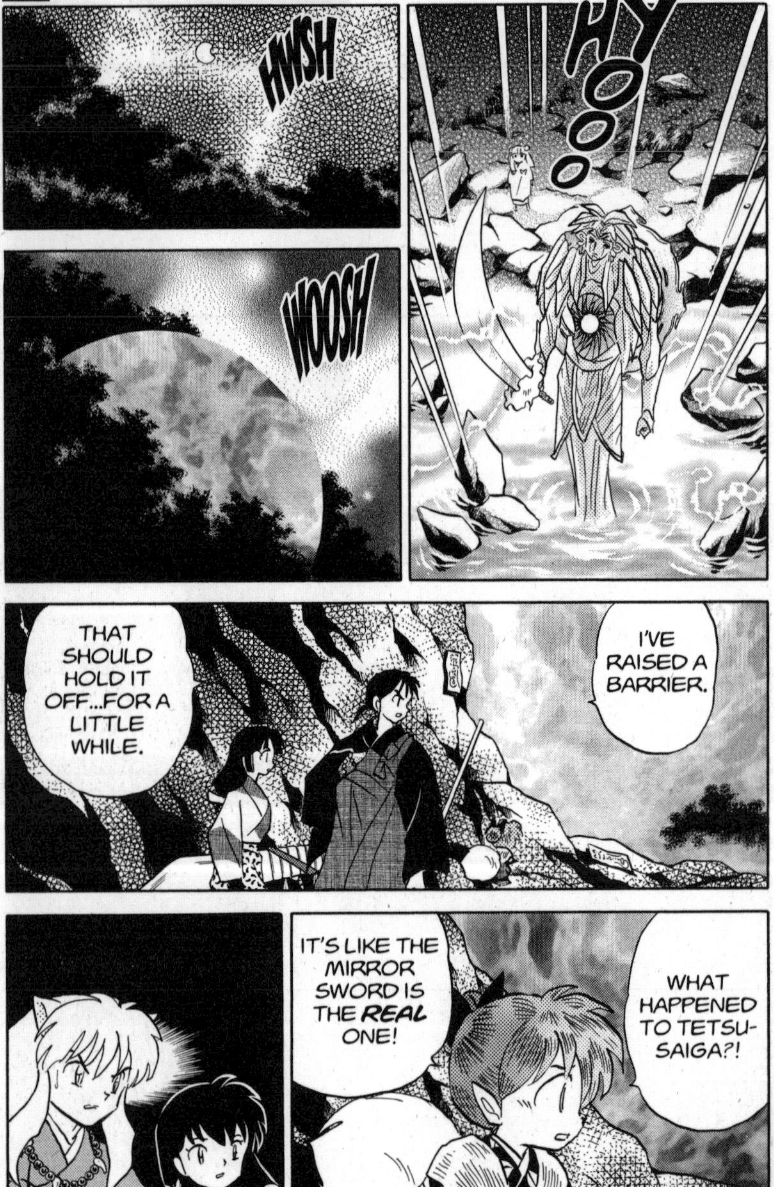
HYOOOO
HWSH
WOOSH
I'VE RAISED A BARRIER.
THAT SHOULD HOLD IT OFF...FOR A LITTLE WHILE.
WHAT HAPPENED TO TETSU-SAIGA?!
IT'S LIKE THE MIRROR SWORD IS THE *REAL* ONE!

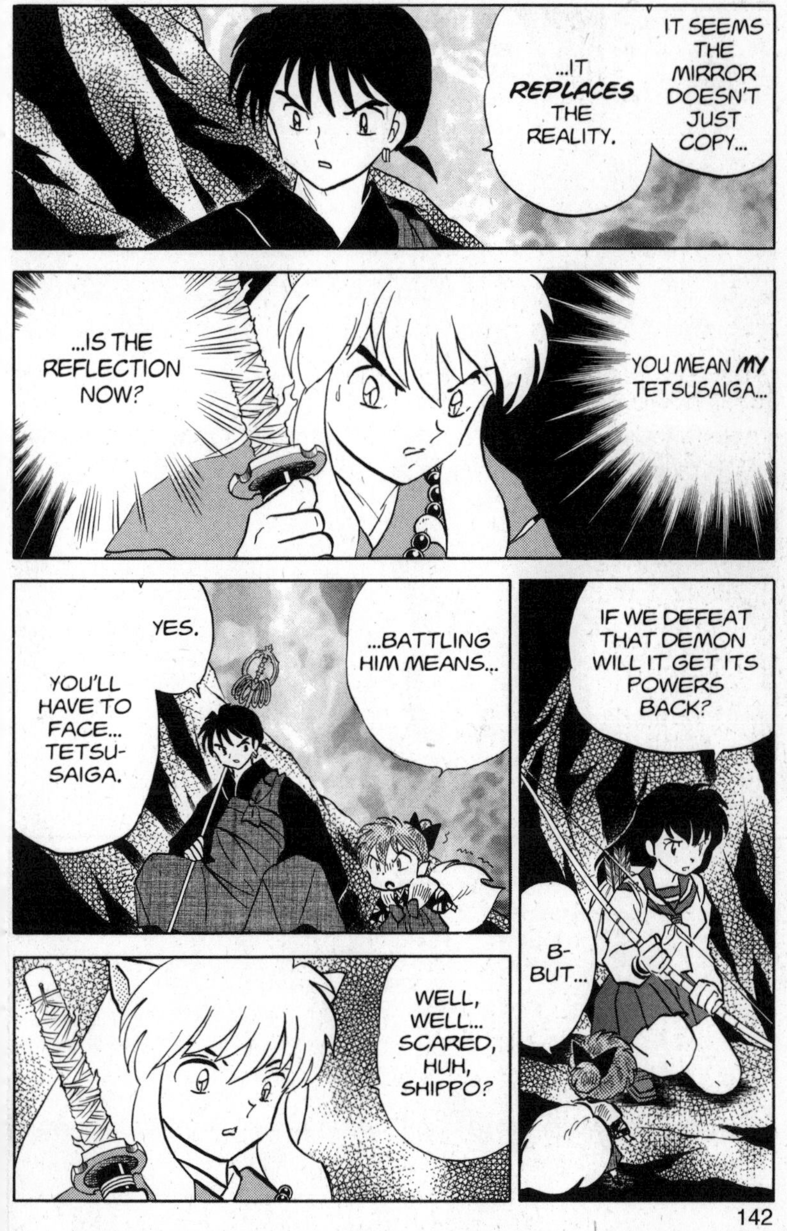
IT SEEMS THE MIRROR DOESN'T JUST COPY...
...IT **REPLACES** THE REALITY.
YOU MEAN ***MY*** TETSUSAIGA...
...IS THE REFLECTION NOW?
IF WE DEFEAT THAT DEMON WILL IT GET ITS POWERS BACK?
B-BUT...
...BATTLING HIM MEANS...
YES.
YOU'LL HAVE TO FACE... TETSU-SAIGA.
WELL, WELL... SCARED, HUH, SHIPPO?

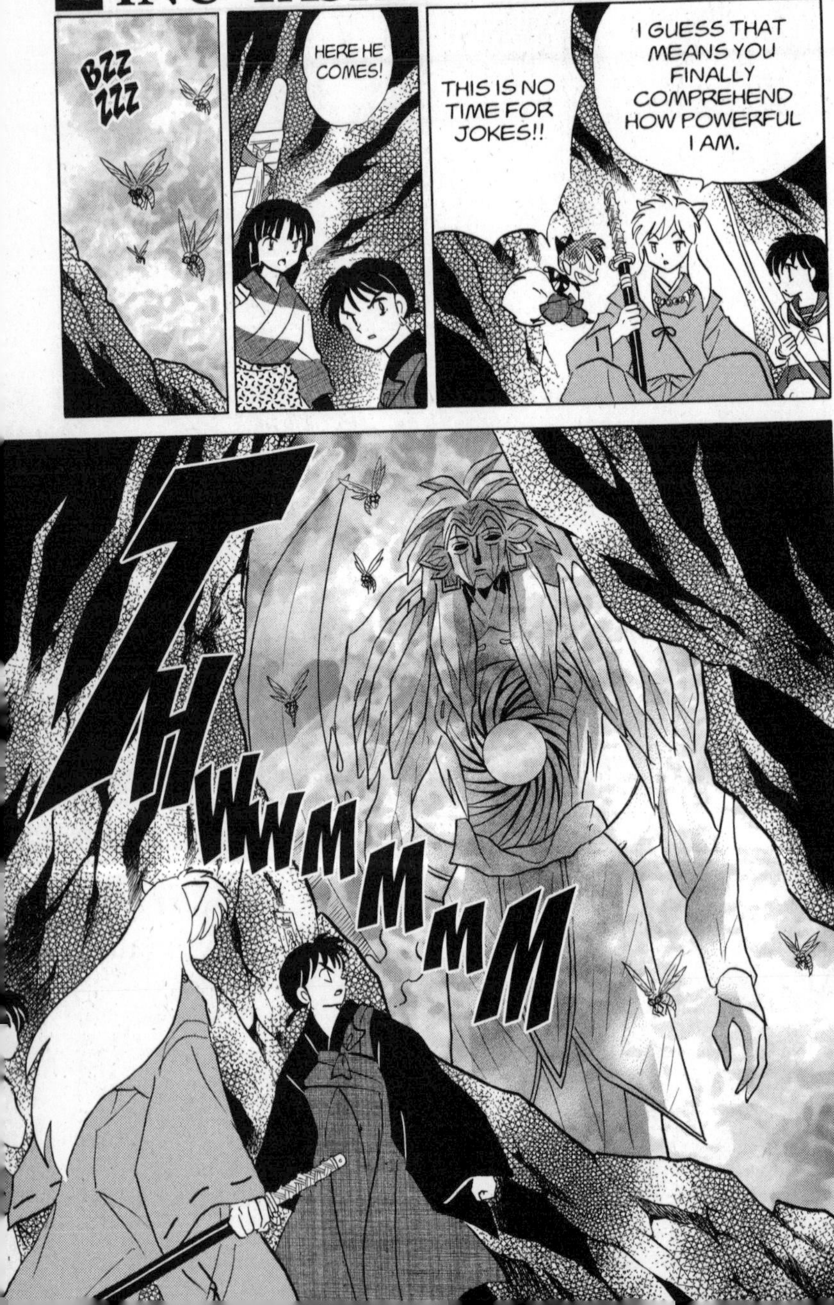
I GUESS THAT MEANS YOU FINALLY COMPREHEND HOW POWERFUL I AM.
THIS IS NO TIME FOR JOKES!!
HERE HE COMES!
BZZ ZZZ
ZHWWWMMMMMM

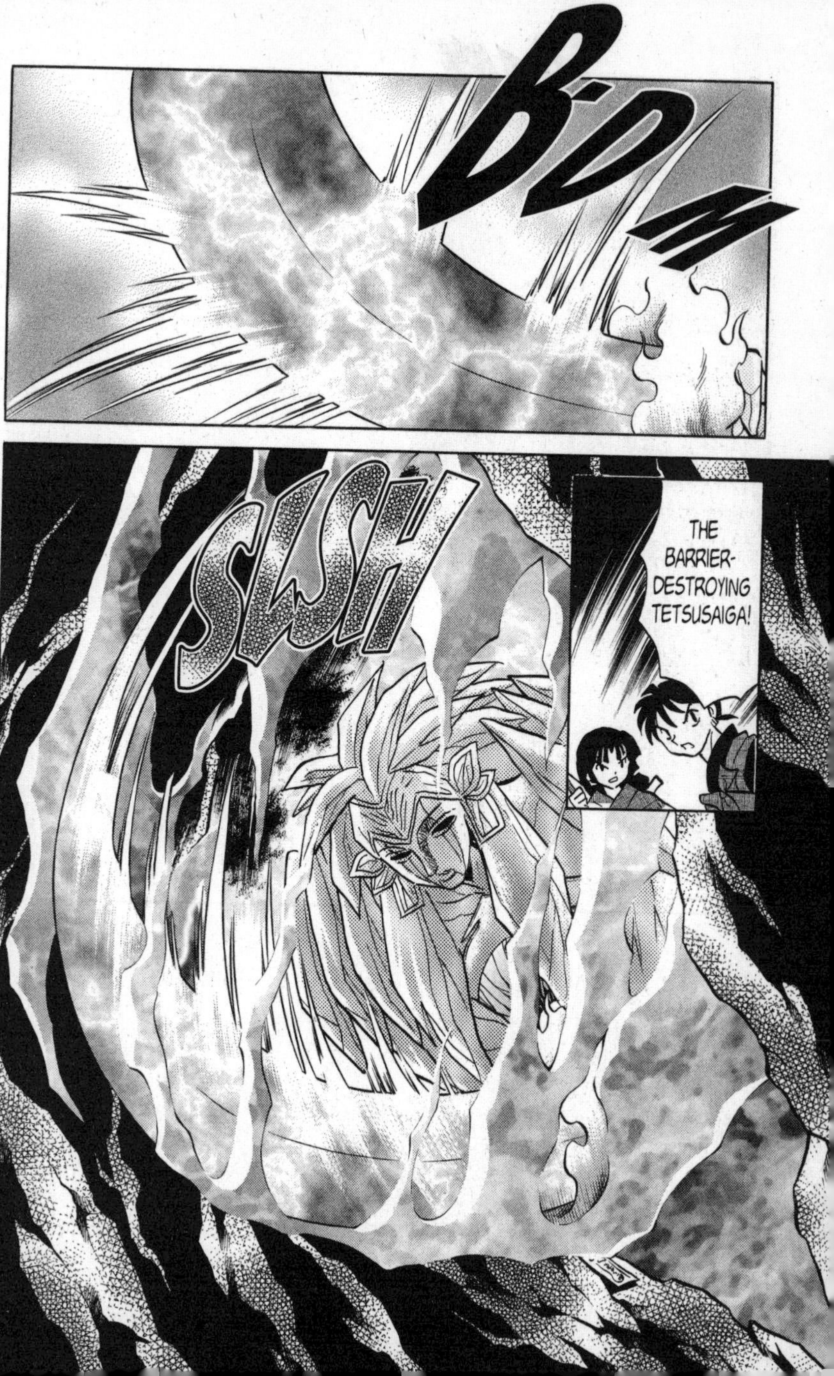
B-DOM
THE BARRIER-DESTROYING TETSUSAIGA!
SWSH

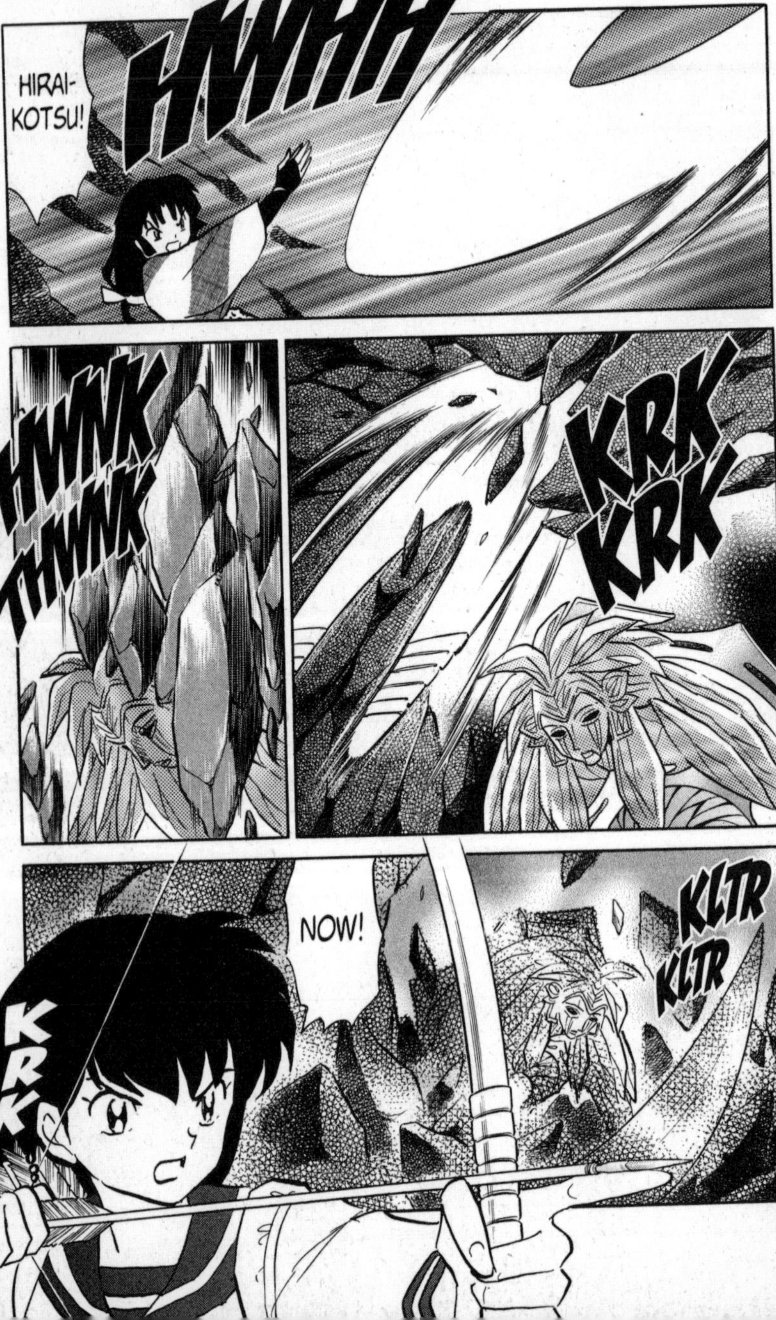
HIRAI-KOTSU!
KRK KRK
THWNK THWNK
KLTR KLTR
NOW!
KRK

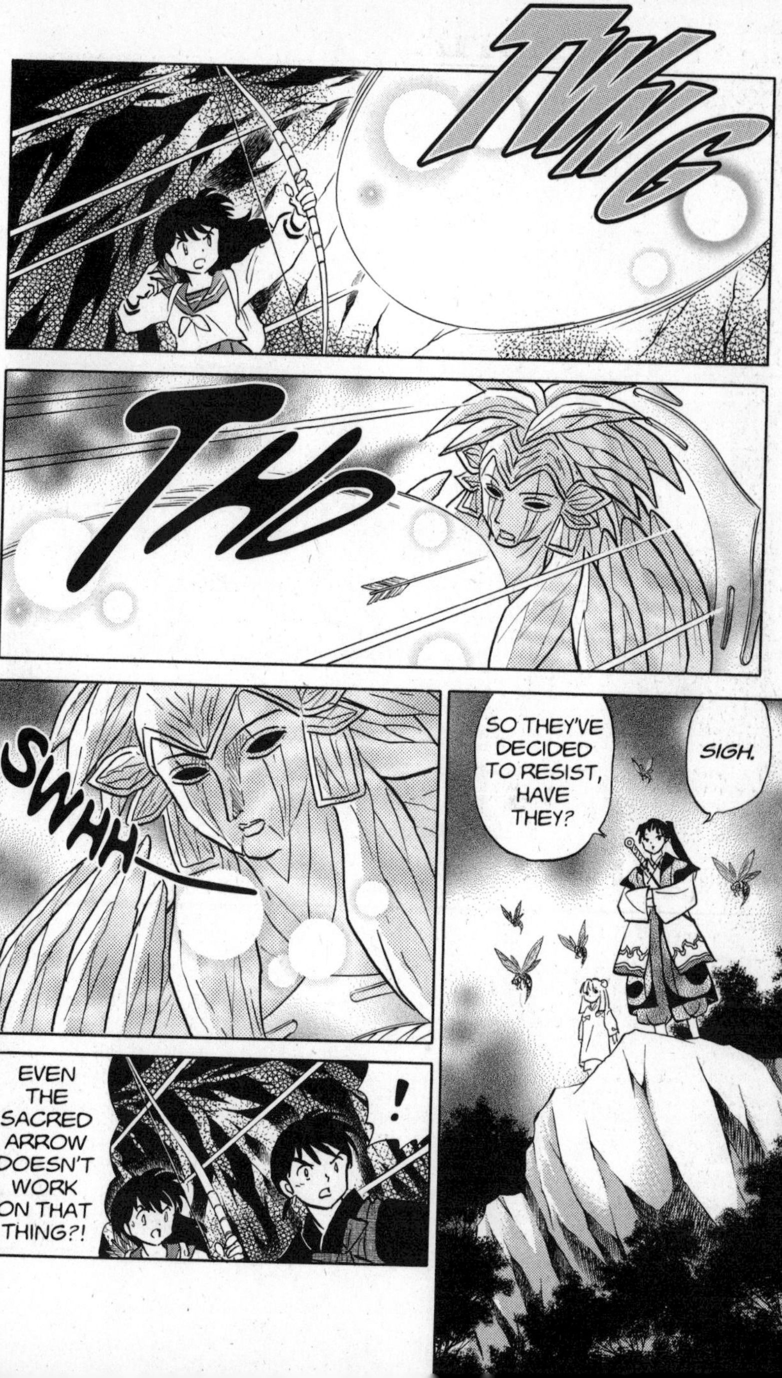
TWNG
THD
SIGH.
SO THEY'VE DECIDED TO RESIST, HAVE THEY?
SWHH—
!
EVEN THE SACRED ARROW DOESN'T WORK ON THAT THING?!

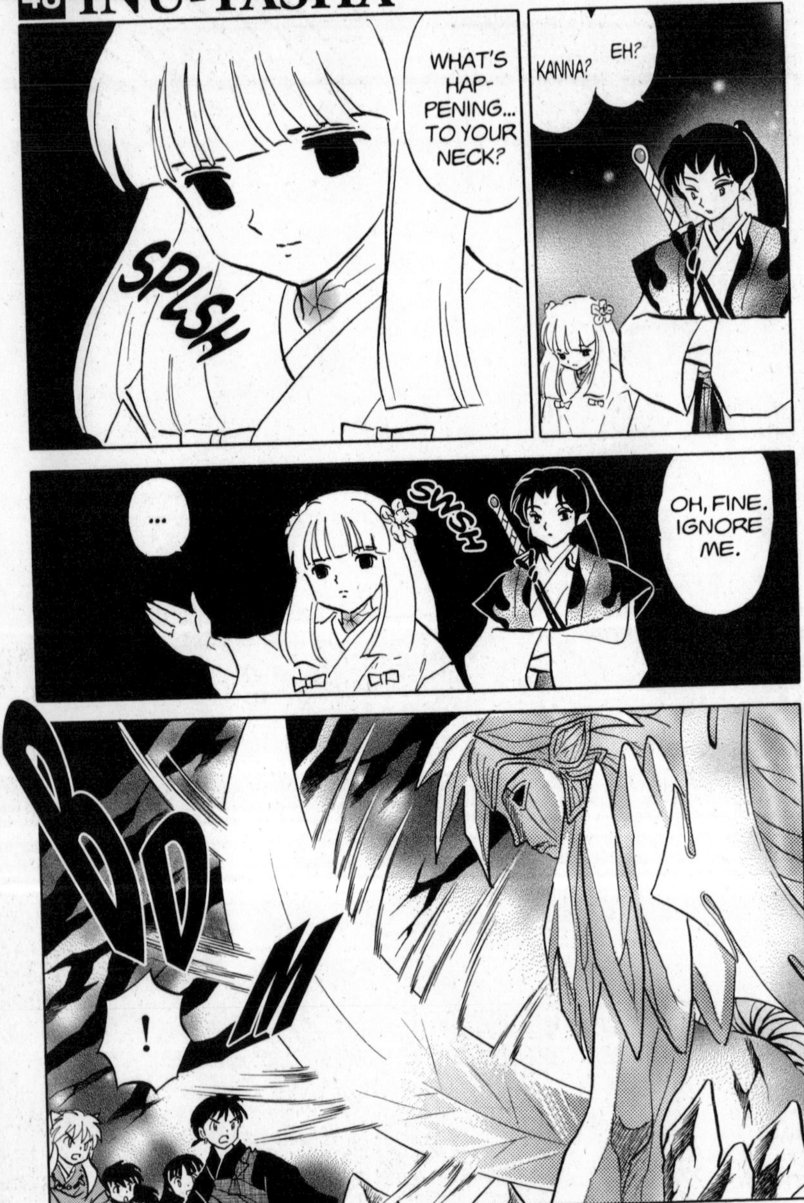
EH?
KANNA?
WHAT'S HAP-PENING... TO YOUR NECK?
SPLSH
OH, FINE. IGNORE ME.
SWSH
...
BOOM
!

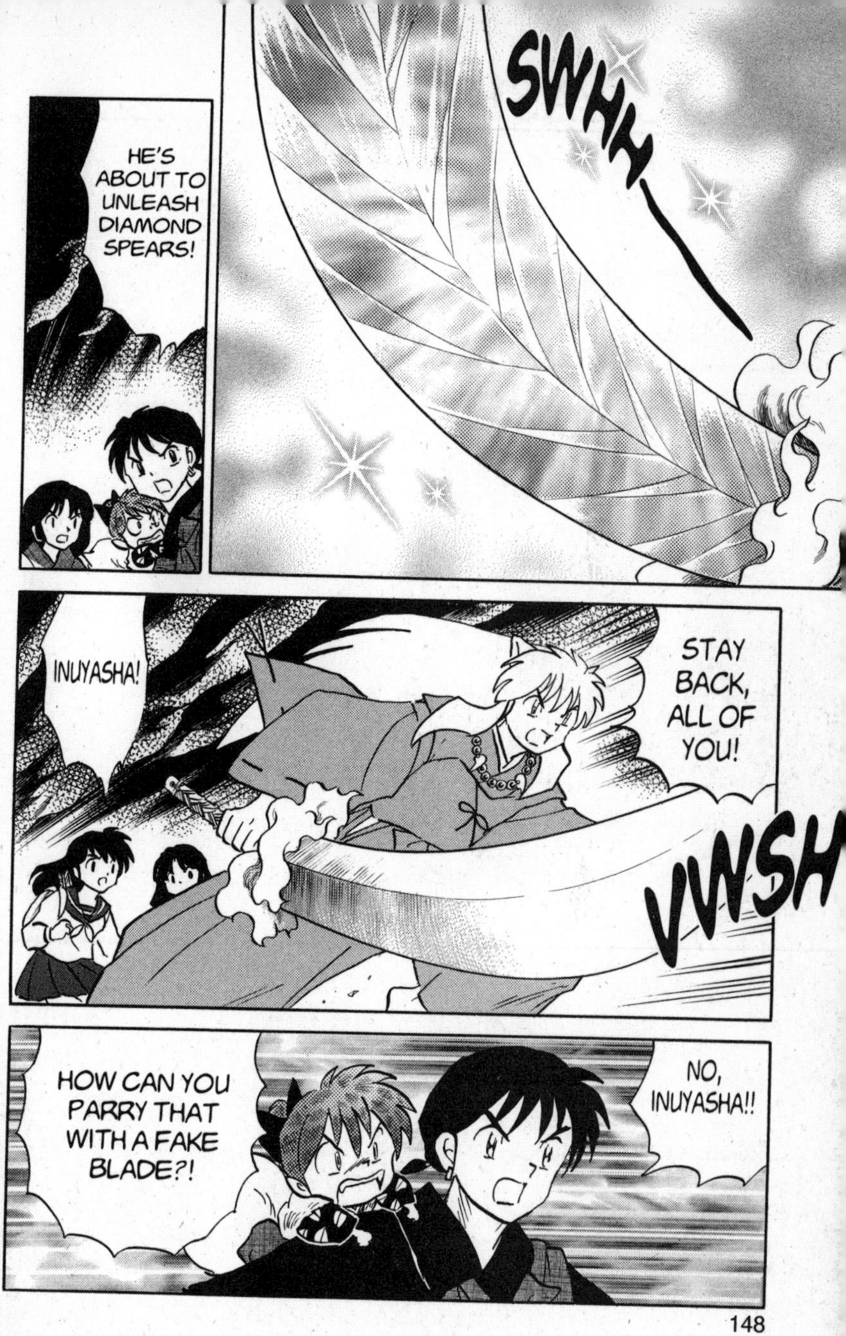
SWHH—
HE'S ABOUT TO UNLEASH DIAMOND SPEARS!
STAY BACK, ALL OF YOU!
VWSH
INUYASHA!
NO, INUYASHA!!
HOW CAN YOU PARRY THAT WITH A FAKE BLADE?!

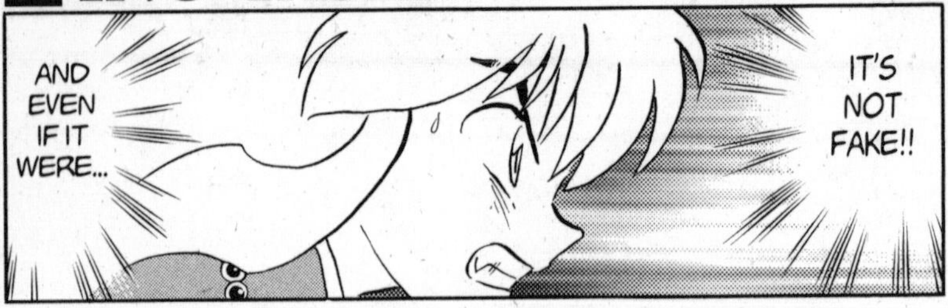
IT'S NOT FAKE!!
AND EVEN IF IT WERE...

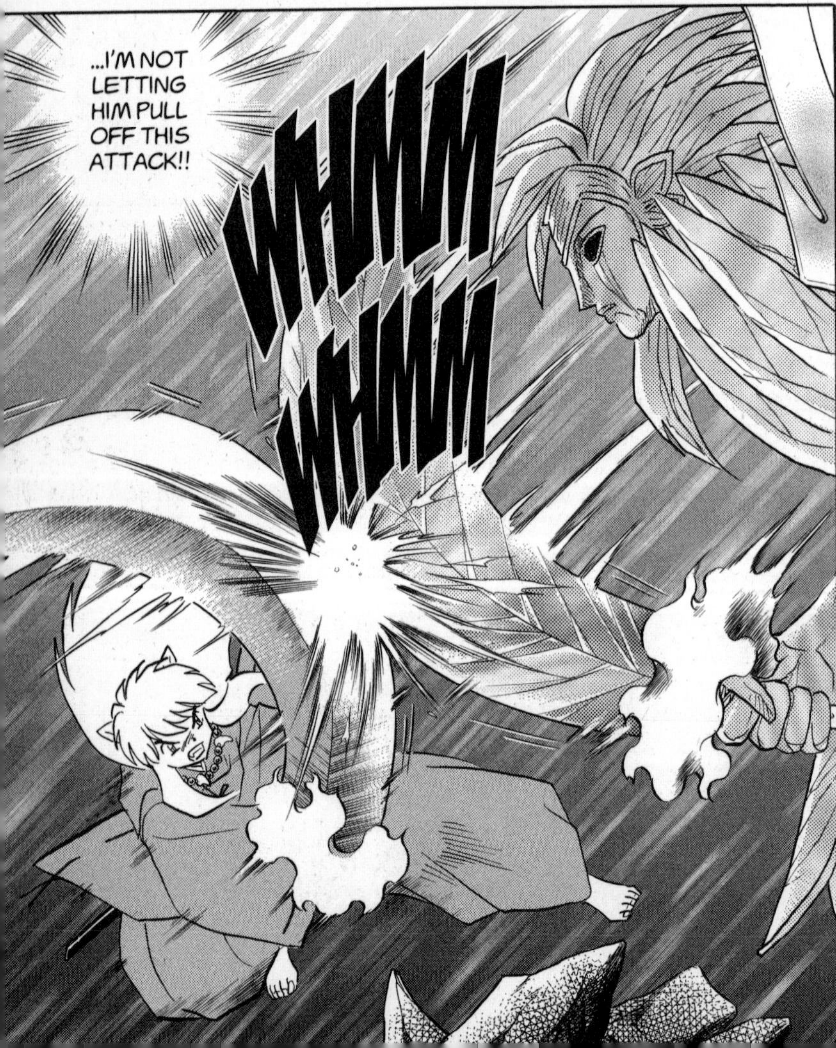
WHMM
WHMM
...I'M NOT LETTING HIM PULL OFF THIS ATTACK!!

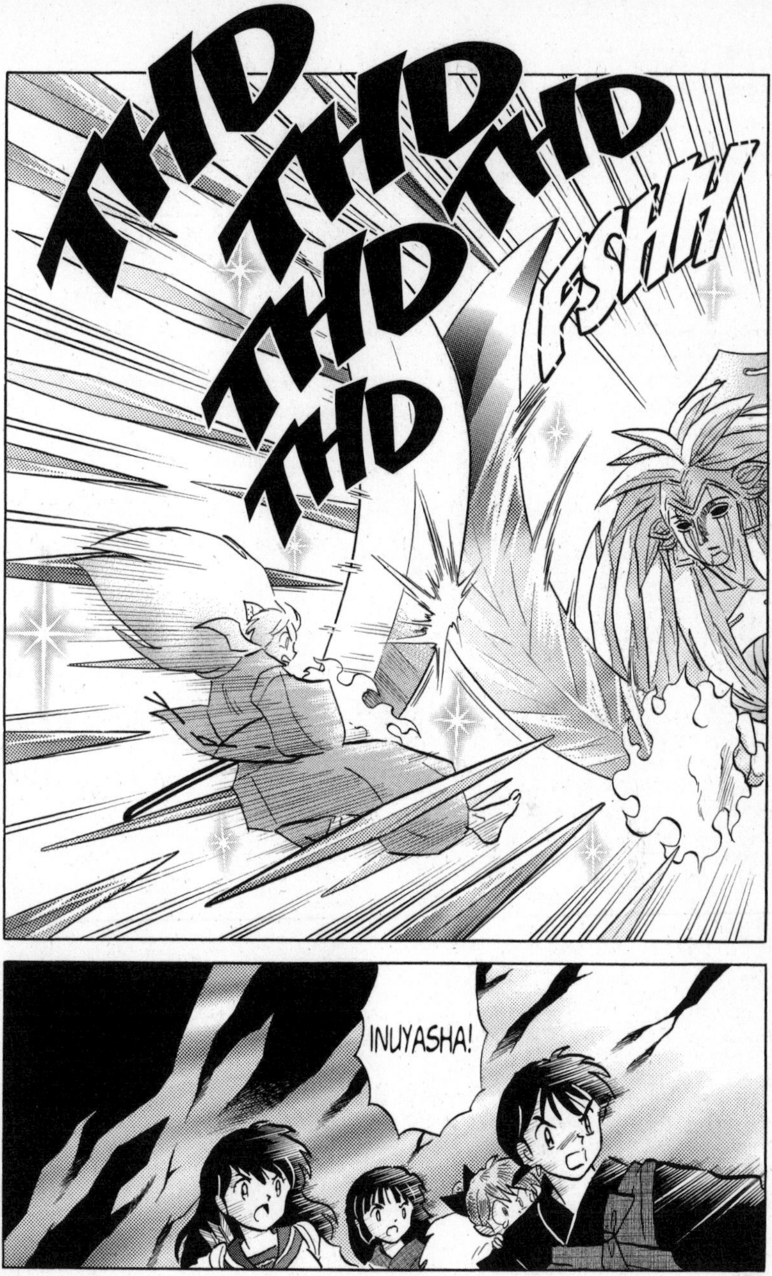
THD THD THD THD THD
FSHH
INUYASHA!

SCROLL 9
INUYASHA'S DEMON POWER

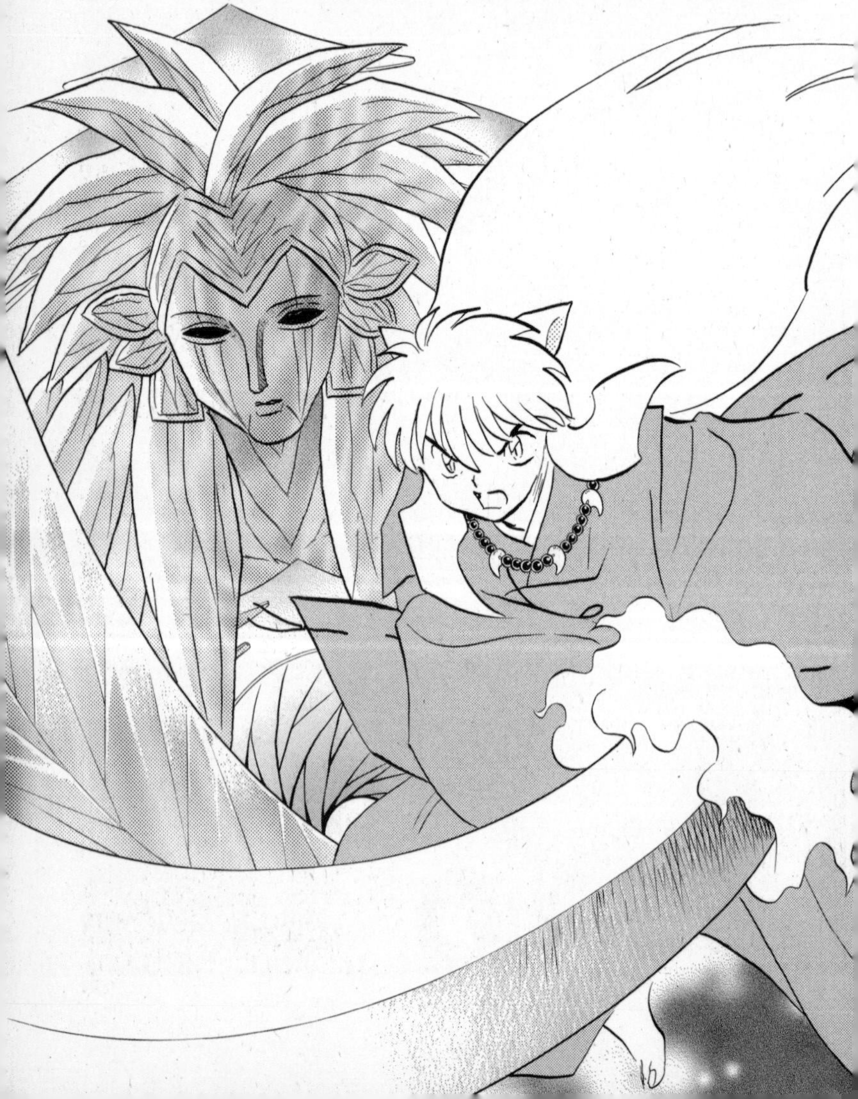

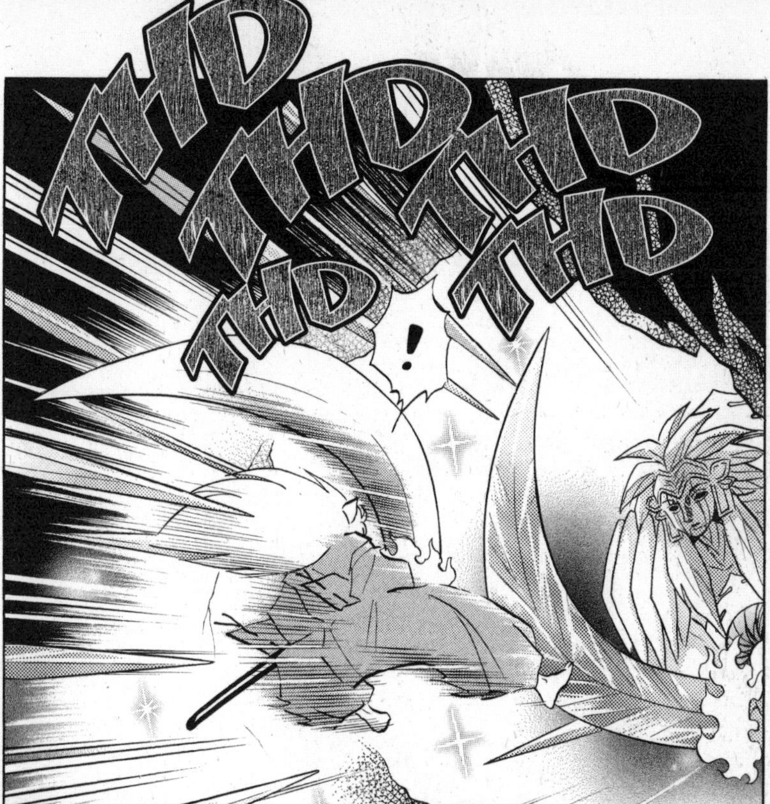
THD
THD
THD
THD
THD
THD
!

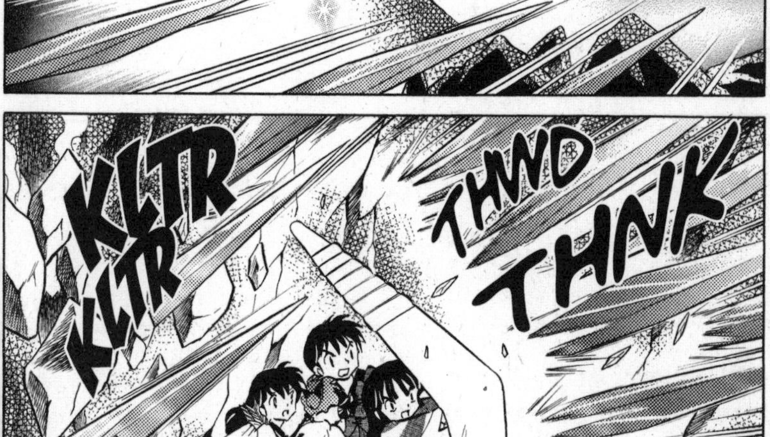
THWD
THNK
KLTR
KLTR

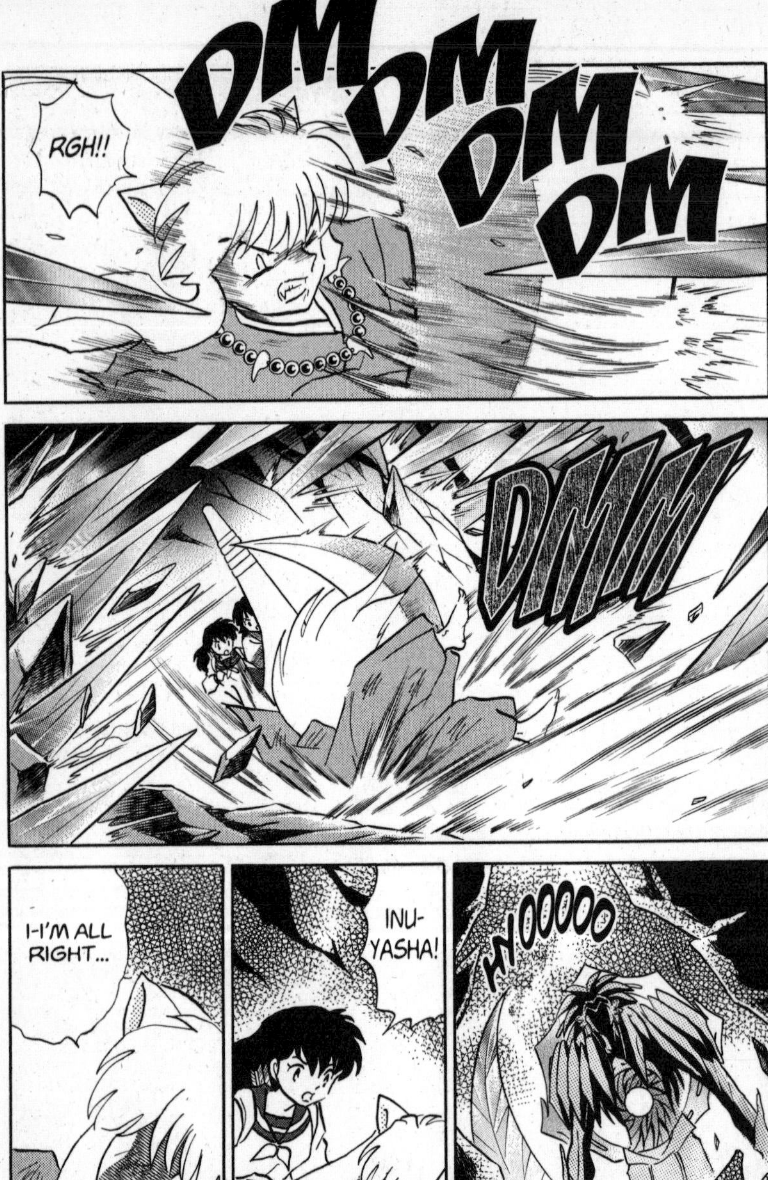
DM DM DM DM DM
RGH!!
DMM
WHOOOOO
INU-YASHA!
I-I'M ALL RIGHT...

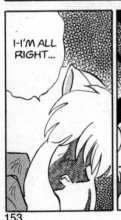

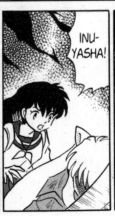

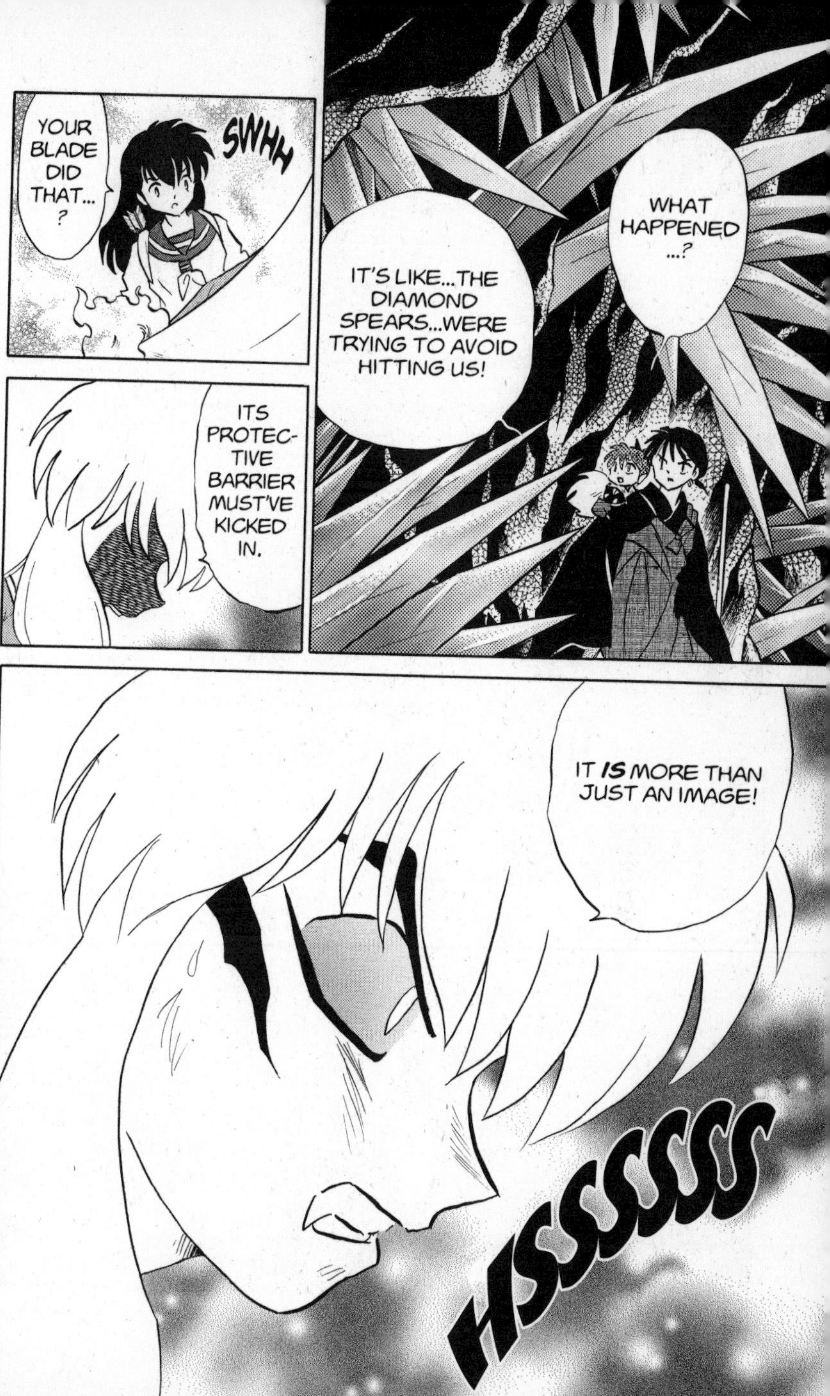
WHAT HAPPENED ...?
IT'S LIKE...THE DIAMOND SPEARS...WERE TRYING TO AVOID HITTING US!
YOUR BLADE DID THAT... ?
SWHH
ITS PROTECTIVE BARRIER MUST'VE KICKED IN.
IT IS MORE THAN JUST AN IMAGE!
HSSSSSS

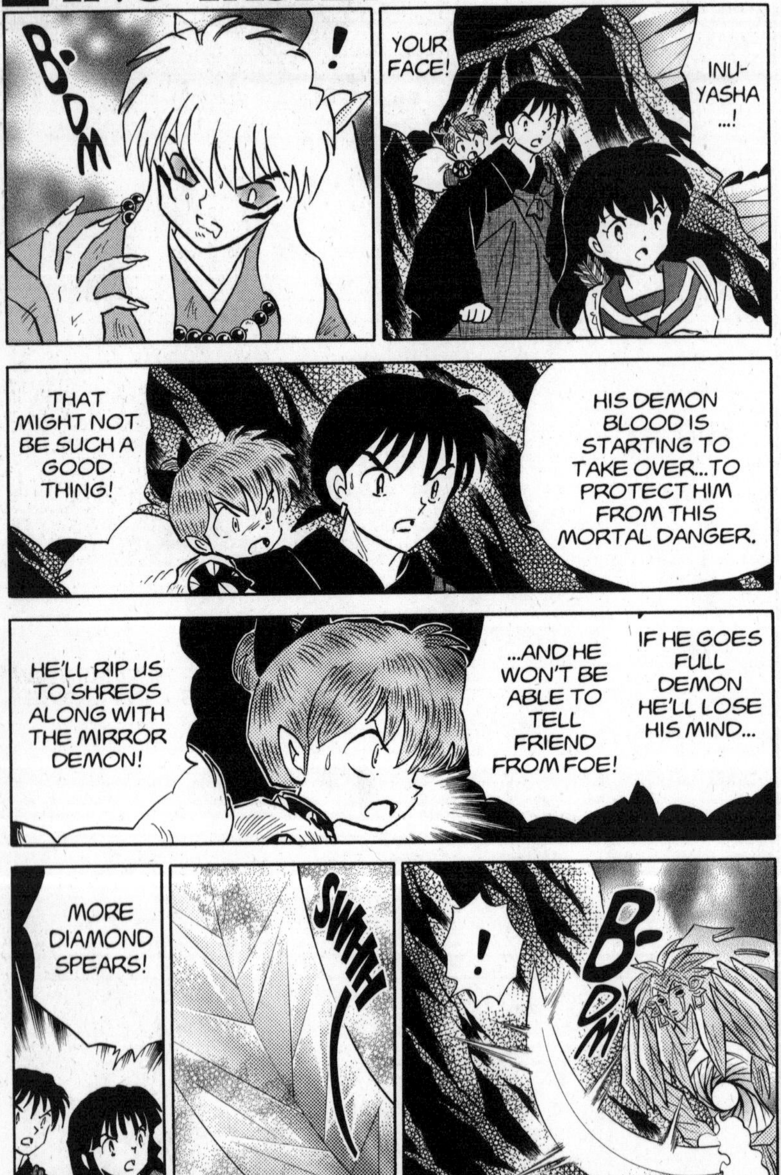
INU-YASHA ...!
YOUR FACE!
!
B-DM
HIS DEMON BLOOD IS STARTING TO TAKE OVER...TO PROTECT HIM FROM THIS MORTAL DANGER.
THAT MIGHT NOT BE SUCH A GOOD THING!
IF HE GOES FULL DEMON HE'LL LOSE HIS MIND...
...AND HE WON'T BE ABLE TO TELL FRIEND FROM FOE!
HE'LL RIP US TO SHREDS ALONG WITH THE MIRROR DEMON!
B-DM
!
MORE DIAMOND SPEARS!

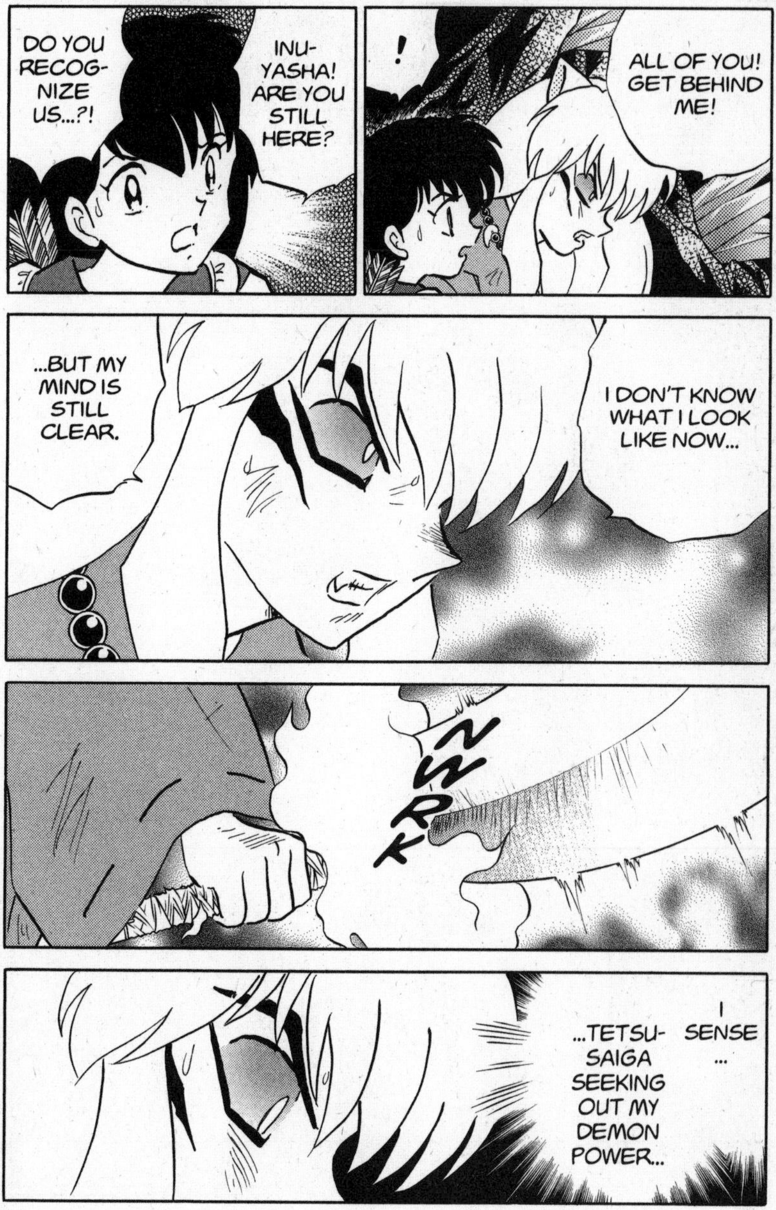
!
ALL OF YOU! GET BEHIND ME!
INU-YASHA! ARE YOU STILL HERE?
DO YOU RECOG-NIZE US...?!
I DON'T KNOW WHAT I LOOK LIKE NOW...
...BUT MY MIND IS STILL CLEAR.
NWRK
I SENSE...
...TETSU-SAIGA SEEKING OUT MY DEMON POWER...

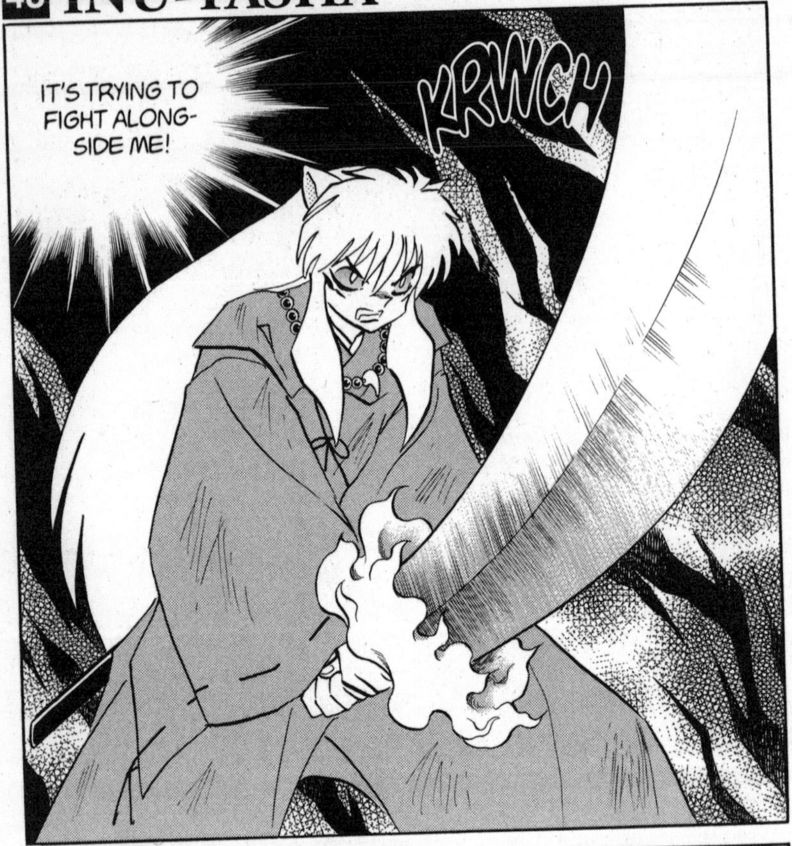
KRWCH
IT'S TRYING TO FIGHT ALONG-SIDE ME!

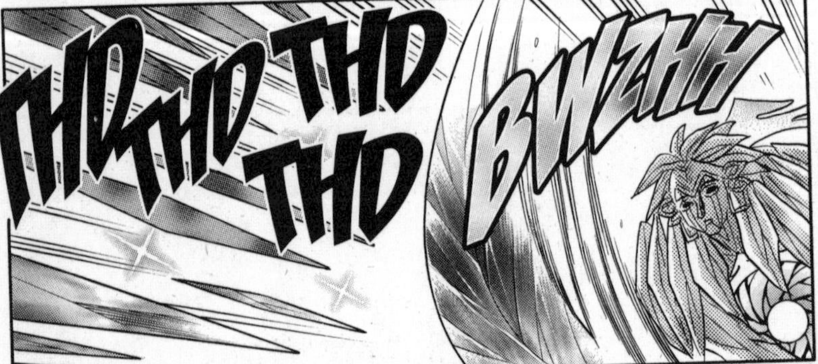
BWZHH
THD THD THD THD

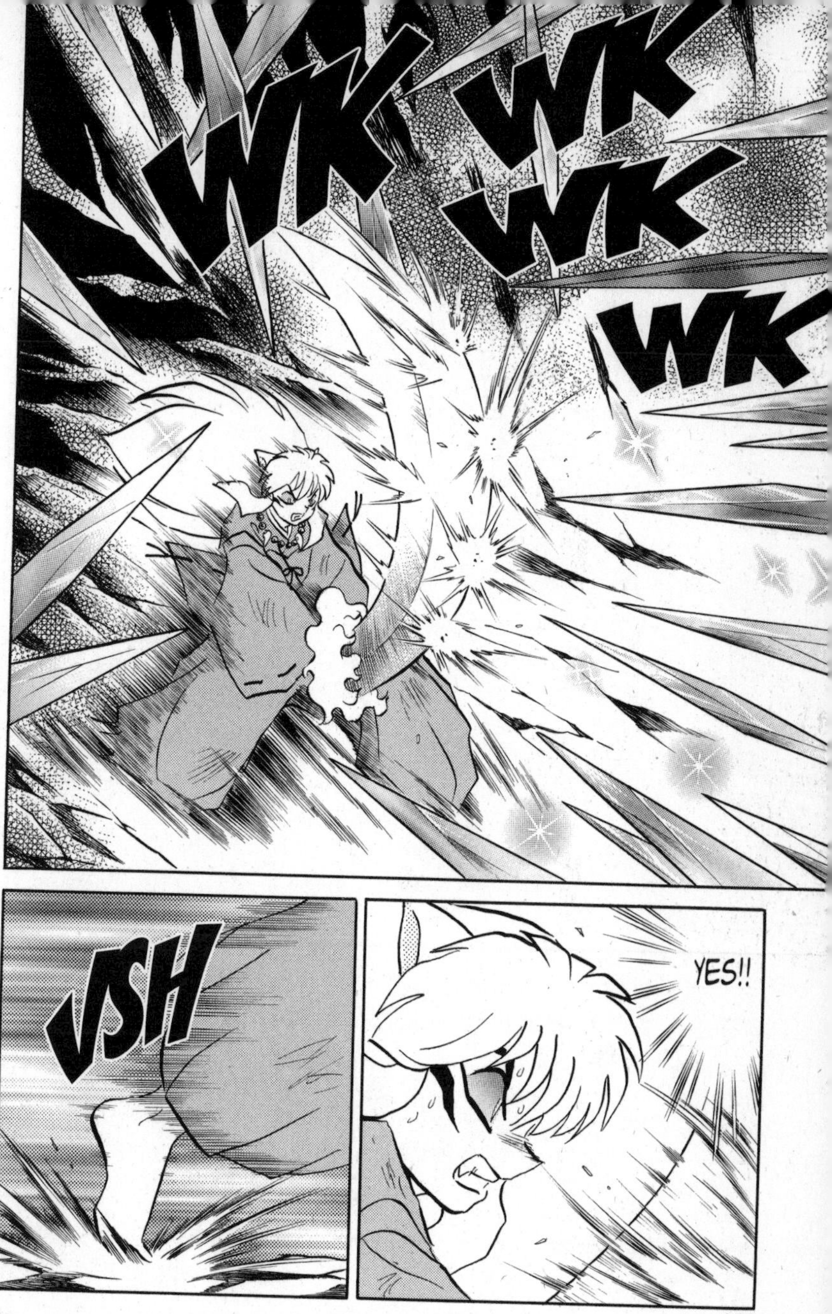
WK
WK
WK
WK
YES!!
VSH

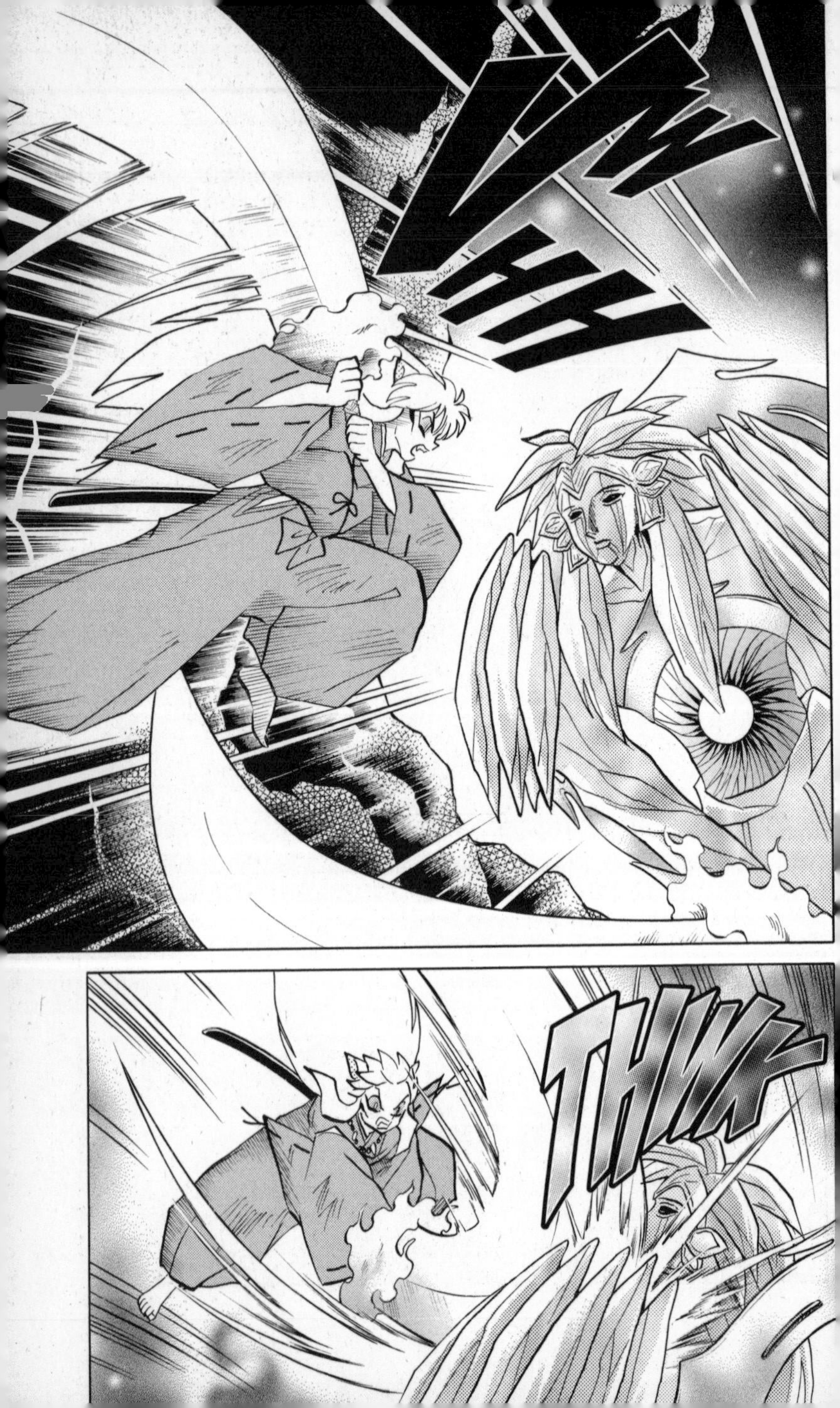
THWK

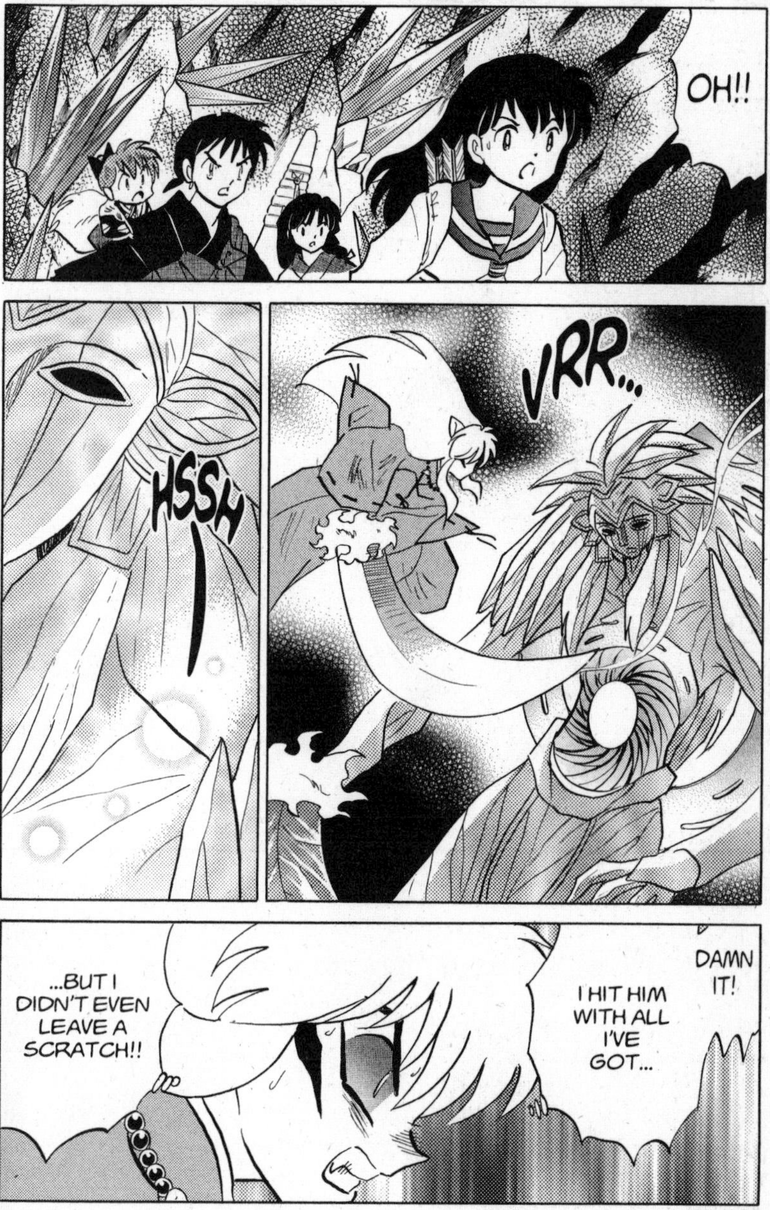
OH!!
VRR...
HSSH
DAMN IT!
I HIT HIM WITH ALL I'VE GOT...
...BUT I DIDN'T EVEN LEAVE A SCRATCH!!

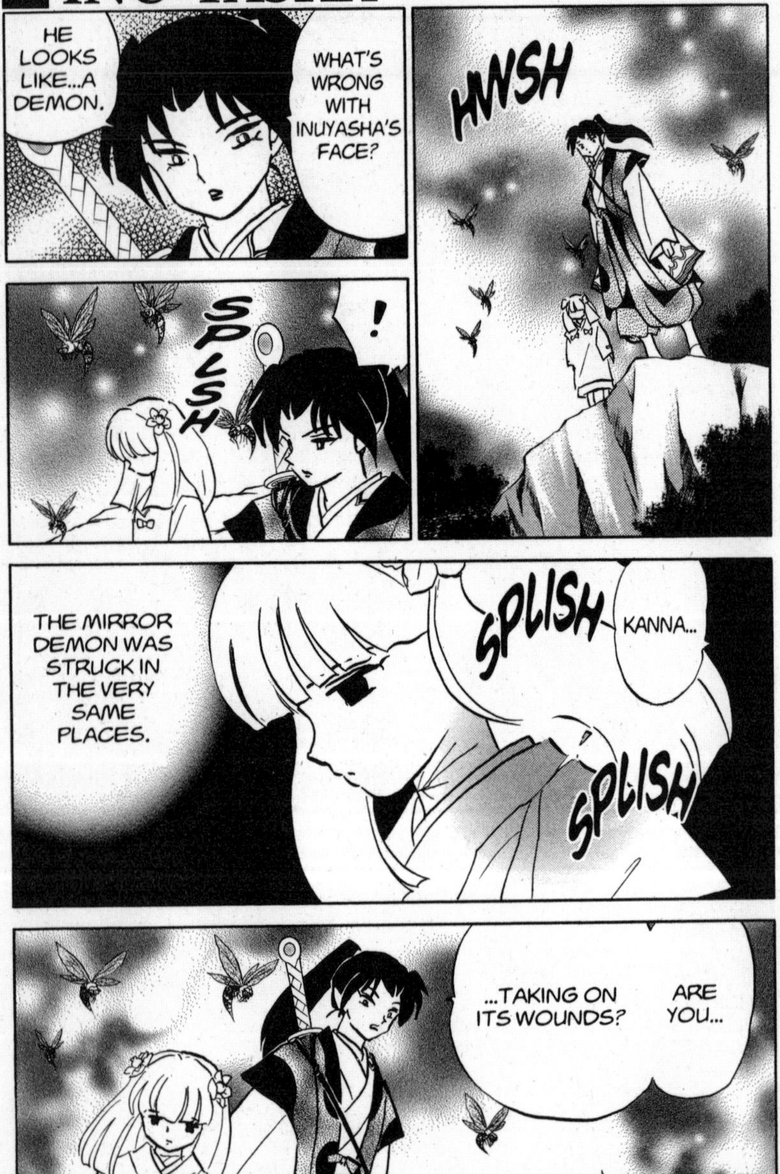
HWSH
WHAT'S WRONG WITH INUYASHA'S FACE?
HE LOOKS LIKE...A DEMON.
SPLISH
!
SPLISH
KANNA...
SPLISH
THE MIRROR DEMON WAS STRUCK IN THE VERY SAME PLACES.
ARE YOU...
...TAKING ON ITS WOUNDS?

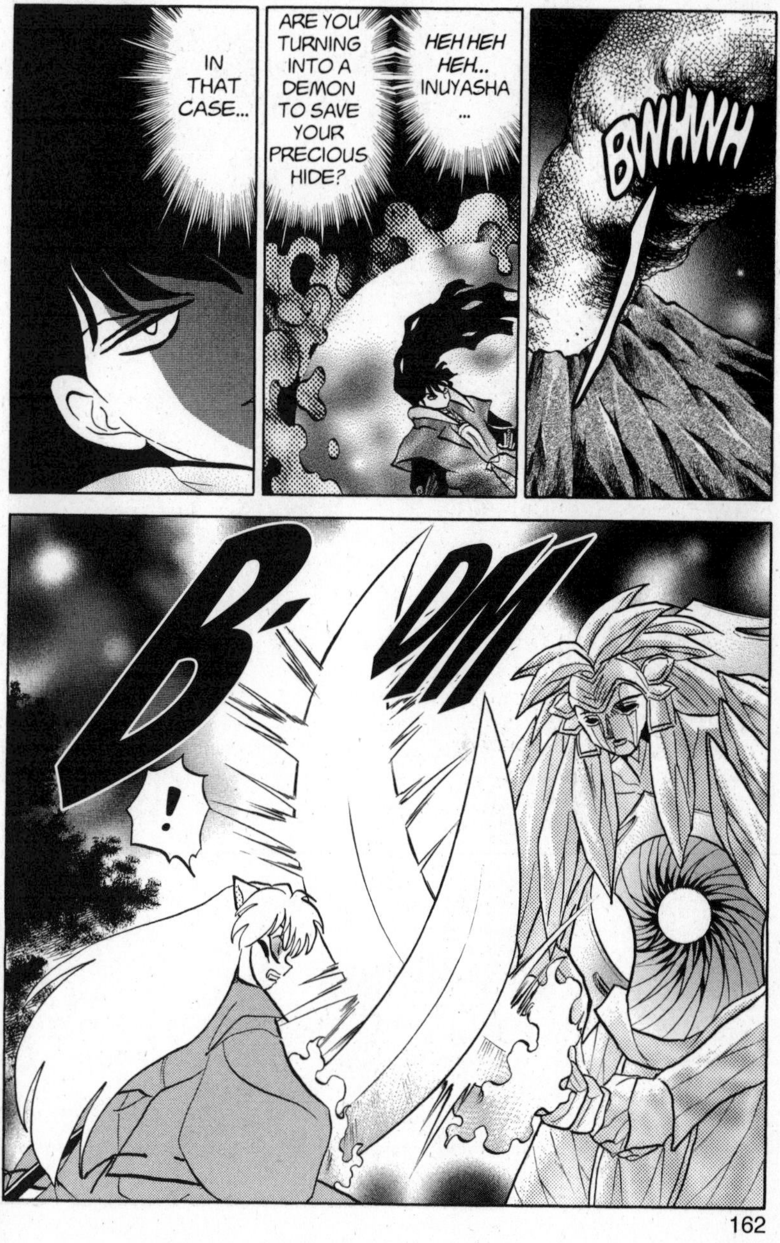
BWHWH
HEH HEH HEH... INUYASHA ...
ARE YOU TURNING INTO A DEMON TO SAVE YOUR PRECIOUS HIDE?
IN THAT CASE...
B-DM
!

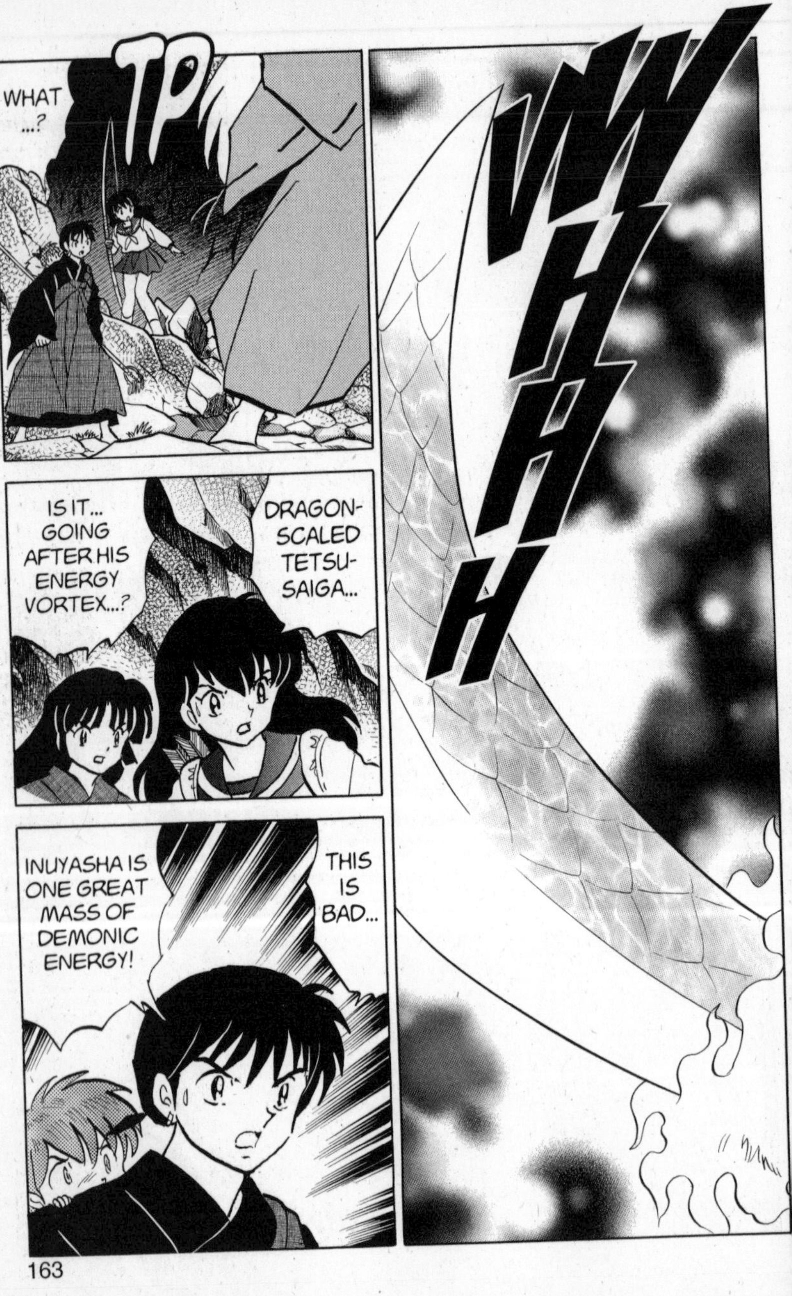
TP
WHAT ...?
DRAGON-SCALED TETSUSAIGA...
IS IT... GOING AFTER HIS ENERGY VORTEX...?
THIS IS BAD...
INUYASHA IS ONE GREAT MASS OF DEMONIC ENERGY!

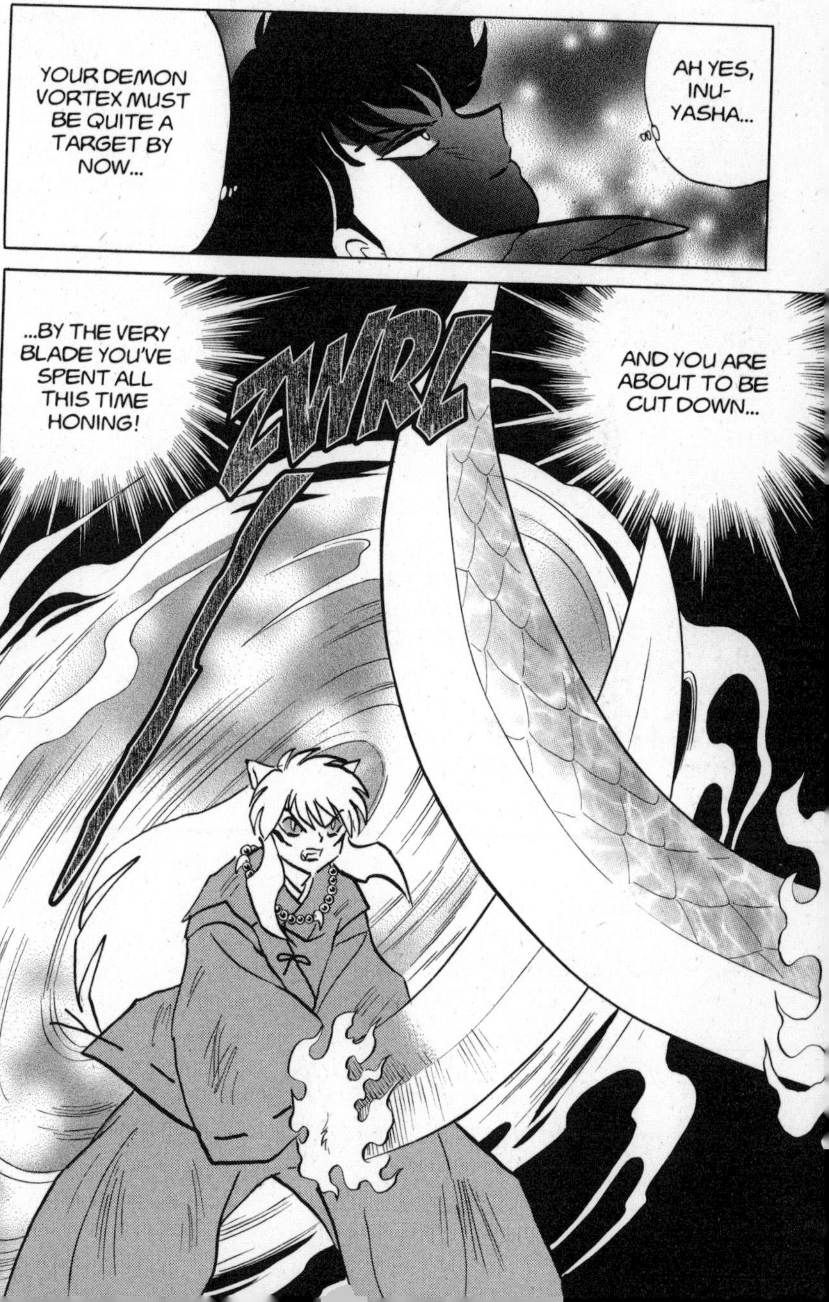
AH YES, INU-YASHA...
YOUR DEMON VORTEX MUST BE QUITE A TARGET BY NOW...
AND YOU ARE ABOUT TO BE CUT DOWN...
ZWRL
...BY THE VERY BLADE YOU'VE SPENT ALL THIS TIME HONING!

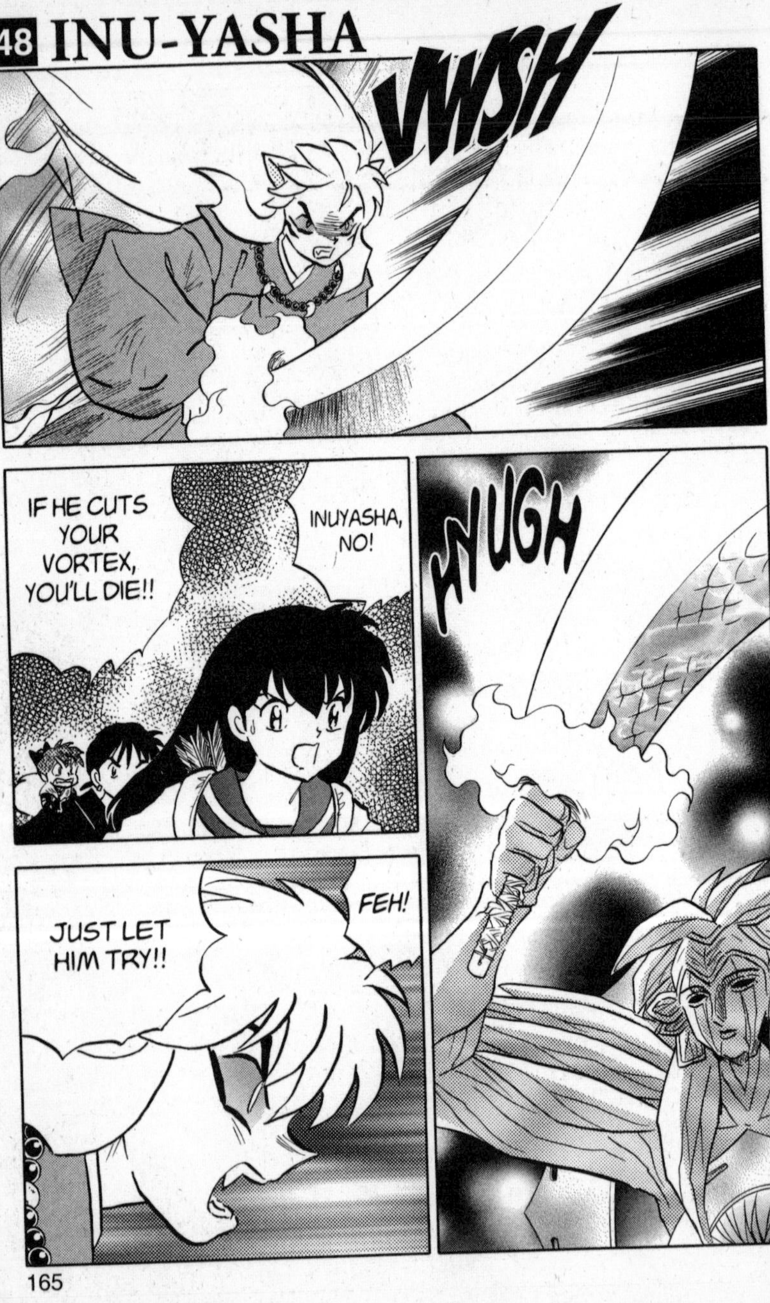
VWSH
HYUGH
INUYASHA, NO!
IF HE CUTS YOUR VORTEX, YOU'LL DIE!!
FEH!
JUST LET HIM TRY!!

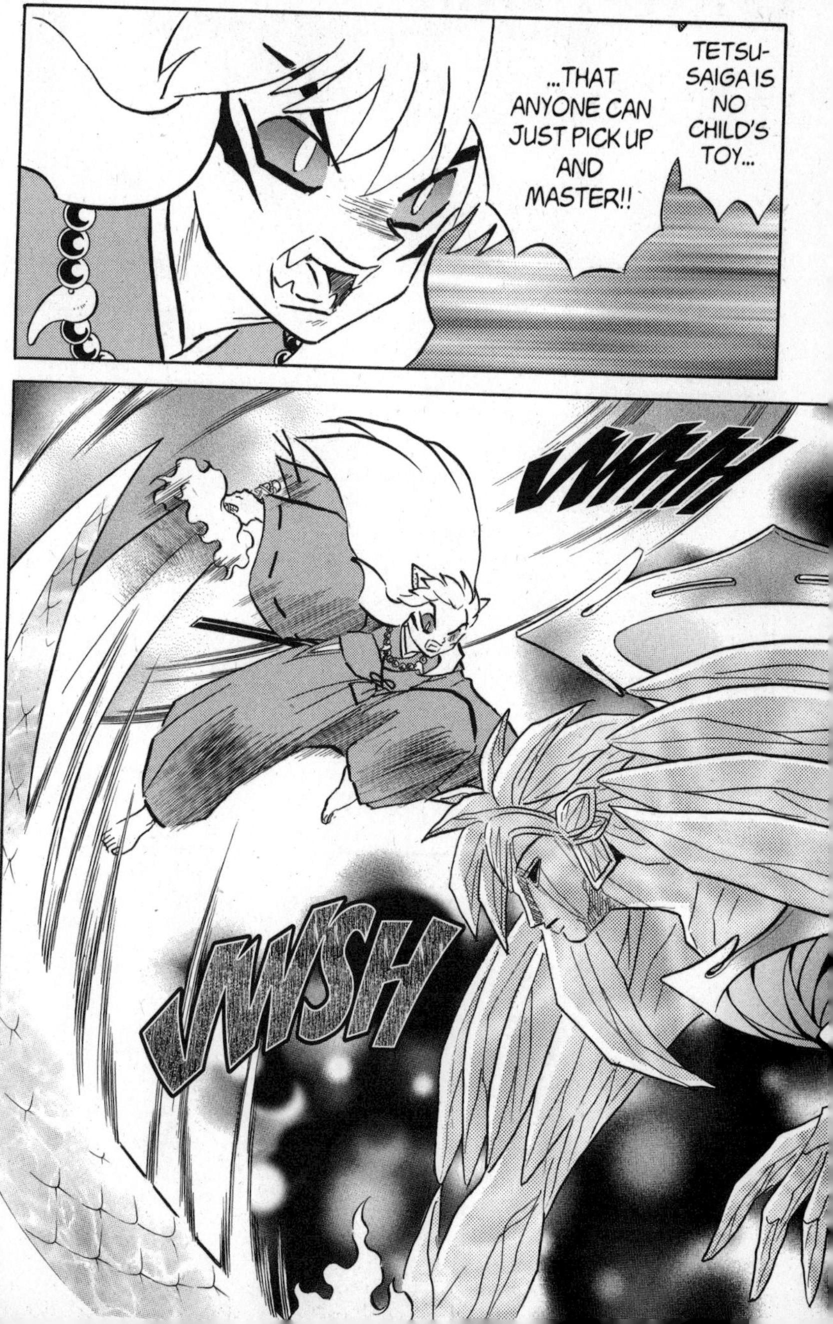
TETSU-SAIGA IS NO CHILD'S TOY...
...THAT ANYONE CAN JUST PICK UP AND MASTER!!
VWSH

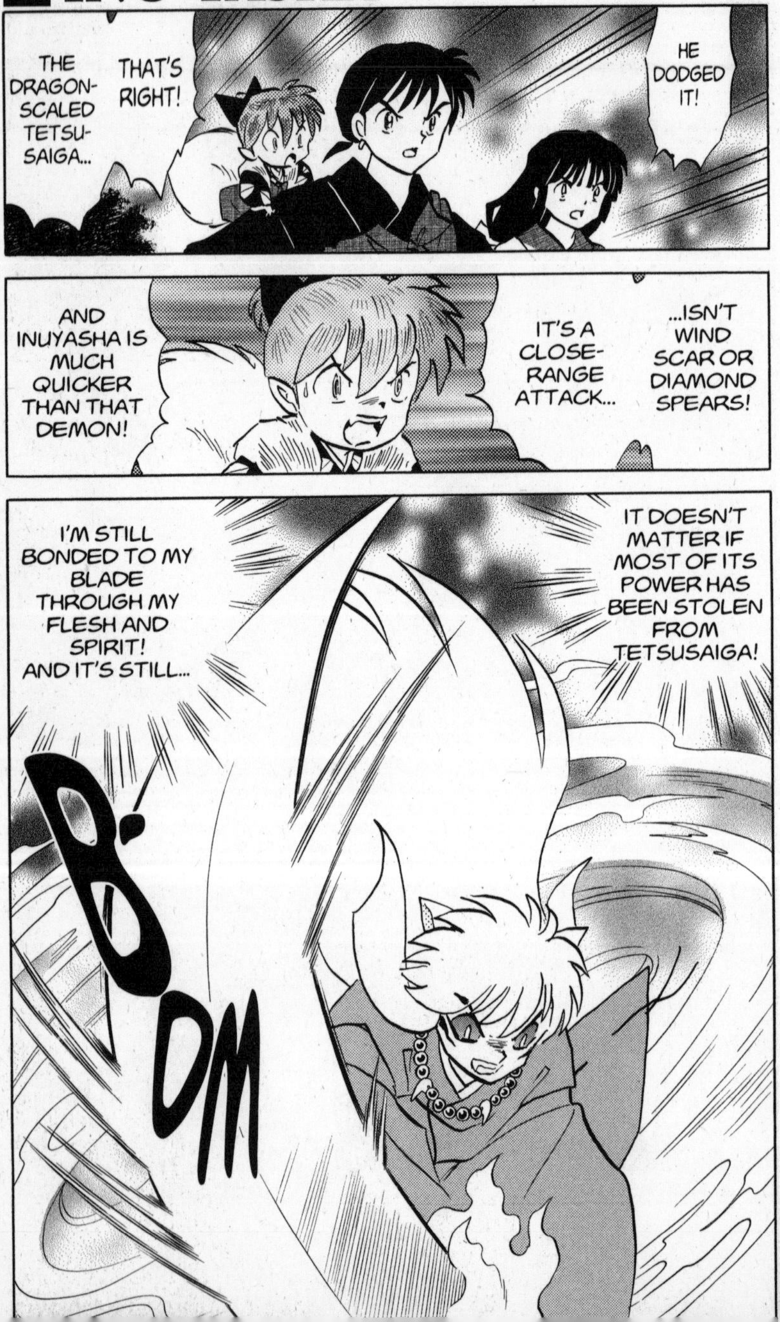
HE DODGED IT!
THAT'S RIGHT!
THE DRAGON-SCALED TETSU-SAIGA...
...ISN'T WIND SCAR OR DIAMOND SPEARS!
IT'S A CLOSE-RANGE ATTACK...
AND INUYASHA IS MUCH QUICKER THAN THAT DEMON!
IT DOESN'T MATTER IF MOST OF ITS POWER HAS BEEN STOLEN FROM TETSUSAIGA!
I'M STILL BONDED TO MY BLADE THROUGH MY FLESH AND SPIRIT! AND IT'S STILL...
BOOM

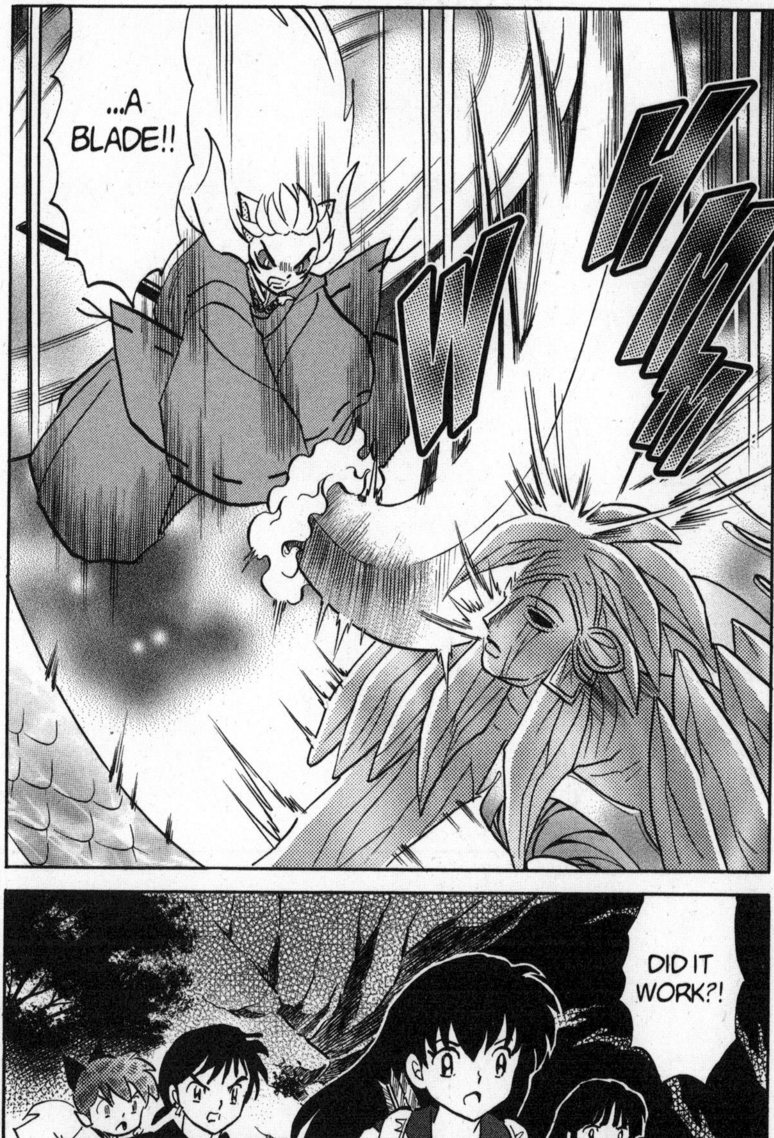
...A BLADE!!
WHAM
DID IT WORK?!

SCROLL 10

THE MIRROR'S SHADOW

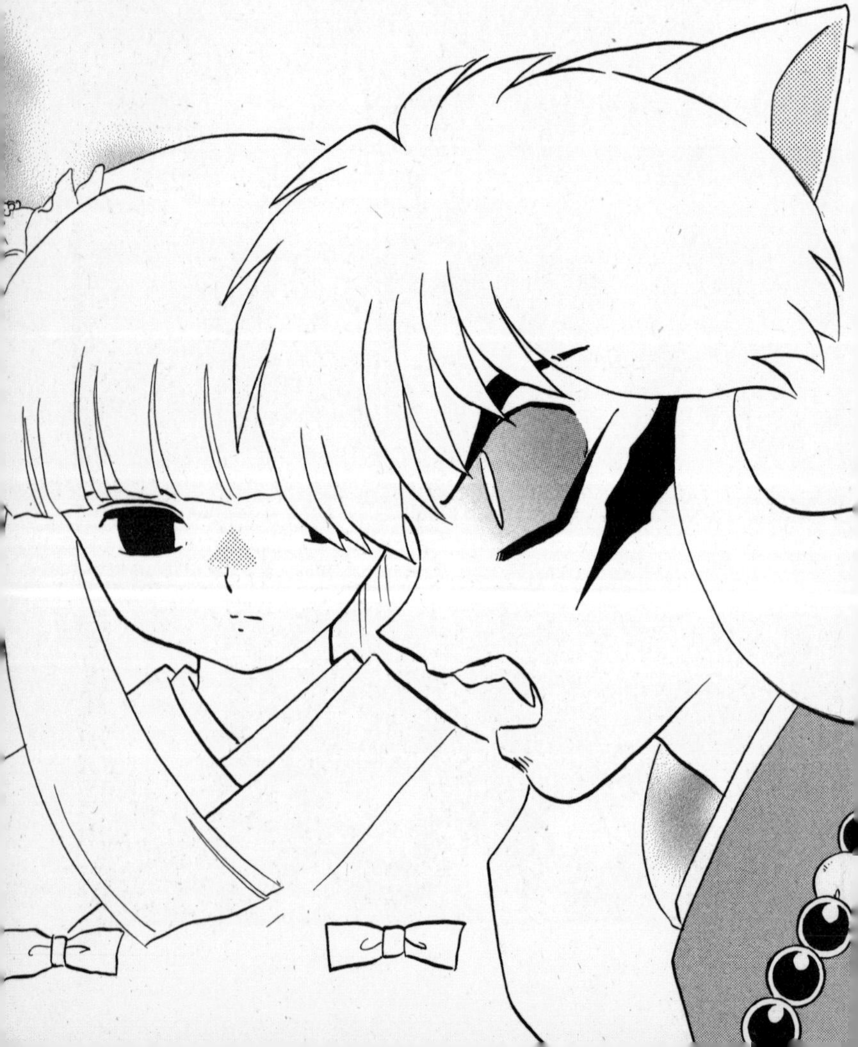

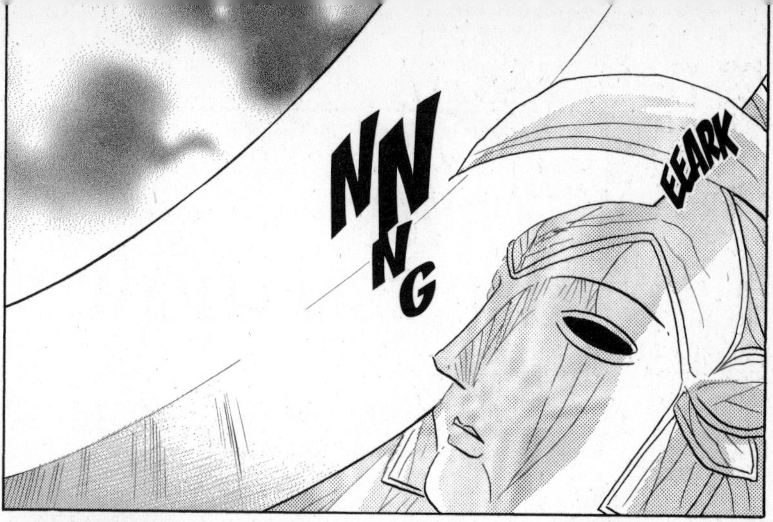
EEARK
NNNG

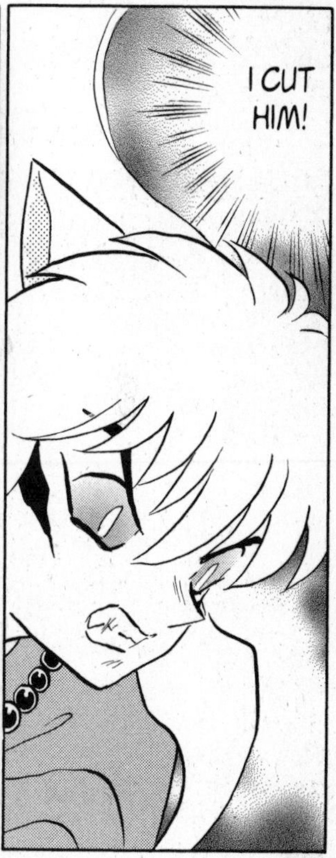
I CUT HIM!

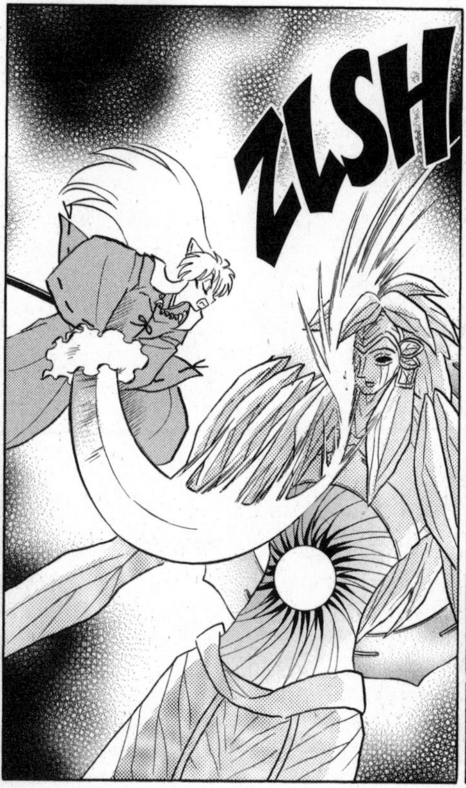
ZLSH

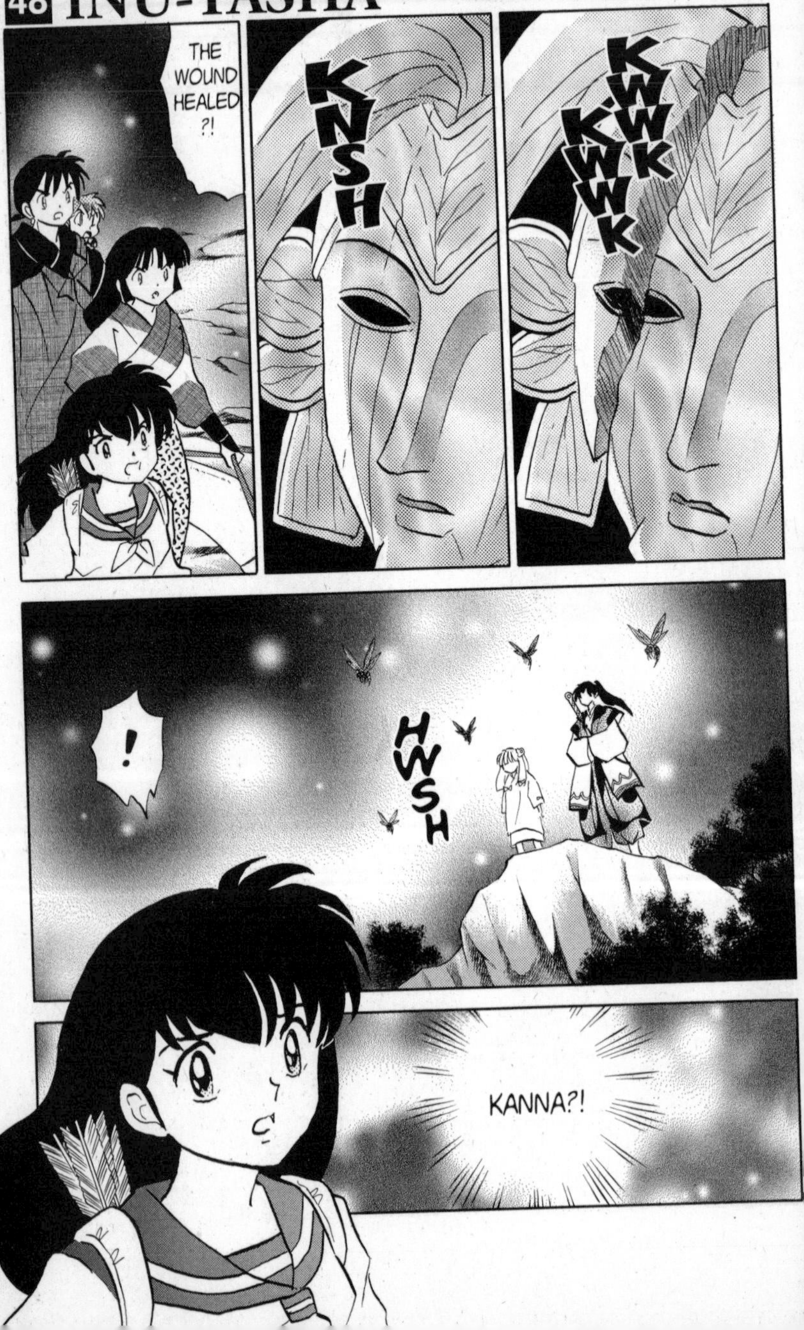
KWWK
KWWK
KNSH
THE WOUND HEALED ?!
HWSH
!
KANNA?!

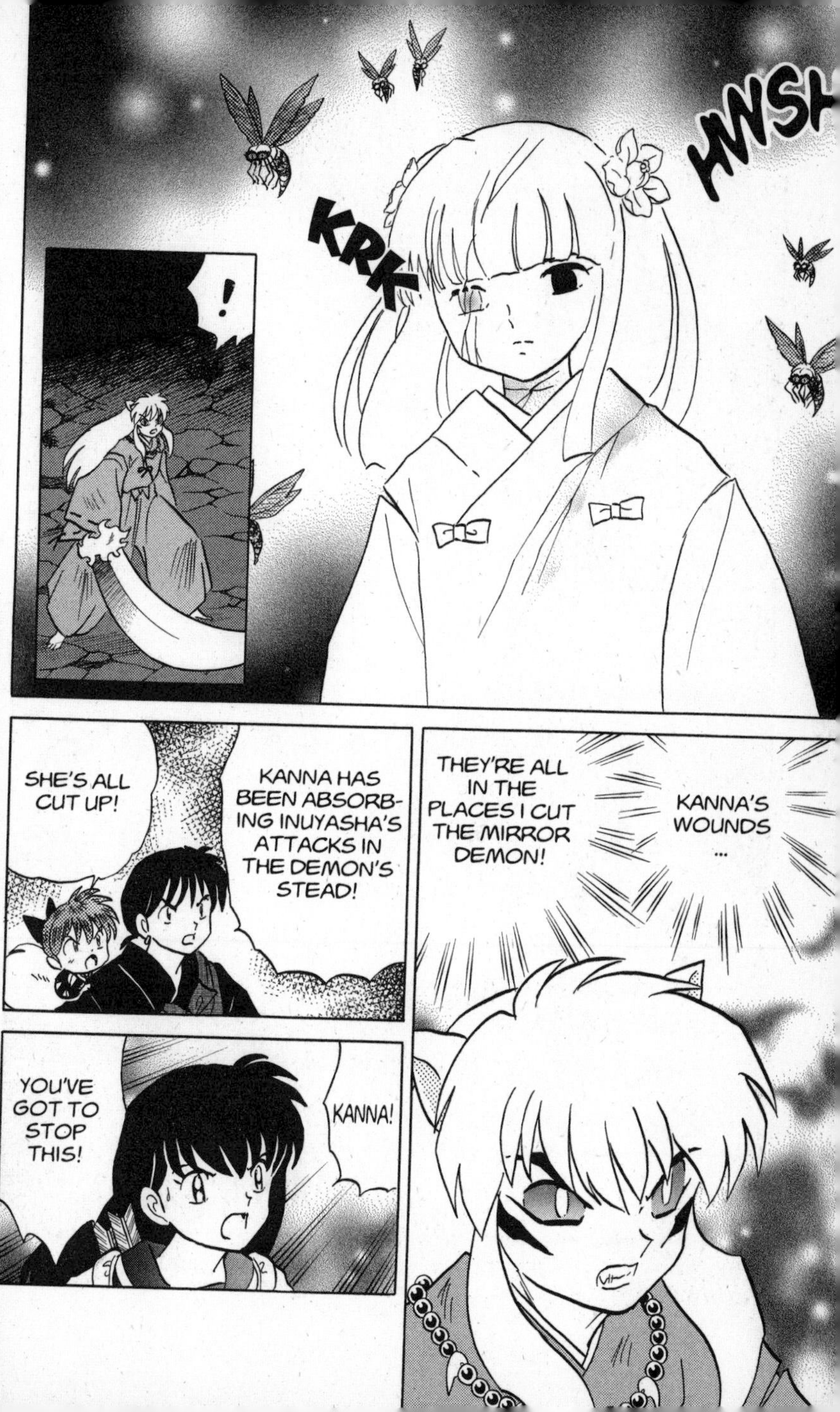

HWSH
KRK
!
KANNA'S WOUNDS ...
THEY'RE ALL IN THE PLACES I CUT THE MIRROR DEMON!
KANNA HAS BEEN ABSORBING INUYASHA'S ATTACKS IN THE DEMON'S STEAD!
SHE'S ALL CUT UP!
KANNA!
YOU'VE GOT TO STOP THIS!

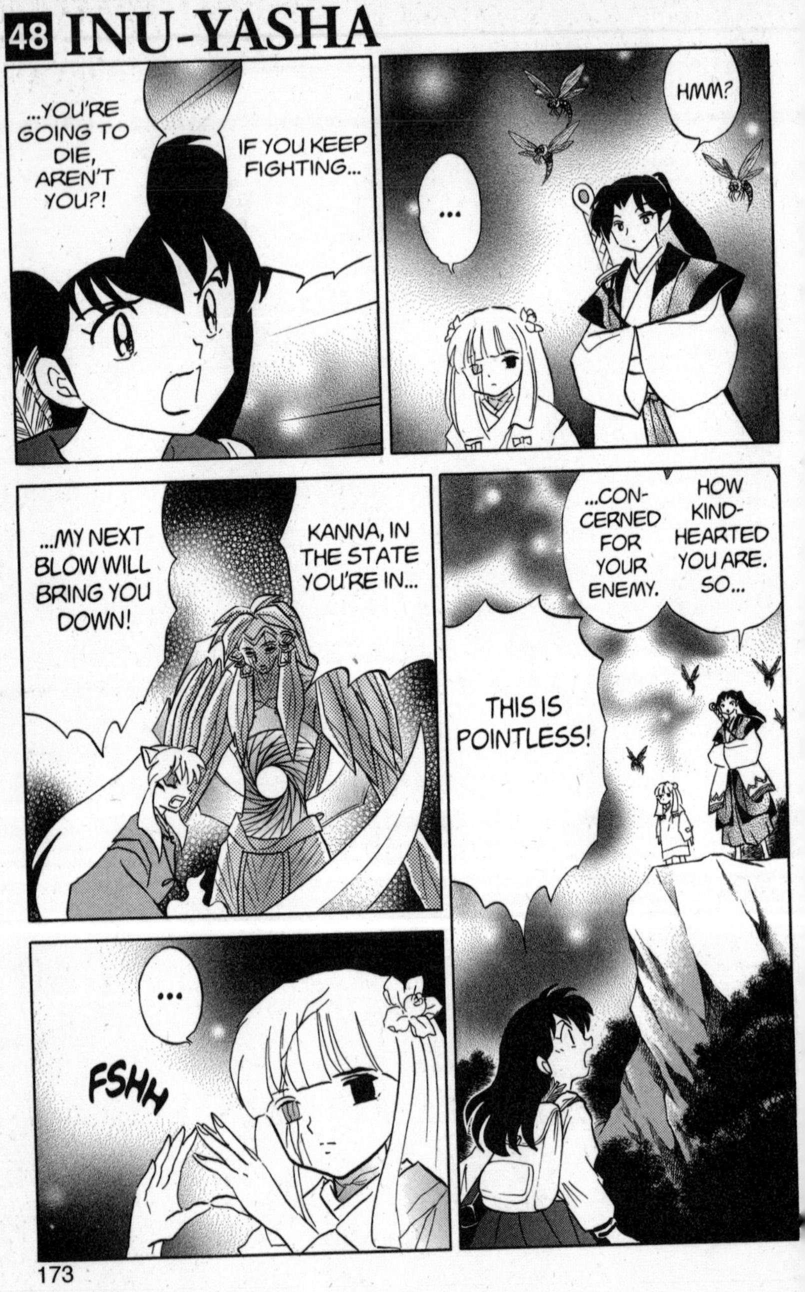
HMM?
...
IF YOU KEEP FIGHTING...
...YOU'RE GOING TO DIE, AREN'T YOU?!
HOW KIND-HEARTED YOU ARE. SO...
...CONCERNED FOR YOUR ENEMY.
THIS IS POINTLESS!
KANNA, IN THE STATE YOU'RE IN...
...MY NEXT BLOW WILL BRING YOU DOWN!
...
FSHH

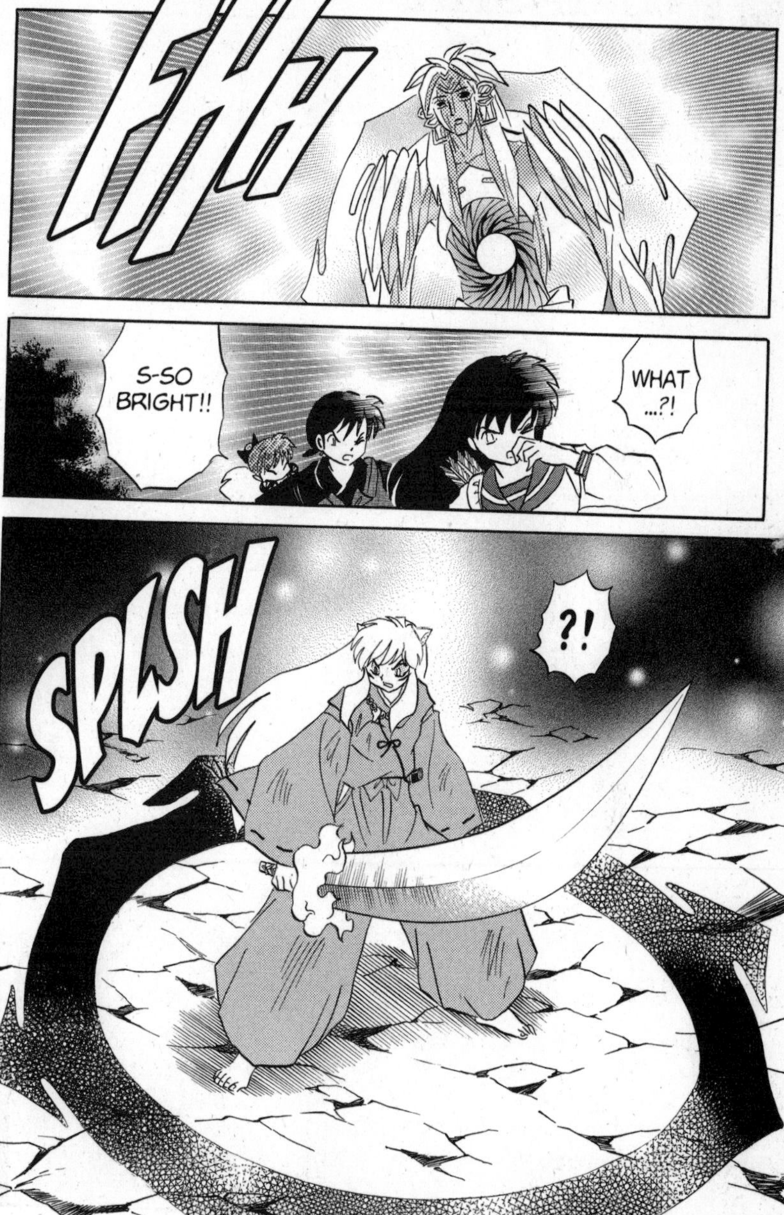
FHH
WHAT ...?!
S-SO BRIGHT!!
?!
SPLSH

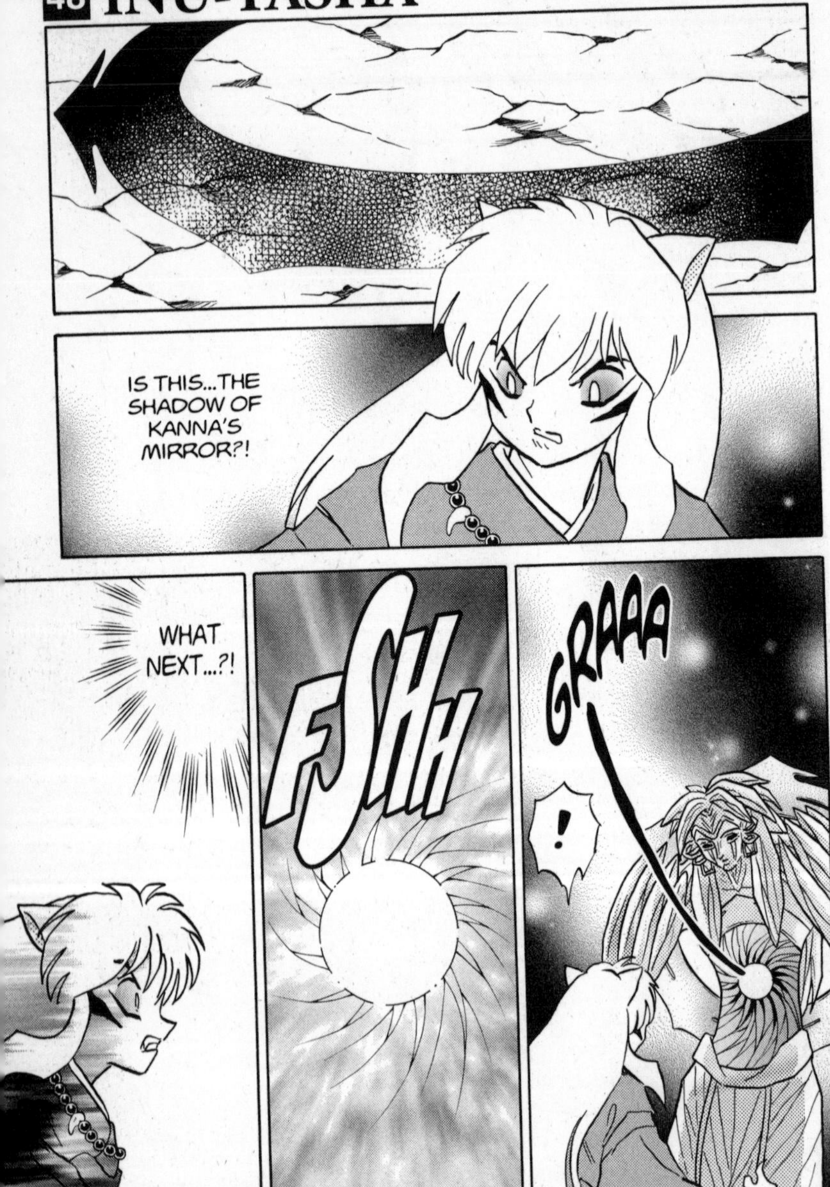
IS THIS...THE SHADOW OF KANNA'S MIRROR?!
GRAAAA
!
FSHH
WHAT NEXT...?!

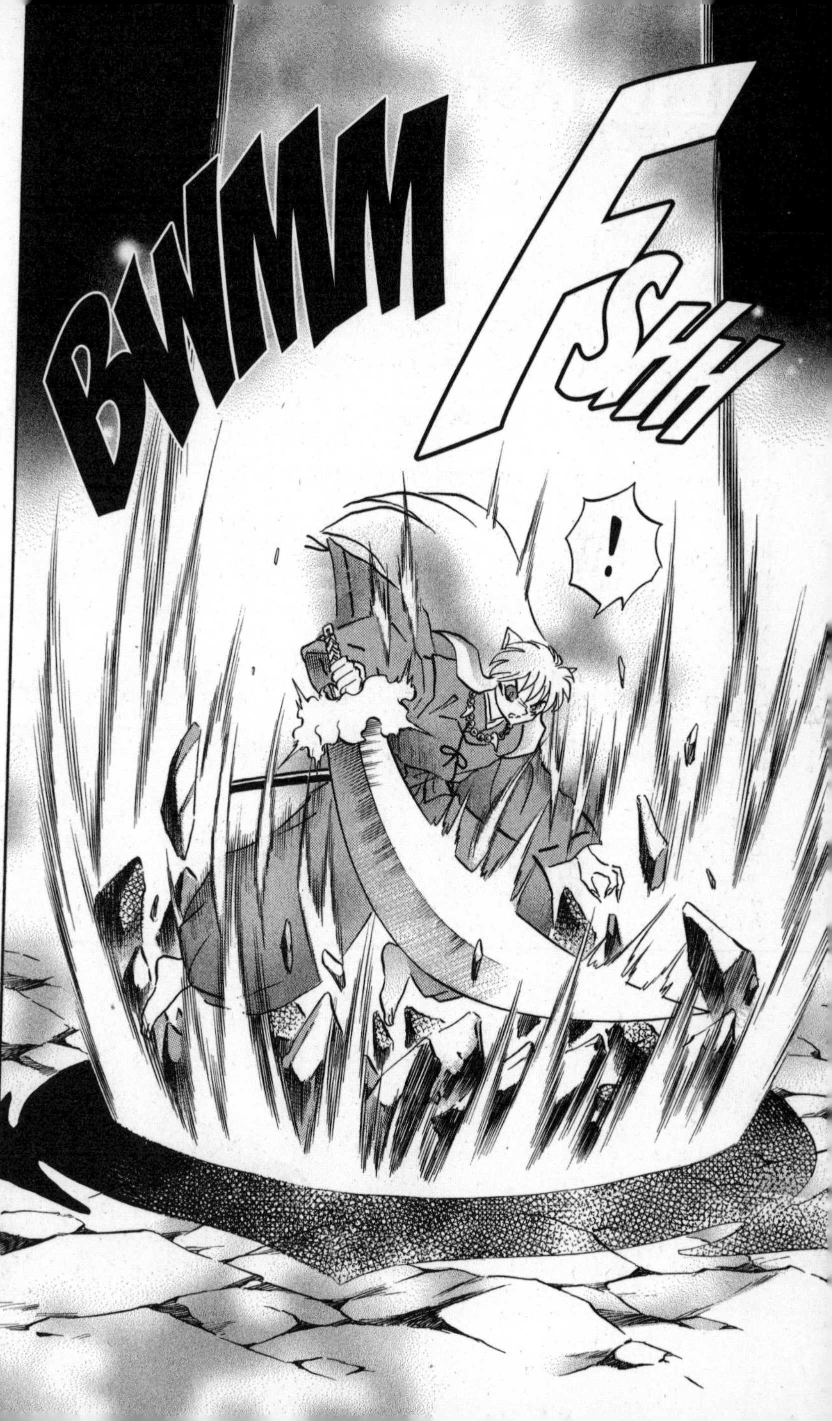
FSHH
BVMMM
!

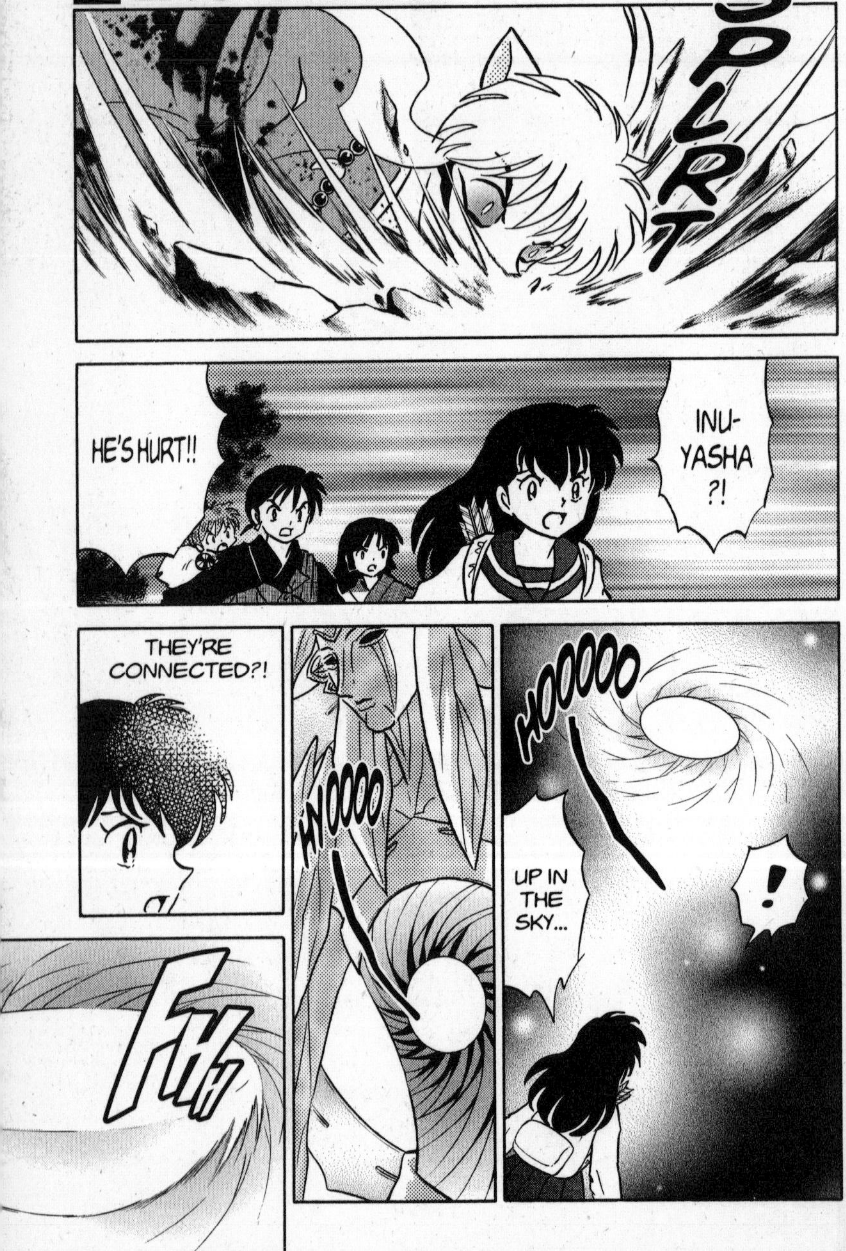
SPLRT
INU-YASHA?!
HE'S HURT!!
HOOOOO
!
UP IN THE SKY...
HYOOOO
THEY'RE CONNECTED?!
FWH

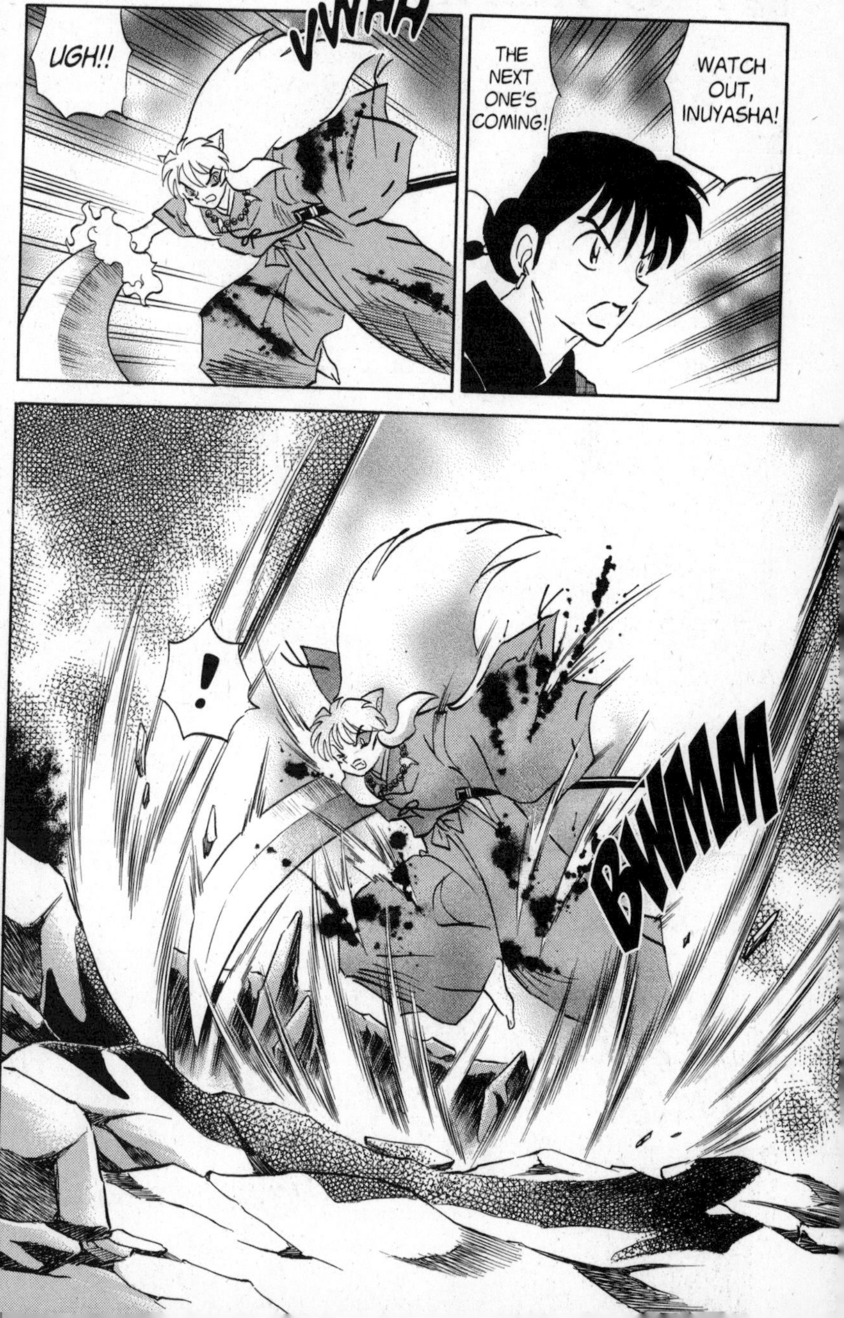
WATCH OUT, INUYASHA!
THE NEXT ONE'S COMING!
VWHH
UGH!!
!
BWMMM

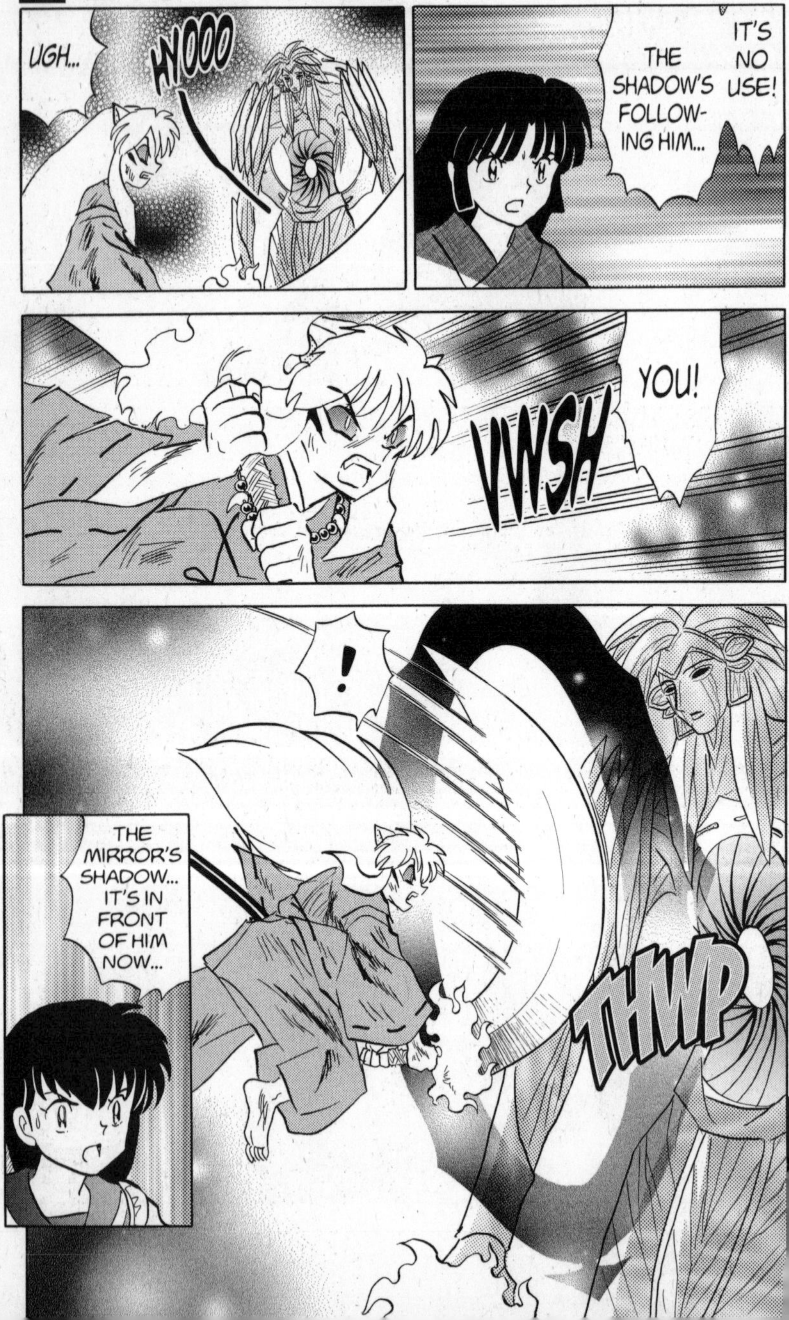
IT'S NO USE!
THE SHADOW'S FOLLOWING HIM...
HYOOO
UGH...
YOU!
VWSH
!
THWP
THE MIRROR'S SHADOW... IT'S IN FRONT OF HIM NOW...

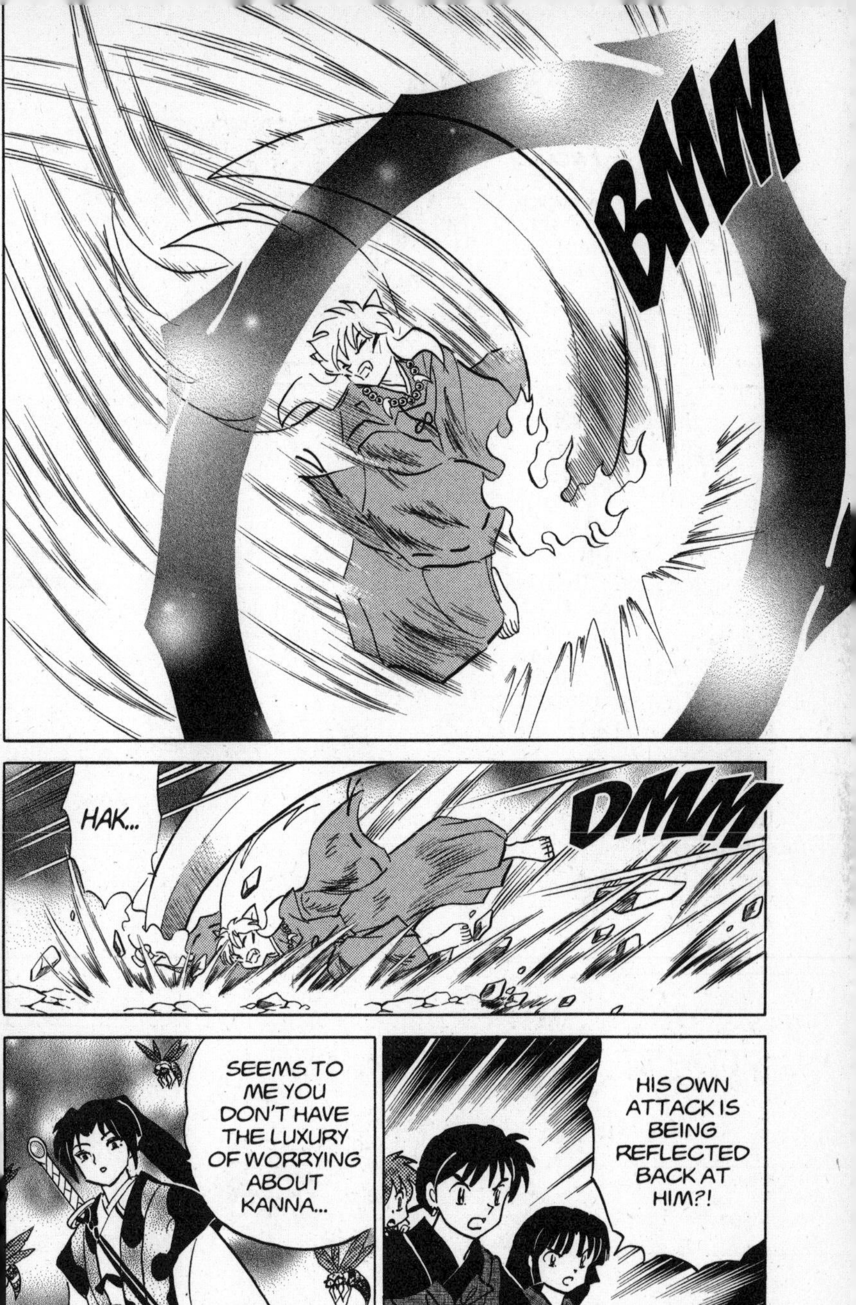
BMM
DMM
HAK...
HIS OWN ATTACK IS BEING REFLECTED BACK AT HIM?!
SEEMS TO ME YOU DON'T HAVE THE LUXURY OF WORRYING ABOUT KANNA...

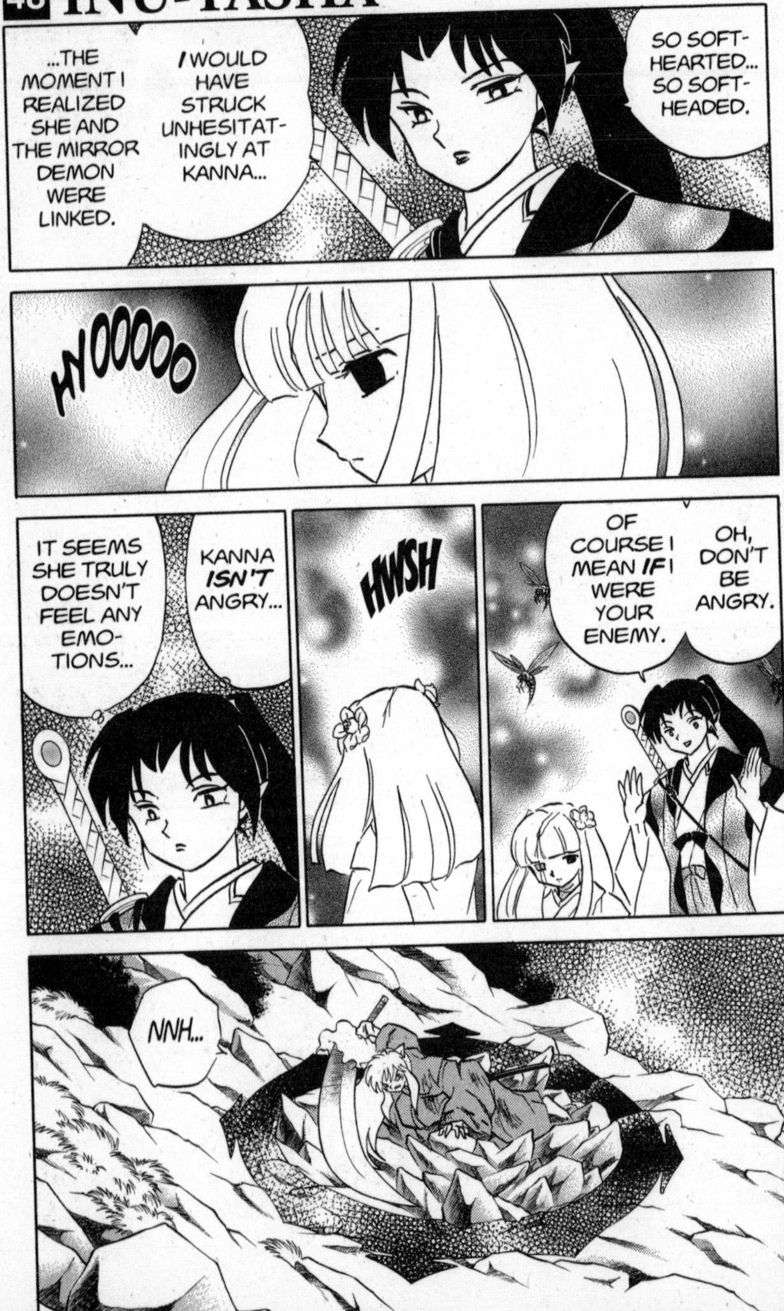
SO SOFT-HEARTED... SO SOFT-HEADED.
I WOULD HAVE STRUCK UNHESITATINGLY AT KANNA...
...THE MOMENT I REALIZED SHE AND THE MIRROR DEMON WERE LINKED.
HYOOOOO
OH, DON'T BE ANGRY.
OF COURSE I MEAN IF I WERE YOUR ENEMY.
HWSH
KANNA ISN'T ANGRY...
IT SEEMS SHE TRULY DOESN'T FEEL ANY EMOTIONS...
NNH...

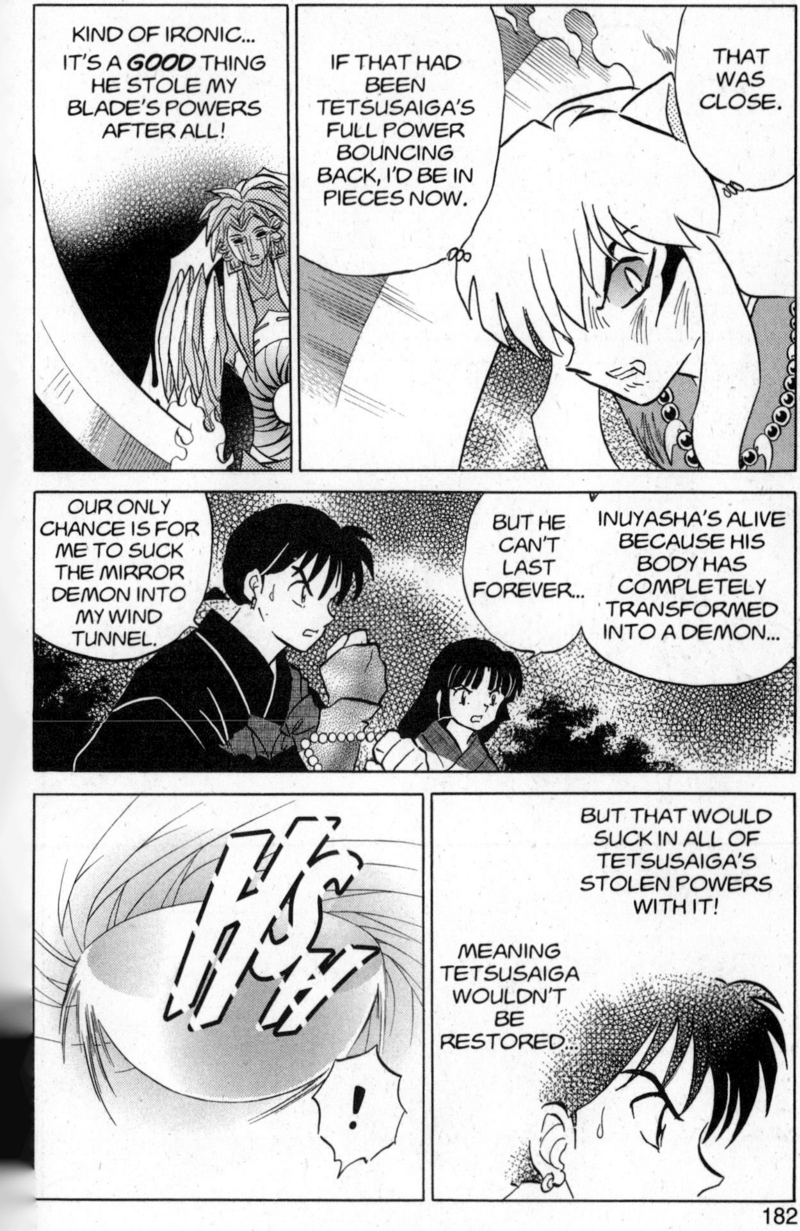
THAT WAS CLOSE.
IF THAT HAD BEEN TETSUSAIGA'S FULL POWER BOUNCING BACK, I'D BE IN PIECES NOW.
KIND OF IRONIC... IT'S A **GOOD** THING HE STOLE MY BLADE'S POWERS AFTER ALL!
INUYASHA'S ALIVE BECAUSE HIS BODY HAS COMPLETELY TRANSFORMED INTO A DEMON...
BUT HE CAN'T LAST FOREVER...
OUR ONLY CHANCE IS FOR ME TO SUCK THE MIRROR DEMON INTO MY WIND TUNNEL.
BUT THAT WOULD SUCK IN ALL OF TETSUSAIGA'S STOLEN POWERS WITH IT!
MEANING TETSUSAIGA WOULDN'T BE RESTORED...
!

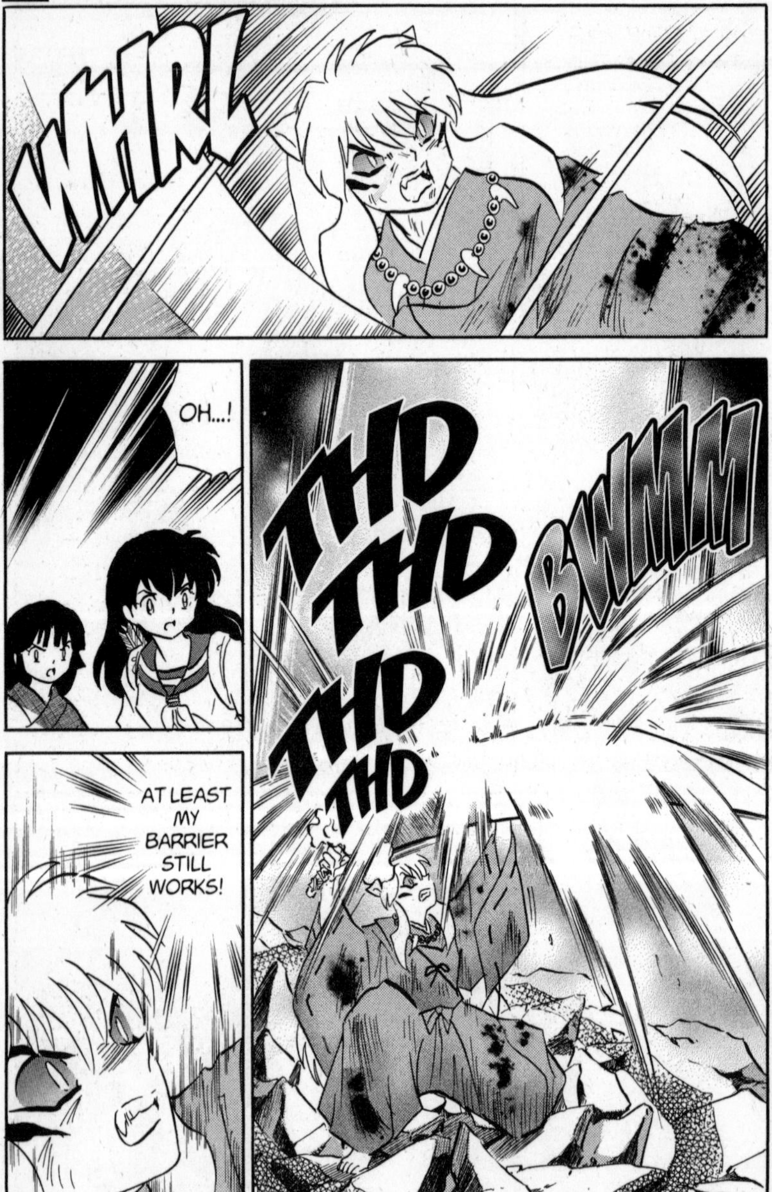
WHRL
BWMM
THD THD THD THD
OH...!
AT LEAST MY BARRIER STILL WORKS!

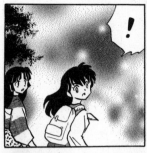

!

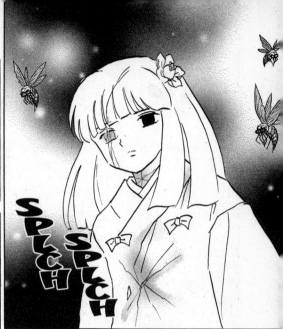

SPLCH SPLCH

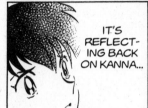

IT'S REFLECTING BACK ON KANNA...

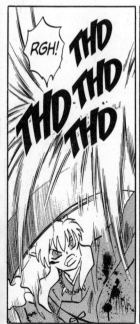

RGH!

THD THD THD THD

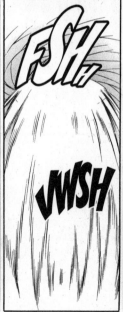

FSH!

VWSH

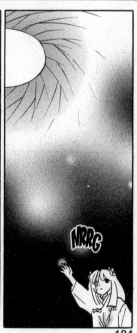

NRRG

184

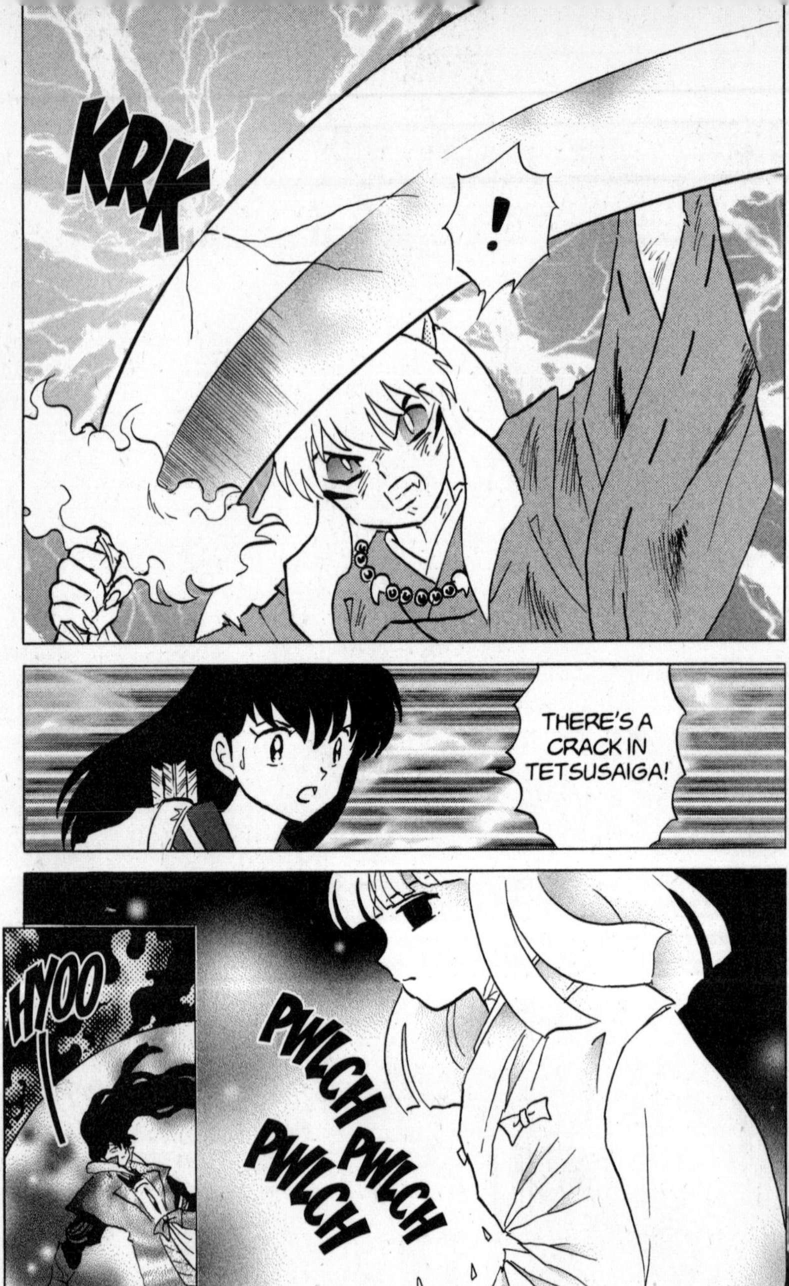
KRK
!
THERE'S A CRACK IN TETSUSAIGA!
PWLCH PWLCH PWLCH
HYOO

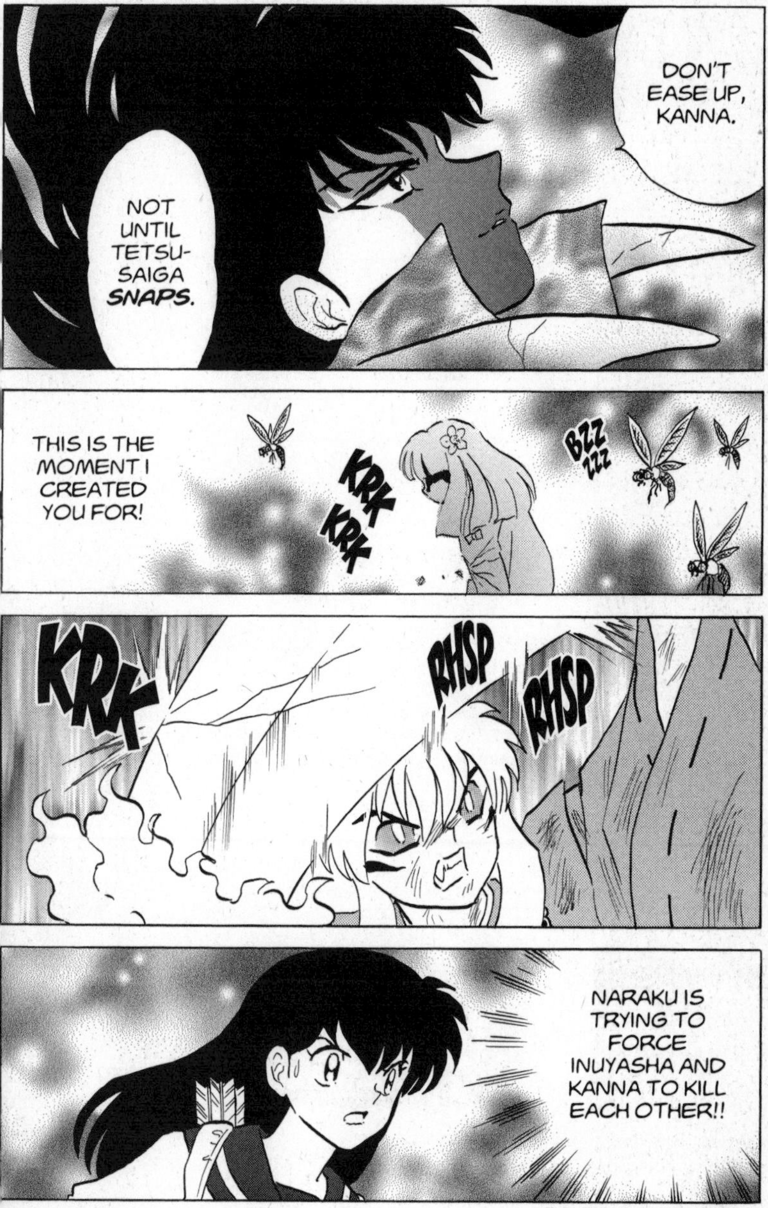
DON'T EASE UP, KANNA.
NOT UNTIL TETSU-SAIGA *SNAPS*.
BZZ ZZZ
KRK KRK
THIS IS THE MOMENT I CREATED YOU FOR!
RHSP
RHSP
KRK
NARAKU IS TRYING TO FORCE INUYASHA AND KANNA TO KILL EACH OTHER!!

TO BE CONTINUED...

INUYASHA

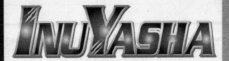

INUYASHA
VOL. 48
Shonen Sunday Edition

Story and Art by
RUMIKO TAKAHASHI

Original Japanese edition "INUYASHA"
published by SHOGAKUKAN Inc.

English Adaptation by Gerard Jones

Translation/Mari Morimoto
Touch-up Art & Lettering/Bill Schuch
Cover & Interior Graphic Design/Yuki Ameda
Editor/Annette Roman

VP, Production/Alvin Lu
VP, Sales & Product Marketing/Gonzalo Ferreyra
VP, Creative/Linda Espinosa
Publisher/Hyoe Narita

Printed in the U.S.A.

Published by VIZ Media, LLC
P.O. Box 77010
San Francisco, CA 94107

10 9 8 7 6 5 4 3 2 1
First printing, May 2010

RATED T+ FOR OLDER TEEN

PARENTAL ADVISORY
INUYASHA is rated T+ for Older Teen and is recommended for ages 16 and up. This volume contains violence.

ratings.viz.com

viz media
www.viz.com

SHONEN SUNDAY
WWW.SHONENSUNDAY.COM

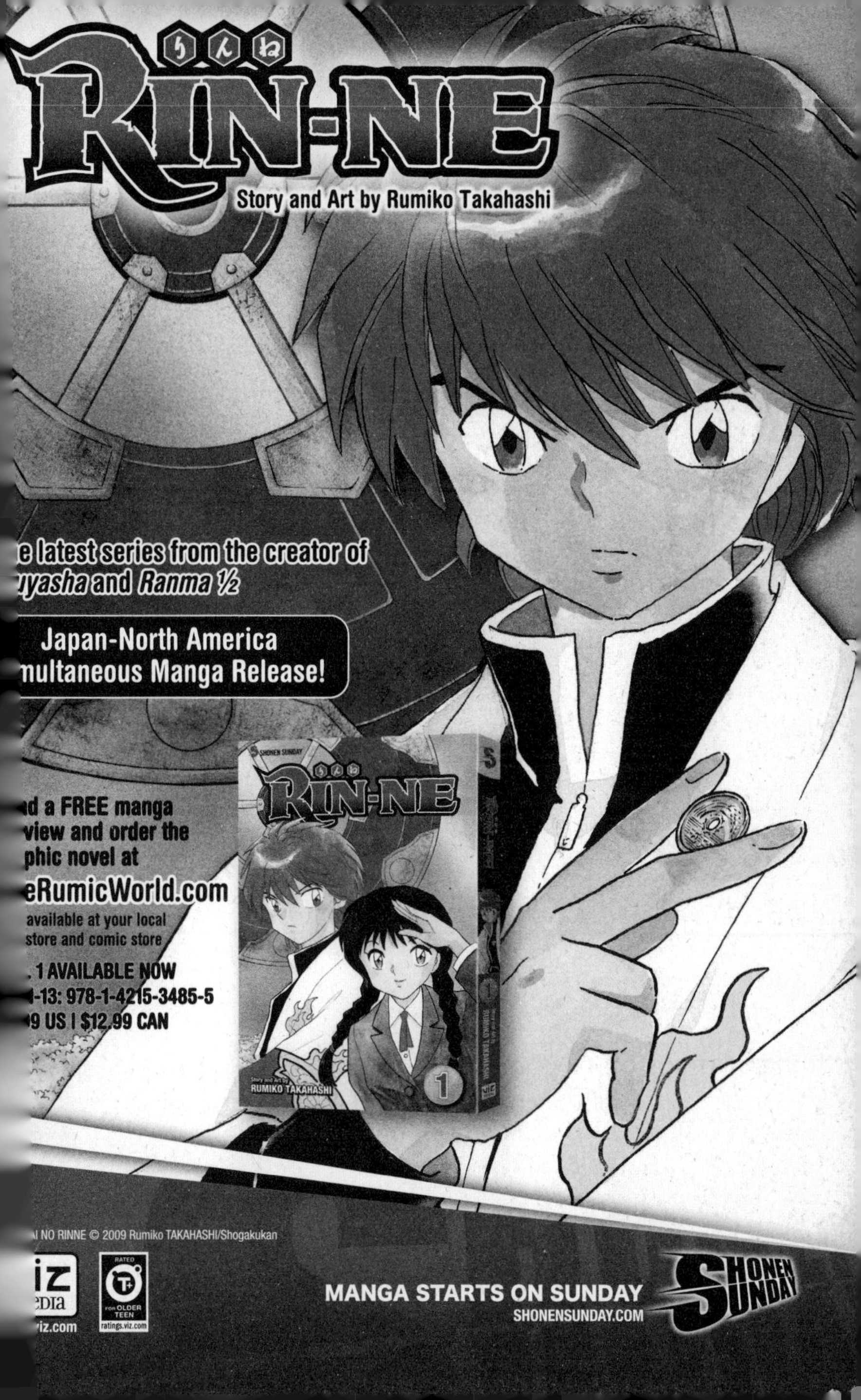
りんね
RIN-NE
Story and Art by Rumiko Takahashi
e latest series from the creator of
uyasha and Ranma ½
Japan-North America
nultaneous Manga Release!
SHONEN SUNDAY
RIN-NE
Story and Art by
RUMIKO TAKAHASHI
1
d a FREE manga
view and order the
phic novel at
eRumicWorld.com
available at your local
store and comic store
. 1 AVAILABLE NOW
-13: 978-1-4215-3485-5
9 US | $12.99 CAN
I NO RINNE © 2009 Rumiko TAKAHASHI/Shogakukan
iz
EDIA
viz.com
RATED
T+
FOR OLDER TEEN
ratings.viz.com
MANGA STARTS ON SUNDAY
SHONENSUNDAY.COM
SHONEN SUNDAY

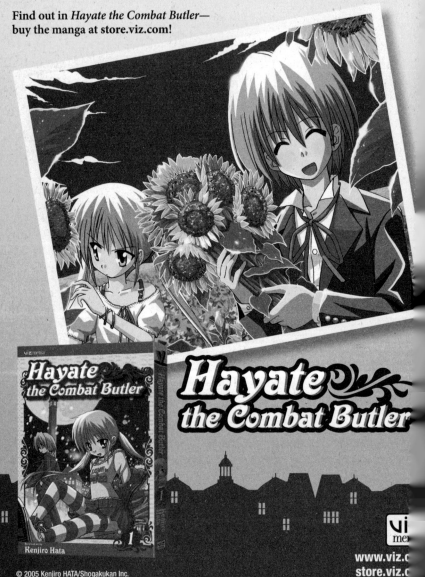

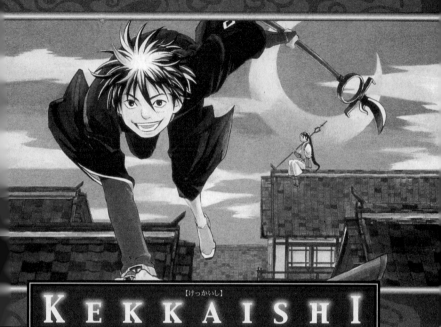
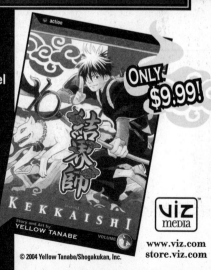

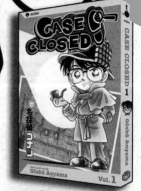

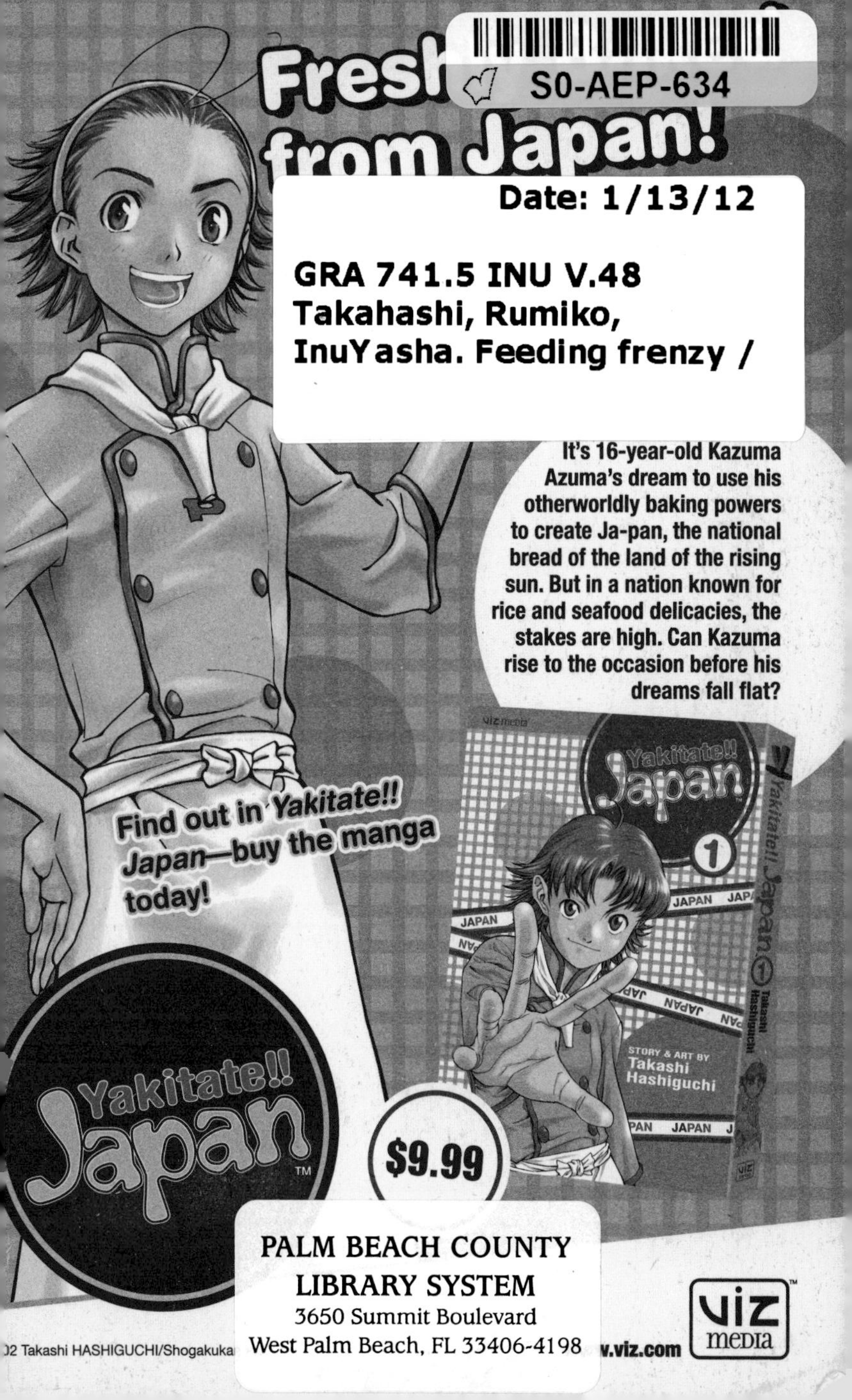
Fresh from Japan!
It's 16-year-old Kazuma Azuma's dream to use his otherworldly baking powers to create Ja-pan, the national bread of the land of the rising sun. But in a nation known for rice and seafood delicacies, the stakes are high. Can Kazuma rise to the occasion before his dreams fall flat?
Find out in Yakitate!! Japan—buy the manga today!
Yakitate!! Japan™
$9.99
viz media
Yakitate!! Japan 1
STORY & ART BY Takashi Hashiguchi
v.viz.com
viz media™